LIVERPOOL

Gangs, Vice and Packet Rats

LIVERPOOL

Gangs, Vice and Packet Rats:
19th-Century Crime and Punishment

Malcolm Archibald

BLACK & WHITE PUBLISHING

First published 2015
by Black & White Publishing Ltd
29 Ocean Drive, Edinburgh EH6 6JL

1 3 5 7 9 10 8 6 4 2   15 16 17 18

ISBN: 978 1 84502 962 3

ALBA | CHRUTHACHAIL

Typeset by RefineCatch Limited, Bungay, Suffolk
Printed and bound by Gutenberg Press, Malta

FOR CATHY

Contents

Acknowledgements   xiii

Author's Note   xv

Introduction   xvii

Chapter 1   A Very Brief History of Liverpool   1

Chapter 2   The Early Years   8

Chapter 3   The Liverpool Police   24

Chapter 4   The Strange Affairs of Ann Crellin   44

Chapter 5   Packet Rats   57

Chapter 6   The Leveson Street Murders   69

Chapter 7   Blue and Red   77

Chapter 8   Contrast: Criminal and Lawman   89

Chapter 9	Death in the Family	116
Chapter 10	Prostitution	137
Chapter 11	Cracksmen and Thieves	152
Chapter 12	Corner Men and High Rippers	171
Chapter 13	Training Ship Trouble	193
Chapter 14	The Irish Have Arrived	201
Chapter 15	The Dangerous Countryside	218
Chapter 16	Liverpool Women	229
Chapter 17	On the Railway	236
Chapter 18	Jack Ashore	241
Chapter 19	Redcross Street Murder	252
Epilogue		264
Select Bibliography		266

'I have visited eight kingdoms on the continent within one year, and in no city or town have I witnessed such scenes of immorality and vice as are daily and nightly to be seen in Liverpool.'

— 'Traveller', *Liverpool Mercury*, July 1861

Courtesy of Liverpool Record Office, Liverpool Libraries.

Acknowledgments

I would like to thank the following organisations and people: the Museum of Liverpool, Liverpool Central Library and Archives, Merseyside Maritime Museum, Lydia Nowak, Production Editor at Black & White, for patiently correcting all my mistakes and Cathy, my wife, for enduring my pre-occupation with crime in yet another Victorian city.

Author's Note

My great-grandfather, William Michie, was a policeman in Liverpool at the time of the First World War and immediately afterwards. He lived in Toxteth, where my grandmother was born. In common with many others, he was an incomer, as his family originated in Aberdeenshire in Scotland. My grandmother returned to Aberdeenshire when she was a teenager and the family connection with Liverpool ended, although she remained a staunch Everton supporter all her life and at times of excitement or stress could break out into broad Scouse.

As a seaman, my father knew the city well. He sailed from here on many occasions during the Second World War and after. My own first visit to Liverpool was in October 1977, when Scotland played Wales at Anfield in a World Cup qualifier. Scotland won, thanks to Don Masson and Kenny Dalglish – and a colour-blind referee who could not tell whose arm struck the ball that resulted in a Scottish penalty. I enjoyed that visit to Liverpool, apart from the score, and remember the bustle and pace of the city well. I also remember the friendliness of the people. That memory remained with me, so when Black & White

Publishing asked me to write a book about nineteenth-century crime in the city, it was with great pleasure that I undertook the task.

This book is the result. It is in no way academic, instead it is intended to give a sample of the variety of crimes within the city and highlight some of the most interesting or most important. It was a labour of love more than pure labour, with the major problem being what to leave out. Nineteenth-century Liverpool was indeed an interesting place in which to live.

Malcolm Archibald

Introduction

In the nineteenth century, Liverpool was Europe's western gateway to the world and Ireland's entry port to England. It was one of the world's greatest port cities, with the 1715 Old Dock being the world's first enclosed commercial dock, but only the forerunner of over seven miles of docks that ran along the River Mersey. By the end of the nineteenth century, Liverpool's docks were granite-built and the most modern and functional in the world. Herman Melville, author of *Moby Dick*, commented that he made:

> sundry excursions to the neighbouring docks, for I never tired of admiring them [. . .] having seen only the miserable wooden wharves and slip-shod, shambling piers of New York [. . .] these mighty docks filled my young mind with wonder.

From here the busy packet ships crossed to New York and Boston, the slave ships to Africa and the Caribbean, the emigrant ships to North America, the immigrant ships from Ireland, the ferries to various ports of western Britain and the trading ships to every corner of the known world. Trade was the life-blood of Britain and much of it passed through the port of Liverpool. The city was a constant buzz of movement, of people passing through, of carts and railway trains, of visitors and hopeful emigrants, of bewildered immigrants and tired dock workers, of seamen and merchants, lodging housekeepers and lonely, waiting wives, of desperate poverty and incredible wealth co-existing side by side in a hodgepodge of excitement and chaos that typified all that was best and worst in the Victorian world.

It is no wonder then that ships and their seamen were often central to crime in Liverpool. There were murders involving nautical wives, muggings of seamen, the disgusting crimps who exploited newly-arrived sailors, prostitutes who preyed on them and needed them to survive, drunken seamen causing trouble and thefts from ships in harbour. But Liverpool crime extended far beyond the dockland areas. In common with every nineteenth-century city there were atrocious murders and clever robberies, but Liverpool also experienced a bank robbery that ended in a manhunt as far as France, terrible teenage gangs and youths who burned a reformatory ship.

The second influence on Liverpool's crime, and one that was also associated with the sea, was the influx of Irish. In the nineteenth century, Ireland was in a state of flux, with an elite who seemed to feel superior to the bulk of the population and the differences between a Protestant minority and Roman Catholic majority. There were constant religious and social troubles that the immigrants often brought to Liverpool with them, and the Orange Lodges tended to provoke confrontations and violence on their marches through the streets of Liverpool.

The combination of religious disputes and poverty had an effect on the Irish communities in Liverpool. It took time for them to assimilate and often they polarised into rival factions as they continued the feuds that they had carried with them across the Irish Sea. Add to that the normal tensions that created problems within any nineteenth-century community – sprinkle on a military garrison who could occasionally drink too much and add the occasional terrorist bomb – and Liverpool could be a lively place indeed, particularly after dark. As in every urban centre of the time, the better off left the town centre to more affluent areas of the suburbs, away from the congestion, dirt and noise. The suburbs had larger houses behind secure garden walls, but the outskirts and environs held their own dangers.

The countryside may have held happy folk memories of more apparently peaceful times, but it held its own danger. Poachers and highwaymen haunted the fields and hedgerows, and for a while the roads between Liverpool and St Helens were infested with a predatory gang known as the Long Hundred, while even places with idyllic names such as Knotty Ash could be targeted by thieves. Nowhere was safe in the days when Victoria sat on the throne and the police were learning their business through hard experience and constant striving.

1
A Very Brief History of Liverpool

Liverpool is undoubtedly one of the world's greatest port cities. In the nineteenth century its location on the west coast of the most industrialised nation in the world, facing Ireland and with easy access to the Atlantic and North America, made it a natural jumping-off point for both trade and emigration. By British standards it is not an ancient city, with most of its growth being in the eighteenth and nineteenth century, but its roots go back to the Middle Ages. It was based around an agricultural settlement called Lytherpul that existed before the thirteenth century, at a time when the area was a hodgepodge of patched bogland and scattered woods, with the River Mersey a blue background and the westerly wind raising great surf rollers on the coast. This would be a wild area with wind and weather dictating the pattern of rural life and poverty guaranteed every winter.

In 1207 Lytherpul was edged into national consciousness when the much-abused King John of England granted permission to create an embarkation port for Ireland. This proved to be a function for which Liverpool was admirably suited and was one of the pillars on which the town and its population rested. However, despite the six streets of this planned new town, Liverpool remained much as it had always been: a small village supported by farming, albeit with the occasional ship visiting from the sister isle. But as time passed, there was a gradual expansion, with mills and minor warehouses added to the village. As the ports of southern England expanded and thrived with European and Mediterranean trade, Liverpool's maritime experience remained limited to the Irish Sea. However, the village gradually evolved to a market town, slightly larger but still content to ease through the passage of the seasons as it had always done.

It was not until nearby Chester lost much of its maritime importance, through the silting of the River Dee, that Liverpool emerged as a locally important port and its destiny altered forever. As Bristol mariners probed the Atlantic and men from the South West plagued the Spanish Main, Liverpool seamen dipped their toes in the coastal waters and wondered what lay beyond. In the seventeenth century Liverpool began to export salt and coal, with the Liverpool mariners operating in the stormy Irish Sea, but not much further. There was a new charter and in the 1640s an explosion of prestige for Liverpool as Civil War ripped through the four nations of England, Wales, Ireland and Scotland. Liverpool at last began to fulfil the function for which King John had designed it: an embarkation port for Ireland. But ironically it was Parliament, rather than the Crown, which shipped troops across the Irish Sea. The clatter of boots and hooves interrupted the quiet market town, the roar of military voices shattered the night and the gleam of steel and raucous laughter of rough men turned the heads of women, who until then had seen none but slow-moving farmers. The population gradually grew and diversified: Liverpool was coming of age.

Trade and strategy invited demographic expansion in the latter decades of the seventeenth century. People moved into Liverpool and began to settle there by choice. Although the south-western ports had fame in Elizabeth's reign, London dominated English shipping until

1700 and more than half the country's trade came in through the Thames. However, trade patterns altered as the West Indies and the North American colonies rose in importance. The Atlantic became a trade highway and west coast ports flourished anew, but not because of royal-licensed piracy. In 1715, eight years after the Union of Parliaments with Scotland and with the country basking in the glory of Marlborough's victories over the French, Liverpool gained her first dock.

For the next two centuries, Liverpool's story was of continual growth as trade dominated all else. The town became a major gateway into England and an important port for exports. Liverpool merchants and seamen broke through the barrier of the constricting Irish Sea and ventured toward the distant horizon. Within a few years they treated the Atlantic highways as if they owned them, with ships participating in the sugar trade, around a hundred in the slave trade, others in the Arctic whaling trade and emigration from Ireland and to North America. In time of war, the deep-water men of Liverpool became privateersmen and scoured the seas for vessels from whichever nation had the bad luck and audacity to oppose Great Britain. Sometimes the privateers over-reached themselves and became victims of warships, but there was always the possibility of capturing a far prize and bringing home a hat full of gold. Money flowed into the town and some men became extremely wealthy. Others manned the ships or serviced the sailors, while there were also those who lived as parasites, stealing from the hard work of their fellows.

There was a sense of truculent independence in Liverpool that not all seaports shared. During the many wars of the eighteenth century, the Royal Navy used the Impress service to forcibly recruit new men. In some places this was not a hard job and seamen were rounded up on land or more often from homeward bound ships. However, in Liverpool the local seamen fought back so successfully that for much of the eighteenth century, Liverpool ships held onto their manpower, while vessels from many other places had to rely on foreign seamen. As the number of ships using Liverpool increased, naturally the sea became vital for the town and had a massive influence in all that happened. But there were many negatives to balance the positives of increased employment and capital.

The slave trade revealed the dark side of human character as Britain, in common with so much of the world, exploited living people for profit. Liverpool ships sailed from the Mersey to West Africa, traded goods with the local African suppliers for a cargo of live slaves, crossed to the Americas and then back to Liverpool. It was a sordid, disgusting and terrible – yet highly profitable – enterprise that made many Liverpool merchants huge fortunes, but it was wasteful of human life. Although the slave mortality rate could be as low as a still terrible 2 per cent, it could also be much higher, and as many as a quarter of the slaving ship crew could die of disease or slave rebellion, but high wages compensated the survivors. Slavery was an accepted part of African culture, but the morality of slaving niggled at Christian consciences until in the latter half of the eighteenth century, there was a dynamic movement to end the slave trade and ultimately the institution of slavery itself.

In 1807, despite the loss of revenue at a time when Great Britain was fighting for her life against the despotic regime of Napoleon Bonaparte, Parliament banned the slave trade. It was a decision that caused consternation in Liverpool as those merchants who had profited from the intense human misery witnessed their source of income drop, while the evangelical Christians were justifiably pleased that they had succeeded in ending a major moral blight.

By that date, Liverpool was already polarising into a town of two extremes. On one hand there were the mercantile elite who boasted addresses in areas such as Canning Street, the very gracious Abercromby Square and Rodney Street – all elegant areas of the Georgian new town. These men drove fine carriages, ate magnificent meals, wore white cravats and evening dress coats, and acted like the merchant princes they were. On the other hand, in the centre of town and around the docks the bulk of the population lived in squalor that would match any city in Britain, if not in Europe. Disease was rife with typhoid, typhus, smallpox and dysentery being a constant threat, while in 1832, cholera cut cruel swathes through the population. There was an escape clause for the wealthy who moved out to the suburb of Sefton Park, but the poor remained in Liverpool's alleys and slums. As was the case in any town with similar problems, many turned to crime. Even as the living conditions within Liverpool deteriorated for masses of people, the Diocese of Liverpool was created in 1880 and the town was elevated to the much-prized status of a city.

The elevation was much deserved. Liverpool's population exploded in the nineteenth century as shipload after shipload of barefoot, ragged, illiterate or semi-literate Irish landed to seek work in the hungry mills and factories. From 82,430 in 1801, the population of Liverpool jumped to over 100,000 in just a decade, then to 129,000 by 1821. In the next ten years, 50,000 more people crammed into the town, joined by another 75,000 by 1841 and then, as famine hit much of Western Europe and particularly Ireland, yet another 70,000 arrived in the next decade. Liverpool was creaking at the seams. By 1881 the speed of growth had slowed, but there were over 700,000 people in the town by the turn of the century. The population had not merely grown: it had also condensed into unhygienic clumps. In the official report of the Royal Health of Towns Commission of 1845, around 18,000 people lived in cellars with no sanitation at all – no wonder disease was rife. In 1884 some areas of the city had a density of 1,200 people to the acre, and that was thirty years after the population density in the city centre had peaked and had started to decline.

When the Industrial Revolution thundered across Britain, many people began to worry about the apparent increase in crime. They looked at the spreading cities and worried about the huge increase of population and the lack of regulation in the sordid streets. As Britain altered from a mainly rural country to a mainly urban one, the old pattern of patriarchal control was eroded and it seemed that only anarchy took its place. The authorities looked with consternation at the urban centres and spoke of a 'criminal class' that lived amongst the apparently respectable people. There were also fears of criminal areas amongst the stinking slums and a desire to rid the country of such undesirable people. The gallows and the transportation ships seemed the best options, and both were well used. Those major and minor criminals who did not end their lives dancing a jig on the wrong end of a rope were herded into ships that sailed to Tasmania or some other part of Australia, and put to virtual slave labour for a number of years or the remainder of their lives.

As Liverpool became one of Europe's major ports, the town attracted criminals who targeted not only the docks and shipping, but also the hundreds of thousands of emigrants who sought a cheap passage to North America. The area around the dockland became arguably one of the most dangerous urban areas in Britain. As hopeful hordes left Liverpool, more people came in, as the destitute from Ireland crossed the Sea in a desperate search for employment or just to escape the horrors of poverty, starvation and disease. All sorts of people came to the docks. There were Down East Yankees in stovepipe hats who chewed long cigars, men from Africa and the West Indies, red-faced, bearded Greenlandmen from the Arctic whaling ships, predatory slavers yellow with fever, stout Prussian traders and seamen from every port in the British Isles, as well as passengers from the packet ships and the truculent, violent packet rats who manned them.

In November 1854 the Rev Isaac Holmes lectured on 'Liverpool in the Dark' in Hope Hall to the Liverpool Church of England Society. He spoke of false weights and measures, of people with contagious diseases selling off their clothes; he spoke of some 9,548 Liverpool people imprisoned during the previous year, 895 of them children. He mentioned that there were over 700 known thieves in Liverpool and added his belief that every street in Liverpool could be visited by at least one criminal every day. Surprisingly, Holmes said that he sympathised with them and blamed society for forcing them into crime.

By that year the old parts of the city had deteriorated. Poorly lit or unlit, the streets were disfigured by houses with broken windows or windows stuffed with rags. It was not a pretty picture to offset the wealth and glamour of one of the world's greatest ports.

As a city, Liverpool was a major success story, but in order to be so, it needed seamen and thousands of labourers who formed the base of the pyramid for the wealthy merchants who looked down on them. At the top, the elite lived in mansions in the Liverpool Parks. These parks were open to the public during the day but locked after sunset. Shipping, industry and wealth, much of it made in the old slaving days, paid for the villas and lavish lifestyles, so there were said to be more millionaires around Liverpool's parks than in London's Belgravia. By that period Liverpool was vying with Glasgow to be the Second City of the British Empire, with the docks central to the lifeblood and economy of the city. The city had expanded in rings around the old central core and the fourteen miles of docks, but although it boasted a vast number of impressive buildings and had an urban identity equal to any, it was also the hub of shocking criminal activity. Trade had brought mixed blessings to the city.

2
The Early Years

Some kinds of crime never change, although the labels may alter with time. The term 'footpad' has a ring of romance to it, when in reality the perpetrators were nothing more than common thugs or muggers, as they are now known. These people had a variety of ways in which to relieve an innocent passer-by of his or her money and valuables, but the end result was usually the same: a victim lying on the ground, bruised and bleeding, and a perpetrator gloating over the loot he had stolen. In common with every other town and city in the country, Liverpool had its share of these predators. The following example both removes any aura of glamour from the term 'footpad' and shows the bravery and decency of some Liverpool Englishmen of the period.

'Damn thee: you little knew Bob Pendleton'

On Friday, 24 April 1818 two footpads haunted the area around the Botanic Gardens, then situated at Mount Pleasant on the outskirts of the town. It was a good area to pick as the gardens provided a plethora of trees, whose shade could be used for cover even on the dim summer evenings. The footpads were obviously professional, for they struck hard and fast, but did not push their luck by infesting the same area. Late that evening they pounced on an unwary man who was walking home to Edge Hill, pointed a pistol at his head and ran away with his watch.

The following morning, Saturday, 25 April, before the authorities had time to circulate details about the robbery, two men sidled into a pawnbroker's shop in Tithebarn Street and pawned the watch. The police re-united the watch with its owner, but at that time they had no idea of the identity of the attackers.

It may have been the same two men who struck on Saturday night at the Everton side of Breck Lane, but this time they chose the wrong victim. Robert Pendleton was a quiet-living but determined man who had never fallen foul of the law. He was walking home along Breck Lane when two men appeared from the shadows. Pendleton did nothing until one cocked a pistol and pointed it at his head, then he came to an abrupt stop.

'How much money do you have?' the men demanded.

Pendleton faced them. 'Not much,' he replied.

'We must have it all,' the men told him, although the words may have been more graphic.

With a pistol an inch from his head, Pendleton had no choice in the matter. 'Then don't use me ill,' he asked, as he placed his hands in his pockets.

The footpads got little spoil from him: a cheap watch, a green-handled knife and two shillings and sixpence in coins. Once they were satisfied and he had nothing left, they fled toward Everton. However, Pendleton was not a man to trifle with. Rather than bemoaning his loss, he decided to do something about it. He was a local man, fit and brave, and he knew the area well. Everton was only some two hundred metres away as the crow flew, but longer by the road. Pendleton vaulted a wall and raced over the fields toward

Everton in the hope of heading the footpads off. When he arrived, there were a few people in Church Street, including a man named William Kelly. Pendleton immediately told Kelly about the robbery and said he hoped to catch the robbers here; would Kelly be kind enough to help?

As he spoke, the two footpads appeared, and Pendleton suggested to Kelly that 'if you will fasten one, I'll fasten the other.'

Kelly must have been a brave man, for he had no hesitation in helping this stranger who had appeared out of the dark. Pendleton and Kelly leaped on the footpads, but the two men were not inclined to submit quietly. Rather than run or submit, both drew shoemaker's knives and stabbed and slashed in frantic retaliation. Unarmed and unprepared for a fight, Kelly was getting the worst of it but he was determined not to give up.

'Damn you, villain,' Kelly said, 'I have fastened on you now and while I have breath in my body, I'll not quit you!'

Despite his brave words, Kelly had numerous wounds gushing out blood and he would have lost the contest had other people not intervened. The first passer-by to help was a man named Robert Woodward, who grabbed one of the footpads by the throat and hauled him away from Kelly. Next was the local watchman who arrived with his staff. He wrestled the footpad to the ground and tied him securely. When three more men came hurrying along to help, the fight was over. Both footpads were overpowered and Pendleton stood up, dusted himself down and said:

'Damn thee: you little knew Bob Pendleton, if thee thought to rob him and get off without a tussle for it.'

The watchman and his many helpers bundled the footpads to the Everton watch house, where they were searched. Pendleton's watch and money were found, as well as some other items that were thought to belong to a man and woman who had been robbed on the Derby Road earlier that evening. The footpads also had a pistol and a number of slugs as ammunition. After questioning, they were found to be two cousins named Daniel and William Fitzpatrick and the authorities believed they had been infesting the roads around Liverpool for the previous few months.

Pendleton and Kelly were both family men, and had been badly stabbed. Pendleton was taken home on horseback but Kelly was carried to the infirmary. Both Fitzpatricks were sentenced to death for highway robbery, while Pendleton and Kelly eventually recovered.

On other occasions, it was usually the authorities who intervened to cleanse the roads of predatory bands.

Everton Highwaymen

Today, any casual mention of the name Everton will probably have people thinking of the prominent football club rather than the locality. It is now just to the north-east of the city centre, but at the beginning of the nineteenth century, it was outside the town of Liverpool, with fields and trees all around. It was an old place, once known as Walton-on-the-Hill, but as Liverpool grew and the town centre became more crowded, the wealthier merchants looked for more space in which to live and some moved out to what is now Everton.

By the early decades of the nineteenth century Everton was 'the Montpellier of the county', a wealthy place with fine trees, commanding views and a population of the merchant elite. Naturally, such a place invited crime as those on the left-hand path of the law looked for rich pickings from the successful.

As the winter of 1812 crept on, the environs of Liverpool were infested by a band of highwaymen. Even more so than 'footpads', the term 'highwayman' has been imbued with a sense of glamour that was rarely deserved. These men normally waited for easy prey who could not fight back, attacked without warning, presented a pistol or two to unarmed and terrified travellers, stole whatever they could and caroused away their profit. Few highwaymen had long careers; they had the reputation of devil-may-care men with an aura of romance and danger, so they often attracted what would later be termed as 'gangster's molls' – a female companion to a male criminal – who would also handle a firearm. Many would have traditional hunting grounds, some would have a local pub or inn where they were well known, and all were playing a very chancy game, for the law hanged highwaymen with great gusto.

The early nineteenth century was a bit of a boom time for highwaymen. The coach network of Britain was nearing its height, railways had not been invented and the turnpike system meant there were toll gates on many roads, so coaches were constantly slowed to pay the toll-keeper.

Many coaches had no brakes, coach companies competed for passengers and speed was everything, but passengers sometimes complained that coaches travelled too fast. In April 1817 the coach from Manchester travelled to Low Hall in a mere two and a half hours, which was an average speed of fourteen miles an hour. At a time when the mail coach moved at seven miles an hour, this speed was shocking and was seen as 'an infamous disregard to the safety of the public.' Putting that in context, coaches were not overly fast and as they often carried merchants, gentlemen and ladies, they were very tempting targets for the highwayman.

Highwaymen were particularly active around the Everton area. Rather than hunt as individuals they operated as a gang, with six rough men specialising in holding up coaches on the dark nights.

Their method was traditional: they stopped the coach by presenting a pistol at the driver and then robbed the passengers. For a while they terrorised the roads in and out of Everton, with people scared to travel in case the highwaymen flitted out of the dark shadows and robbed them, but eventually they caused so much disturbance that the authorities decided to do something about it.

It was obviously no use just sending out patrols that the highwaymen could avoid, so the authorities decided to be clever and adopted a Trojan Horse manoeuvre. They knew the modus operandi of the highwaymen, and knew what type of target they preferred to go after, so created a trap for them. The town constables hired a coach, filed into it and slowly drove around the roads leading to Everton, hoping to attract the attention of the highwaymen. After a few uneventful trips the trick worked and the gang surrounded the coach. They presented their pistols and gave the usual demand to stand and deliver, but rather than a coachload of terrified travellers, they faced five determined constables, armed and ready to retaliate.

The constables threw open the doors of the coach and opened fire, so the night became hideous with the bark of large bore pistols, muzzle flares and the reek of white powder smoke. Taken by surprise, the highwaymen reeled back, with some spurring their horses into the night. Others were less fortunate, as the constables raced out of the coach to confront them. The constables arrested two of the highwaymen, Tobias Toole, aged thirty-four, and thirty-two-year-old William O'Bryan on the spot, while twenty-year-old John Davies and two men known only as Clancy and Newton managed to escape. Clancy was never caught but Davies and Newton, alias James Rogers or Timothy O'Bryan were picked up within a few days.

William O'Bryan had also been known as Thomas Dwyer. Using an alias which was not an uncommon ruse in the nineteenth century. In an age when personal documentation was not always accurate, criminals could change their name if they operated in different parts of the country, thus avoiding detection. All the captured highwaymen were hanged at Lancaster Castle in April 1813, which was the normal end for many of their type.

Arrest of Huffey White

Huffey White was one of the most notorious criminals of the early decades in the nineteenth century. He was a bank robber and a highway robber, as well as a man renowned for escaping from the prison hulks. By 1809 he was already well known when he appeared at the Old Bailey and was sentenced to be transported for life. He escaped from the prison hulks before long and returned to his old habits. In 1810, he was arrested at Stockport and sentenced for transportation once more. Sentencing White was one thing, but holding him secure was another and he slipped ashore from the hulks again, and continued to make a nuisance of himself until he was later arrested for robbing the Paisley Union Bank. He slipped free yet again, and robbed and looted his way through much of England.

Using the name Wallis, he robbed the Leeds Mail Coach; he was known in Birmingham; he was nearly caught in Bristol, where the Post Office put a reward of £200 on his head. In the spring of 1813 he looked toward Liverpool for his next criminal venture.

However, the Liverpool authorities were not inclined to allow such an evil man to infest their city. Although Huffey White was a vastly experienced crook, the Liverpool constables were also good at their job. Only the previous autumn they had caught Dwyer's gang, who had infested the roads around Liverpool and now they were on the alert for Huffey.

As was normal, the police depended heavily on informers, and one of these men whispered that Huffey White and a man named Richard Haywood were working in the Liverpool area. The police asked their network of informers to be on the alert and heard that there were two suspicious strangers lodging in Scotland Road.

Three Liverpool head constables: Edward Preston, Thomas Parkinson and Stephen Clayton, together with four sub-officers, hurried to Scotland Road to arrest White and Haywood. However, the people of Liverpool were not to be cowed by any show of authority and the woman who ran the lodging house refused to allow them in until they told her who they were. She was still reluctant until they informed her that unless they gave access they would kick the door in, whereupon, she stood aside.

Leaving Clayton with the sub-officers outside, Parkinson and Preston pushed past the woman and ran down to the cellar, where the cheapest rooms were let. Haywood saw them coming and tried to escape, but Preston and Parkinson stopped him, pushed him against the wall and began to question him, none too gently. The constables were too preoccupied with Haywood to notice White, until he roared out of an adjacent room, punched Parkinson full in the face and threw himself up the stairs. Haywood wrestled free and also dived for escape. Parkinson staggered and fell but Preston was quicker, thumped Haywood to the floor and threw himself on top.

Preston and Haywood wrestled on the ground for a few moments and then Preston drew a small double-barrelled pistol from his pocket, and smacked Haywood over the head half a dozen times. Although the blood flowed freely, Haywood still fought back. In desperation, Preston fired a shot over Haywood's head.

'For God's sake,' Haywood said, cowering from the blast of the pistol so close to his ear, 'don't murder me!'

'I'll blow out your brains unless you yield!' Preston replied, and pressed the muzzle of his pistol to Haywood's head.

Not surprisingly, Haywood surrendered. Only then did Preston call for help from the men he had left outside.

In the meantime, Parkinson had also been busy. Although White had smacked him on the nose, he still managed to grab at the thief's legs as he ran past. White fell and Parkinson struggled with him and bit hard on his hand. When the remainder of the police thundered in, they arrested both White and Haywood.

With the prisoners secure, the police tore the house to pieces to see what they could find. They looked in the cupboards and under the mattress; they rummaged through the clothes and they even lifted the flagstones in the cellar. It was under the latter that they found the evidence for which they were looking. They found a number of dark lanterns; the type favoured by burglars as they had been modified to send only a thin beam of light, so the burglar could see where he was going but there was little chance of the light being seen by others. There were also a large number of skeleton keys, suitable for opening many locks and simple tools such as jemmies, drills and augers. The police lifted the lot, including the woman who had answered the door, and left. It had been a good day.

Huffey White, however, survived to have a long and lucrative career before his eventual and perhaps inevitable execution at Northampton in 1841.

Bodysnatchers

By the third decade of the nineteenth century, Britain was a nation in turmoil. There was mass unemployment in the wake of the Napoleonic War, political upheaval as thousands clamoured for electoral reform, the spread of industrialisation and a growing fear of crime. There were highwaymen on the roads, footpads in the dark streets, pickpockets sliding through the crowds and burglars with a hundred ways of relieving householders of their property. Yet of all the assorted hordes of criminals, probably the most reviled were the bodysnatchers, the resurrection men.

Although the Edinburgh pair, Burke and Hare, has achieved fame for their murderous exploits, resurrection men infested every corner of the country from the Scottish Highlands to the festering alleyways of London. It was a period of technical and medical advances, and teachers of anatomy needed fresh corpses on which to demonstrate the workings of the human body to their students. The law of supply and demand dictated that, with the various medical schools hungry for fresh meat, somebody must find them and often there was little scruple about how the corpses were obtained. It was difficult to obtain a body legally: people hanged could be dissected, as could children who died before they were baptised or some orphans who were not subject to apprenticeship. The other method was by unearthing newly buried corpses, hopefully before decomposition had properly set in. But relatives were not keen to allow their loved ones to be dragged from their graves and cut open in front of an interested audience of students.

Hiding behind the rationality and science of the age was a Celtic knot of interwoven religion and superstition. Many people believed that when Judgement Day arrived, the dead would rise from the grave in the same condition in which they were buried, so if they were dissected by an anatomist, their hopes of successful resurrection were vastly diminished.

The high prices paid for illegally obtained bodies created a number of grave robbers. Some were professionals who specialised in digging up the dead; others were purely local and would go for one or two operations and then sicken of the trade. Naturally, there were defences against such ghouls. Graves were dug deeper than the customary six feet and layered with branches to hamper the urgent spades of resurrection men, mort stones, or huge stone slabs, were placed on top of new graves until the contents were too decomposed to be worth unearthing, locked mort houses, or dead houses, were used to store the newly dead and, most effective of all, volunteer guards were placed at graveyards, hunting the hunters.

But those who sold the bodies had their own repertoire of tricks. A mort stone was a sure marker for a fresh corpse, coffins could be opened from the end as well as the top, so circumventing the difficult top layers of digging, and guards were not always alert in the dark hours of a winter night. Or so the bodysnatchers hoped.

Raid on St John's

At about two in the morning of Monday, 21 October 1824, the four watchmen in St John's Churchyard, Old Haymarket, heard a suspicious noise in the furthest corner of the graveyard. There were only three possible reasons for somebody being in the graveyard at that time of night: a courting couple, a wandering drunk or a grave robber. The watchmen hoped for the first two, but suspected it was the last. At that time the place was in darkness, with the gravestones not even shadows in the night, so although the watchmen tried to peer into the gloom, they saw nothing. The watchmen split up, with one pair moving toward the noises and the other standing guard at the entrance to trap the supposed grave robbers.

The watchmen inside the graveyard found that the robbers had dug up two bodies and had them placed in flour sacks near the wall at St John's Lane. At that point, the wall was lowest and the bodies could most easily be passed out of the graveyard. However, the watchmen either made too much noise or the grave robbers were very alert, for when the watchmen came close the robbers leaped over the wall and into the lane. The second pair of watchmen saw their shadowy shapes, shouted a challenge, broke into a run and pursued. One of the bodysnatchers escaped, but the watchmen chased the other along St John's Lane through Hood Street and caught him in Murray Street. He was a baker by the name of Armstrong and immediately professed his innocence, but his coat and boots were covered with mud from the graveyard so the watchmen had no doubts. Armstrong was handed to the police and was safely locked away in Liverpool's main bridewell. In Liverpool a bridewell meant a police station with cells, whereas in other towns it was a place of lesser punishment than prison: a house of correction. There were a number scattered around the town, each holding the ne'er-do-wells of its own area.

The noise of the scuffle had awakened Mr Holden, the Church

clerk, and he had the foresight to grab a lantern before he ventured into the graveyard. The light bounced from gravestone to gravestone, cast long shadows from the church walls and only highlighted the overall gloom. Holden saw two discarded spades lying beside the two disinterred bodies. He knew that both bodies had been buried only that Sunday, so were still fresh and eminently suitable for the anatomy lab. When he learned that there was a gig standing at the foot of London Road, with a horse in harness all ready for a quick getaway, Holden knew that this was not some drunken escapade, but an organised raid on the graveyard. He had not seen the gig, but he knew his job and was well aware who was most likely to be involved in the bodysnatching trade in Liverpool.

There was one major suspect at Concert Street, off Bold Street, so Holden gathered a posse of watchmen and walked there, with the night gradually fading as dawn threatened the eastern sky. It was about five in the morning when the drumbeat of horse hooves clattered down Bold Street and the grumble of wheels warned of an approaching vehicle. Holden ordered his men to hide and they waited until the gig had passed before they emerged. When the gig stopped at a house, Holden led his men forward; he recognised the driver as a man named William Stewart, who was long suspected of being involved in the resurrection industry. Holden asked him if he had been digging up dead bodies.

Stewart denied any such thing, but he also refused to say where he had been with his gig at that time in the morning, so Holden had him arrested and taken to the bridewell. After both prisoners were questioned, some of the story came out. Armstrong, who had been arrested at the graveyard, had hired the horse and gig at six the previous evening in Leeds Street. The intention had been to dig the bodies up, cover them in the flour sacks, load them on the gig and sell them to an anatomist.

Alderman Gerard heard the case and gave an interesting statement. He said that personally he thought that unearthing dead bodies was essential for the advancement of medical science, but it was his job to prosecute those who break the law, so he sent them for trial.

Stewart was a known professional gravedigger who had already attempted to bribe a watchman with forty shillings at the St John's burial ground. Although that was more than two weeks' wages for a labouring man, the watchmen refused. Stewart did not just rely on chance, but attended the funerals around Liverpool, so he was fully aware of the freshest graves and the best bodies to unearth. Both he and Armstrong were sent to Kirkdale Jail for six months and fined £50.

But that sentence did not deter the Liverpool resurrectionists ...

The cellars in Hope Street

The Rev Mr McGowan was a well-respected man in the Liverpool of the 1820s. In addition to his religious duties, McGowan also ran a school for boys in Hope Street. This street no longer exists, but the memory of what happened here is still remembered. Underneath the school building there was a brace of cellars, one large and one small, connected by a heavy wooden door. The door was never locked, with only a wooden bar holding it shut, so the more inquisitive of the boys were in the habit of moving from one cellar to the other, just for the fun of the thing. In August 1826 the boys were a bit annoyed to find the door locked. They told McGowan, but he reminded them that the tenant of the second cellar had every right to lock his side of the door, and the boys accepted the explanation.

However, after a few days the boys became aware of a strange smell seeping from the second cellar. The smell strengthened and the boys complained to McGowan, who explained that it was mould, and opened the windows of the schoolhouse. The smell remained and increased. The boys endured, gagged and no doubt made typical young boy comments. They got into trouble for looking out the window rather than working at their lessons, but saw some men carrying sacks into the house next door. The smell got worse, coming in waves and gusts. The boys saw a man trundle next door with a handcart full of casks and the smell intensified, so concentrating on their lessons became next to impossible. The smell remained lingering in every corner of the building.

Being boys, and therefore nosy, they wondered what was happening. They watched every movement and got access to the cellar by devious means, and saw two men making up more casks. Rather than sneak around in the shadows, the boys came closer and asked what the casks were for.

'What do you think?' the men asked, but gave nothing away. A few moments later they chased the boys out of the cellar. Other people were equally curious about these coopers who banged away in the closed cellar. They asked the same question, but were given different answers. The casks were apparently to be used to hold anything from whale oil to herring. There was an air of mystery around the cellars in Hope Street.

But however busy the coopers appeared, the tenant of the cellar seemed reluctant to pay his rent to McGowan. A Scotsman named William Gillespie acted as a go-between between John Henderson, one of the tenants and McGowan, and however full of charm and excuses, his pockets seemed empty of money. McGowan asked in vain for his rent, and still the smell and the sound of hammering continued. McGowan was a patient man, but even he was unhappy. He tried to find John Henderson, even visiting his home in Caroline Court, but without success.

In the meantime, the stench continued to pervade the house, but there was a major discovery in the docks.

A number of seamen were loading a fishing smack at George's Dock. They were loading three barrels of salt to be sent to Leith, but the stench from the barrels made it obvious that there was more than just salt inside. The seamen complained to the master, who opened a barrel and investigated: rather than salt to preserve fish there were pale and naked human bodies.

Horrified, the captain opened all three barrels and found more bodies, all naked; eleven in total, a mixture of men, women and even some children. The sight was shocking, so he called in help.

Robert Boughey of the Dock Police was given the daunting job of tracing the bodies and finding who had sent them. In these days before the creation of the uniformed Liverpool Police, Boughey was very much untrained, but he was enthusiastic and all the evidence suggests he was a very capable man. He set to work as quickly as he could and followed a logical line of enquiry. He found the carter who had carried the barrels to the dock, and was told the barrels had been picked up from the schoolhouse in Hope Street. Boughey marched to the house and rapped on the door, probably with a mixture of apprehension at what his reception might be, indignation, disgust and anger.

Rev McGowan answered the door and explained that although he owned the cellar in question, he had rented it out to a Greenock man named John Henderson.

'What does John Henderson do for a living?' Boughey must have asked.

'He is a fish oil merchant,' McGowan told him.

'Have you the key?' Boughey wanted to know. But unfortunately, McGowan did not have the key: there was only one and Henderson had full control.

'In that case,' Boughey decided, 'I'll force the door.'

McGowan did not seem pleased at the prospect, possibly because his property would be damaged and possibly because he knew, or at least suspected, what Boughey might find. He began to bluster, issuing threats of calling lawyers and prosecuting Boughey. Despite his calling and his charitable teaching, the good reverend may not have been as innocent as his clerical collar suggested. Either Boughey saw through the façade, or he was just intent on solving the mystery of the eleven bodies, for he ignored McGowan and booted the door open.

What he found inside shocked him, used as he was to dealing with drunken seaman and all the vices and horrors of the dark alleys around the docks. The cellar was littered with a variety of barrels and sacks, many of which contained bodies. In all there were twenty-two adult bodies in that cellar as well as a barrel full of the bodies of dead children, pickling in brine.

Even at a time when bodysnatching often received media attention, this was a terrible discovery. The police investigated further, checked the local cemeteries and asked the relatives of recently deceased if their loved ones were safely interred. It seemed that the majority of the bodies had been unearthed from the cemetery in Cambridge Street, but the police also suspected that some had never been buried. They thought one of the officials from the Cambridge Street workhouse had sold the bodies of people who had died there. As the inhabitants of the workhouse were paupers, the unemployed and the unfortunate, there was often nobody to care for the deceased, so it would be relatively easy to sell the dead.

The idea of a workhouse official selling the bodies of those who died in his care was not as far-fetched as it may sound. According to Gilbert Henderson's report for the 1832 Royal Commission into the operation of Poor Relief, Liverpool's workhouse could hold as many as 1,750 people and had a rigid regime of twelve-hour working days picking oakum, the proceeds of which helped maintain the establishment.

The eventual outcome of Boughey's investigation led to the arrest of two men, of whom one, Donaldson, was sentenced to a year in jail. The other, Gillespie, was released. Henderson was never traced but the smell would soon dissipate from the schoolhouse and the scholars would be able to return to their studies.

Liverpool in the early years of the century was a lively place, but times were a-changing.

3

The Liverpool Police

In common with every other British city, Liverpool gained its police force in the nineteenth century. That is not to say that the people of Liverpool had been without any form of crime prevention. There was the Night Watch, the Corporation Constabulary and the Dock Watch, each of which had a specific role and a specific area of expertise. Unfortunately, none of the forces was blessed with a good reputation.

Hugh Shimmin wrote a number of articles about Liverpool policing in the nineteenth century and stated that the Night Watch were a 'terror to nobody and an amusement only to mischievously disposed lads.' However, Liverpool was not alone in that. The Night Watchmen in most British cities had the ubiquitous nickname of 'Charlies' and were figures of faint fun to the career thieves, although they were probably fairly proficient in escorting drunks and vagrants to the lock up. The Liverpool Watchmen frequented sentry boxes to protect them from the night wind, which made them splendid targets for rowdy youths who liked to overturn the boxes on top of the Charlies and keep them prisoner inside. They carried clumsy lanterns to pierce the gloom of the unlit streets and long staffs to defend themselves. They were also reputed to resort to drink to ease the burden of their lives. The youths of the town treated the Charlies with so much contempt that in January 1820 several teenagers were jailed for attacking the Watchmen and often people had to use diverse methods to protect their property, from hanging bells on the windows attached to a large central bell, to arming the butler with a blunderbuss gun.

Sooty footprints

In November 1816 a young man named Michael Fennigan took a fancy to burgling a house in Pool Lane. He waited until three in the morning, when even the most enthusiastic of late night revellers had returned from the pubs and the streets were empty and dark, then carried a ladder into the yard beside Mr Howie's house. Placing the ladder against the wall, he climbed to the roof and slithered down the chimney to the room beneath. The room was directly above Howie's grocery shop, and Fennigan descended the steep stairs, leaving a trail of sooty footsteps in his wake.

He had either found keys in the room above, or had come provided with false keys, for he opened the door to the shop. There was a dog lying on the floor, but it seemed to be asleep, for it made no sound as Fennigan opened the till and took out £47. Unfortunately for him, his trail of sooty footprints was easy to follow and a Watchman picked him up not long after. They were ponderous and often inefficient, but the Watchmen were useful from time to time.

But even so, they were not the best people to defend the respectable of the growing city of Liverpool against the criminal element that at times threatened to take over. At frequent intervals, the Watchmen had to cope with the savage pub fights that could break out at any time.

Batting Liverpudlians

In June 1828 there was a fight outside the Seven Stars pub in Lower Chisenhale Street, when a number of men began to argue, and then started a mass brawl, in which one man was killed. The supposed killers fled, but one was found in August at Newton and locked in jail at Lancaster.

On Monday, 19 August 1828 there was a fight in a pub in Vauxhall Road. Once again it started with an argument between a number of men and ended when a corkcutter named Joseph Hughes challenged a blacksmith named James McGinnis to a fight. For some reason the brother of the smith, John McGinnis, offered to fight in his brother's place. They met at the Brickfields in Vauxhall Road and hundreds of spectators gathered to watch the fight.

Both men had been drinking heavily so the fight was short, if brutal. The corkcutter hammered John McGinnis into insensibility within a few moments and the defeated man was carried off to Portland Street, where he lodged. He was badly hurt and died, so the police began a search for Hughes. The corkcutter did not try to hide but gave himself up right away.

Varieties of law keepers

By day, a force known as the Corporation Constabulary was meant to curb the lawless, but allegedly those who actually remained on their designated beat were notorious for taking bribes to turn the other way if there was criminal activity.

The remit of the third force, the Dock Watch, did not extend beyond the area of the docks. They were formed in 1811 and had the unenviable task of watching for petty pilfering, as well as ensuring that drunken seamen did not brawl too often or fall into the dark waters. It may have been frustration at the inept behaviour of the Night Watch, but the Dock Watch had the habit of arresting the Charlies and tossing them into the lock ups at the docks, alongside the reeking seamen.

By 1832 there was a fourth force, the Parks Police, who had proved themselves inept when a thousand-strong mob besieged the cholera hospital in Toxteth Park, but redeemed themselves in subsequent years when they protected all the green spaces of the town.

Types of crime

As well as the expected crimes of violence and overt theft, there was covert theft by fraud and deception that blossomed at any sporting occasion. For instance, in the Maghull races in June 1834 there were thirty known gaming tables and the following month, the Aintree race meeting was a haven for gambling, legal and illicit.

The roads were crowded with vehicles: from the four-horse drag filled with members of the swell mob, the gambling elite, to the humble dung cart filled with the lower orders and pulled by a single worn out hack. There were also horsemen and pedestrians. The crowd was down on previous years because the magistrates banned any gaming tables. In the terminology of the day, the 'blacklegs, swindlers and their allies' made a living by preying on the unwary. However, there were thimble riggers on the roads and by-ways, and in Clayton Square there was one room noted for gambling, but where on previous years the door had stood open for crowds of gamers, now there was only a smooth-tongued man who informed the hopeful that there were gentlemen upstairs who had paid a guinea subscription for a private game, and more than fifty men were there. The authorities had managed to lessen gambling, but not stop it completely.

There was always robbery of course.

In the autumn of 1835, the suburbs of Liverpool were hit by a gang of robbers who prowled the streets looking for any house that appeared unguarded and worthy of a visit. On 9 October that year, they tried

Prescott Road, moving into the house of Miss Johnson, right beside St Anne's Church. They got about £12 in cash as well as a fine watch with a gold chain that could easily be pawned in any of the less reputable pawnbrokers in town. On Wednesday, 15 October, they were in Knotty Ash Lane where they escaped with silver plate and linen.

It might have been that same gang that appeared at Broad Green and attempted to rob the house of a Mr McCammon. However, McCammon was more alert. He heard them outside, opened his window and blasted the general direction with a double-barrelled shotgun. He saw around seven men scurry out of the dark and lift the man he had hit, so gave them the second barrel as they ran. McCammon watched but there were no more disturbances for his house that night.

On Friday, 23 October, they came again, this time to Brunswick Road. Having been successful on two occasions, their confidence had increased and they took the time to slice out half of one of the panels from the house of a Mr Rose and were in the process of entering when they heard a noise from inside. Leaving the house un-robbed, they fled to Marsden Street where they had better luck and burgled a house of a fowling piece worth £6. They collected some other items, but one of the inhabitants was up and moving around, so they fled again. Like so many burglars, these men were never caught. Liverpool needed an efficient police force.

Watchmen's success

The Watchmen, however, were not always unreliable. On Thursday, 12 October 1835 Robert Shaughnessey, one of the night patrol, was on his beat in Toxteth Park when a middle-aged couple hurried up to him. They told him that they had heard somebody moaning and were afraid to investigate. Shaughnessey walked to the place and found a man lying on his back, badly injured and 'beaten out of all resemblance.' Although he had a watch, a snuffbox and a single shilling in his possession, his right pocket had been cut away, a sure sign that he had been robbed. Shaughnessey had him taken to the police office and then to the infirmary.

The police discovered that he was James Hurst, married to Anne, and he had come to Liverpool from Bristol around two months previously. They did not intend to stay in Liverpool but hoped to emigrate to America, in the meantime lodging at the house of Mr McKean in Redcross Street.

There was another lodger named John Maginnis in the house, and he remained there when the Hursts relocated to a rented cellar and kitchen across the road. The night of the attack, Maginnis had called on Hurst and asked him if he wanted to see some cheap furniture in Vauxhall Road. Hurst agreed and that was the last Anne saw of her husband, until the police notified her he had been attacked.

There was no hesitation in arresting Maginnis, who had a fresh scar on his face. Maginnis denied any assault and said that he had spent the night with his partner, Margaret Reece, who had given him the scar. Margaret neither confirmed nor denied Maginnis's statement.

The police took Maginnis to the infirmary and asked Hurst to say what had happened. Hurst tried to rise from the bed and shook his fist at Maginnis, so the police had to restrain the still badly injured man. Hurst said that Maginnis had taken him to a lonely part of Vauxhall Road and asked for money. When Hurst refused, Maginnis knocked him down. Hurst remembered nothing else until he was found by the police. He had broken jaw and cheekbone, and a large dent in the back of his skull, where he had been struck with a heavy instrument. In this case the Watchman had proved eminently capable of doing his job.

Beginning of the police

In June 1834 the Commissioners of the Watch decided to appoint four policemen to patrol the streets of Liverpool by day, to 'prevent street nuisances and police the various by-laws. That was a pointer that the authorities were taking crime worries seriously and an indication of greater things to come.

However, such a piecemeal arrangement might have been adequate for a small town in the eighteenth century, but with nineteenth-century expansion and the onset of industrialisation, to say nothing of increasing trade, Liverpool needed a more efficient and modern police force. In the early 1830s crime was thought to be increasing; there had been unrest over the political situation, trade was not great and the streets were dangerous with footpads and desperate unemployed men. It was no wonder that in April 1835, a bill was produced for the Liverpool Day Police, with the mayor and four commissioners in charge.

Finally, in 1836 the Liverpool City Police were formed as a fresh start to combat crime. Superintendent Michael James Whitty, once of the Night Watch, filled the ranks with the best men from the Night Watch and Corporation Constabulary. Whitty was a Roman Catholic Irishman, a journalist and one of the most popular men in the city. He had the unenviable task of creating an efficient police force out of some very rough material, and with boundaries that had expanded to take in Everton, Fazakerley, Kirkdale and Walton-on-the-Hill.

Whitty surveyed his 360 men, issued them with stout batons and ordered them to clean up the crime and disorder that was rife in the city. The influx of so many blue-coated men with top hats and long batons had an immediate effect, and within the year the batons were recalled but the job of the police continued.

With the 1836 formation of the Liverpool Police, the town was split into two divisions, North and South with the boundary running from the Mersey along Water Street, Dale Street, Shaws Brow (William Brown Street), London Road and Prescott Street. Each division had their own bridewells: the North had one in Exchange Street East and one in Vauxhall Road, while South

Division had Duncan Street East and the pragmatically named Brick Street.

The men had a regular, steady job at a time when such things were scarce, but they were hard worked, with twelve-hour days, no days off and a wage of eighteen shillings, which was about average for a working man. There was a high turnover of officers, who had to be literate and pass a medical before being issued with their uniform, plus a truncheon and pair of handcuffs. There was a definite promotion grid, from third-class constable to first class, and possibly to sergeant and above.

Police at work

Even with the prospect of a steady job and promotion, it was no fun being a policeman in Liverpool in the 1830s. At about half past four in the morning of Sunday, 5 June 1837 Constable Robins was on duty in Hill Street when he heard a terrible noise of shouting and hurried to the spot, to see an altercation between a group of men. Robins urged them to break up and go quietly home, but instead the men ganged up on him. The constable sprang his rattle to summon assistance as he was heavily outnumbered.

Knowing that more police were on their way, the men ran to a nearby house in Wolfe Street, slammed shut the door and tried to barricade themselves inside. Robins watched where they went and when his colleagues arrived, he led them to the house. Robins was first through the door and reeled back when somebody cracked him over the head with an iron fender. The other police officers tried to force their way in, but the defenders were powerful men and had the advantage of a fixed position. The police recoiled, battered and bruised.

At that point, Inspector Hatch arrived with a larger number of police. A civilian had come to the station to tell him that there was a riot and he had come as fast as he could. The increased body of police kicked open the outer door and charged inside. The group of men had retreated to the head of a flight of stairs and were waiting there, jackets off, shirtsleeves rolled up and bedposts and staffs as weapons. Hatch immediately recognised five of them: Michael McGrave, John Doyle, John Curtfield, Michael Kelley and Hugh Keenan. All were known bad men with a reputation for violence and disruption. Hatch knew that a frontal assault on such men would bring casualties to his officers, so tried to negotiate.

'If the man that attacked the constable gives himself up, the others can go free,' Hatch said, and added that the criminals could not win for the police would just continue to come until they had their man.

Keenan gave the reply: he pushed to the front of the men and said: 'You bloody bastards! If you come one step forward I will have your life.'

'I won't stand to hear Mr Hatch threatened in that way,' Constable James said, and mounting the stairs, he landed a mighty blow on Keenan's head with his truncheon that knocked him to the bed. Unfortunately, one of the other defenders intervened and knocked James on the head. The defenders threw him bodily down the stairs. A second policeman rushed up to take his place but was also knocked down. Keenan, recovering from the constable's blow, swung a mighty whack at Hatch with an iron rod. Hatch parried but the force of the blow felled him to the floor.

Once more the police withdrew, leaving the group of men as masters of the situation, but Hatch was not done yet. He sent for more reinforcements and a ladder. While Hatch and his men remained in possession of the ground floor of the house, the third group of police clambered up the ladder to the roof, broke open a skylight and swarmed inside, to overpower the men.

All five were arrested and later imprisoned, but it was an example of how a minor incident could escalate in the Liverpool of the 1830s.

Statistics

The police faced some sort of danger every day, for the idea of a uniformed police was not popular with the working classes and, when fighting drunk, many men and women would consider the police as a legitimate target for their frustration. The police themselves were no angels, with over 600 instances of drunkenness between the 574 men in 1839 alone, but as drunkenness was common among the general population, perhaps that should not be surprising. The majority of police did not stay long in the position, with many leaving after one year. The stress of the job mixed with the poor pay and unpopularity must have been powerful disincentives for remaining as a police officer.

However, Liverpool Police became more professional year on year. As well as preventing crime and arresting criminals, the police had a vast number of duties from ensuring there were no obstructions in the streets to preventing suicides. The night shift was always the more active, as that was when the pubs came out and the prowlers, burglars and footpads were more likely to be on the hunt.

Superintendents on the job

In 1843, the year before Whitty retired, the police added firefighting to their duties. With Whitty's retirement, Henry Miller was the new Superintendent of Police. He arrived on the steamer from Glasgow in April 1844, and announced his arrival as Whitty arranged a march-past of the entire force for his inspection. However, in a six-month spell, he managed to reduce the efficiency of the force and make himself unpopular for his authoritarian attitude.

Miller was replaced by an ex-Metropolitan policeman named Matthew Dowling. He had a tough baptism of fire, with riots in the streets almost immediately after he took office, but things improved when the veteran Whitty came out of retirement to give a hand. Even so, the situation was so bad that the army had to be called out to help the police, but eventually Dowling and Whitty got the unrest under control and then there were just the usual crimes of murder, assault and theft for the police to worry about.

The next major worry was in 1848 when, as well as the possibility of a Chartist revolution, there was an outbreak of highway robbery outside Liverpool. Dowling was not a man to bow down before circumstances and met fire with fire. He armed fifty men with cutlasses and sent them to patrol the roads. Other officers remained within the town, where there was also danger.

For example, on 5 December 1848, a band of three men dressed like railway navvies were seen lounging around Bootle Lane. Passers-by gave them a wide berth, but the beat policeman watched them closely, sure that they intended robbery or worse. He signalled to his closest colleagues and they waited, hoping for something more active than merely moving beggars along or checking on unregulated midden heaps.

When a horse-drawn cart moved slowly up the lane, the three jumped on it and demanded money, but three police officers ran up to stop the highway robbery. The men showed fight, but when the police drew the cutlasses they then carried, the would-be robbers surrendered at once.

In 1852 Captain John Greig became Head Constable of the Liverpool Police. He remained in office for nearly thirty years as a social reformer, as well as a law enforcer. In 1857 he promoted the idea of more open spaces for the people of Liverpool. Many lived in terribly overcrowded streets with no access to light or fresh air, but over the next couple of decades new parks opened up around the town. One of the more significant was Newsham in 1868, which was the model for New York's Central Park. Newsham was not merely a lung for the overcrowded inhabitants of the town, for Queen Victoria and High Court judges stayed in Newsham House when they came to visit

Liverpool; quite a contrast from the congested streets in which so much of the population existed. There were more parks later: in 1870 Stanley Park was opened and Sefton Park in 1872, all under the auspices of John Greig.

The most drunken town in England

The Liverpool police had more to worry about than green spaces. There was the rising drinking problem. In the 1860s there was increasing concern that Liverpool was the most drunken town in England. A survey of some of the major industrial and trading towns found that while Plymouth had one drink-related arrest for every 361 people, Bristol had one for every 245 people, Birmingham one in 231 and Newcastle one for every ninety-five, Liverpool had an arrest for every thirty-three.

The Instructions for the Liverpool Constabulary Force said: 'although a constable is always to act with firmness, he is never to interfere needlessly. If a drunken person is disorderly, he is to persuade him to go home; if, however, he is riotous and will not go, he is to call for sufficient assistance and convey him as quietly as possible to a station.'

Handling drunks remained a problem throughout the century. At this period the police wore uniforms modelled on the Peelers who patrolled London. They wore a dark blue swallow-tailed coat with brass buttons and the number of the officer on the shoulder, also in brass. They wore dark blue trousers in winter and white in summer, held up by a stout black leather belt with an ornate buckle decorated with the Liverpool coat of arms. To complete the picture was an official armlet and a leather top hat.

The top hat was not purely for decoration. The effect was to make the men look taller, which might have been impressive to the criminals and gutter scourers that infested every city in the country. Additionally, it also served a secondary purpose of protecting the head of the wearer. It is not easy to strike somebody on the skull if they have a tall leather hat balanced there.

Indelicate policeman

Despite their practical and smart uniform, sometimes the police could be less than delicate in the manner they handled the public. John Murphy would vouch for that. Not that he was any angel himself. In October 1867 he was a cab driver in Liverpool, but unlike most who had a special bond with their horse, Murphy was often seen hitting and abusing the animal. One version of the subsequent story claims that on the night of 10 October 1867, George Twiss, the Night Inspector of the Royal Society for the Prevention of Cruelty to Animals, approached Murphy in Williamson Square and spoke to him about the proper care of horses. Murphy did not appreciate the free advice and responded by punching and jostling Twiss for his pains.

Twiss sought help and returned with Constable O'Boyle, who asked Murphy for his name and address, and when he reached for his notebook, according to O'Boyle, Murphy shouted: 'What is it to you?' He then punched him to the ground and began to kick him, as a crowd gathered and seemed to encourage the attack. Constable Cross had heard the disturbance and hurried to help. He grabbed Murphy at once, turned him around and threw him face first onto the ground, in which position he arrested him.

Murphy had friends who told a different story. There was a fellow cab driver named Nicholas Wright who claimed to have witnessed the whole thing. Wright said that Twiss had been checking the horses and came near to Murphy and accused him of 'thrusting something at him.' When Murphy denied it, Twiss had said 'I will have satisfaction' and left, to return with the policeman. When they arrived, Twiss held up his official lamp close to Murphy's face. Murphy asked him to lower the lantern, but then, according to Wright, the policeman O'Boyle had punched Murphy full in the mouth and Twiss had begun to kick him at the same time. While they were doing so, another policeman arrived and joined in, with the attack being so vicious and sustained that the police broke one of their official batons over Murphy.

A cab-owner named William Watson also witnessed the events. He said that Twiss was examining the horses, which he was legally entitled to do, when he accused Murphy of throwing something at him. Murphy denied the charge and Twiss brought over Constable O'Boyle, who punched him in the mouth. The second constable joined in, kicking Murphy on the legs and groin. Watson agreed that the police had broken a staff over Murphy's back. When a further two cabmen each gave independent and supporting evidence at the hearing, it became obvious that it had been the police who had been the aggressors in this case. The charge against Murphy was dismissed.

'A sort of ulcer among the police force'

Not all police were angels. Although the police were guardians of law and order, and formed the first line of defence between the respectable and the sinister armies of the underworld, there were occasions when temptation got the better of them and they joined the other side. Perhaps that was natural for some people whose lives were always on the grey fringe between good and evil, and who were not overpaid for what was a dangerous and often thankless job.

In October 1878 the ship *Antiope* was berthed in Salthouse Dock, in the southern dock system of Liverpool. She was in the final stage of loading and nearly ready to sail for Australia in just a few days time. However, there were still a few items to get on board, including a large bale of cloth. The bale was carted to the dock and left on the quay in the normal manner, and that was the last known about it for quite some time. One day it was there, the next it was gone, so the port authorities believed the bale had been loaded, and the ship's captain thought his cargo was intact. Yet, that single bale was to be a significant factor in uncovering a network of police corruption.

As a major port, Liverpool docks was a natural target for thieves of various types, from the normal petty pilfering, which would be expected, to major theft. However, the port employed a dedicated body of professional police who normally kept a lid on the worst excesses. And then in 1878 and early 1879, it became apparent that there was a massive problem at the docks. Ships left the port and when they were far out to sea, the captain discovered that their stores had been tampered with. Sometimes even the stores that had been checked by the Customs Officers and were secured by a customs seal were missing. As the customs seal was placed on valuable stores such as tobacco and spirits, the thieves would make a good return for their labour, while the morale of the crew would plummet when they discovered that such luxuries were missing. This was no act of petty pilfering by a sneak thief, but something much larger.

Every week there were complaints and reports going to Chief Constable Greig of thefts and depredations. Greig selected the best of his detectives to investigate what was becoming a major worry, and ordered his dock police to be extra vigilant. Although there were some arrests with a couple of dock workers accused of minor theft, ships' masters continued to complain, and the detectives were not much further forward. Despite everything that the professional guardians of the law could do, it was mere chance that led to the initial breakthrough.

On 29 December 1878 police Inspector Jackson had seen a number of men behaving furtively in the narrow alleys just outside the docks. Knowing about the thefts, Jackson watched them for a while and realised that they were carrying what looked like sacks. He yelled a challenge and four of the men fled, but the fifth ignored him. Jackson ran forward and the man glanced round, saw him watching and ran, with Jackson in hot pursuit through the narrow streets. There were a confusing few moments of tag in the dark, but eventually Jackson collared one of the suspects and held him tight.

The police discovered the suspect was named Humphrey Cronin and the sack held bottles of wine and spirits. The police investigated Cronin's known colleagues and friends, and gradually rounded them up, to be eliminated from enquiries or investigated further. When one man named Albert Jones was brought in for questioning, he turned informant and opened up an entirely new line of enquiry.

According to Jones, there had been five people involved in this theft. Jones and Cronin, together with John Flood and Peter Davies, met a labourer named James Tomkins by the Salthouse Dock. When the men boarded the barque *Delscey*, destined for Callao in South America, Cronin took charge. He was a marine storekeeper but also doubled as a shipkeeper, the watchman who was left to care for a ship when nobody else was on board. He was therefore a man with responsibility and in whom a great deal of trust was placed. In this case, the trust was misplaced as Cronin unlocked a padlock on the hatch cover, slid it open and guided them below. He had no fear of the police: Flood and Davies were both constables in the dock police. They took off their uniform coats, so they were partly disguised. Cronin knew his way around *Delscey* and led them to the lower hold, where the wine and spirits were stowed. Drink was always a popular choice for thieves as there was a ready market and it was portable.

The thieves were quite relaxed: they knew there was no possibility of discovery, so after sampling some personal refreshments, they packed dozens of bottles into sacks and brought them ashore. They were cheerfully carrying them to Cronin's house when they noticed Inspector Jackson watching them. Once again, Cronin took the lead. He ushered them into a narrow entry, 'Come in here,' he said and three of the men followed. Unfortunately, Tomkins was partly deaf and continued to walk.

Jackson raced up, but rather than Tomkins, he grabbed Cronin, who slipped free and ran, but was eventually caught again. Jones ran to Cronin's house and removed anything that he thought might be incriminating. But by that time the police had Cronin under arrest and were interrogating him.

Around the same time, the police had another slice of luck. Somebody had accidentally dropped a package of iron from the quayside into the dock and one of the dock gatemen was given the task of fishing it out. However, instead of hooking the iron, he caught the canvas wrapper of the bale of cloth from *Antelope*, complete with the maker's marks. The wrapper had been weighed down with stones and cast into the dock. Until that moment nobody had known that the bale had been stolen, and now the police began further enquiries.

Two policemen, Constable John Flood once more and Constable William Hough, together with another shipkeeper named William Edmonston and the ubiquitous Humphrey Cronin had stolen the bale from the quayside. Edmonston had been the shipkeeper on *Antelope*, Flood and Hough were the local beat policemen and this time Cronin had helped in the theft and acted as the receiver, the man who sold the stolen goods on. At first they had not intended to steal the entire bale, and had cut off only one segment of cloth, but when they realised they could not make the bale back up so stole the whole thing. They carried it, roll of cloth by roll of cloth, to the engine house at the Albert Basin, then whistled for a cab to take it to Cronin's home.

Albert Jones, the man who informed on his colleagues, was an ex-policeman who had been dismissed for being absent from his beat. There seemed no code of honour among the thieves and the more the police asked, the more they learned. The police marked constables John Flood, Peter Davies and William Hough off their list of decent officers. They listened as Jones admitted to having been a petty thief for a number of years, but only after he met Cronin did he move to a higher level.

Two of the criminal police were ex-seamen and therefore skilled at climbing masts and rigging, so it was nothing to them to clamber over the highest railing and fence to get at the cargoes. On at least one occasion the police members of the gang had robbed a ship, and then put the blame on innocent dockers. The criminal police arrested the dockers and charged them with the theft, but fortunately the legal process sought more evidence and the men were released. However, the resultant suspicion lost them their jobs and a lot of trust until the truth was revealed months later. Jones claimed that having police on their side made it easier to steal from the cargoes of ships in the dock, but his unsupported word was not enough to prove his story or give evidence enough for an arrest.

Detective Inspector Cozens was handed the case. While he could not uncover every theft over the past several months, he could concentrate on the two most obvious: the wine and the bale of cloth. Rather than just the few bottles that Jackson had uncovered, the thieves were accused of taking eighteen cases of wine and spirits, each holding twelve bottles. The bottles were apparently to be sold to a forty-two-year-old publican named William King, whose premises were on the corner of Park Road and North Hill Street. King was yet another ex-policeman, but had been booted out of the force for some misdemeanour. He had been a cow-keeper for some years and finally became a publican; at the initial hearing he resolutely denied any knowledge of Jones or the sixty bottles of stolen alcohol. However, at the trial in April he changed his plea to guilty.

At the hearing in January 1879, Jones said that Cronin had repeatedly admitted having 'done something' at the docks and asked him to come along, so 'something could be done', meaning that they could steal something. He hinted at many more thefts from the docks, but the trial concentrated only on the two. The accused were all found guilty. The police were given seven years penal servitude each; Cronin and Tomkin five years penal servitude, and King was given fifteen months with hard labour. The judge said he feared there were others among the police who were also dishonest, a 'sort of ulcer among the police force [. . .] that must be rooted out.'

Although the warning was clear, the bulk of the Liverpool police were honest men. They were not angels, but dedicated men performing a herculean task in very difficult conditions. A few bad apples did not contaminate the entire force, but, if anything, served to highlight the basic honesty and decency of the thousands of men who did not turn to the criminal path. More often the police were dedicated to their job and were the victims of countless acts of aggression.

Police on horseback

In 1880 Liverpool officially became a city and the next year, with John Nott-Bower as Head Constable, it obtained a number of wagons that would carry a body of men to quell riots or fights. In 1886 Nott-Bower also brought mounted police into the city, an innovation that proved invaluable in helping stop civic disorder. Liverpool was the first city after London to have such a unit. Often the mounted police did not have to act; the sight of these tall, purposely grim-faced men on powerful horses was enough to quieten down riotous youths and bring angry men to their senses.

As ordinary beat police knew little about working on horseback, Nott-Bower asked the experts. Troop Sergeant Stephen Sales of the 7th Hussars was brought in, given the rank of Inspector and handed the formidable task of creating the mounted police out of nothing except Nott-Bower's idea. He proved a good choice. He selected and bought eight horses that year. However, he was not in charge for long, with Sergeant Major James Nimrod Race of the 13th Hussars appointed as superintendent soon after.

The Mounted Section had a number of duties including the transport of prisoners, patrolling the streets and policing crowds, as well as acting as despatch riders in the days before telephones or even telegraphs were common. It must have been quite a sight to see a blue-uniformed man pushing his horse to the limit through the narrow city streets. In the closing years of the century, the men of the mounted section were not ordinary policemen who were taught to ride, but were recruited exclusively from the British cavalry regiments, so they were already expert riders and used to the discipline of a uniformed service. By 1896 there were thirty-six tough mounted police in Liverpool, based in Hatton Garden and ready to deal with any emergency. The police horses were hard worked animals: as well as crowd control and patrol duties, they also pulled the fire engines and ambulances, and the carriage of the Chief Constable – his open phaeton in summer and closed brougham in winter. These horses were as highly-trained as the men.

Nott-Bower added other instruments to the police armoury as he made use of the then new-fangled gadget, the telephone. He was said to have stated that 'there were streets in the Scotland Road Division which were unsafe for respectable people to enter and where even the police could not patrol alone.'

Bower did his best to end this state of affairs. In his time, the richer citizens of Liverpool demanded more protection for their persons and their wealth. His horse patrols and improved communications helped make the Liverpool Police one of the most efficient forces in the country.

In 1902 Leonard Dunning took over as Chief Constable, but by that time pay and conditions had improved and the number of crimes had diminished, either through better policing or because the overall morals of the population had altered, or there was better education and job prospects than in the desperate days of the 1830s and 1840s. There was even a pension scheme!

Police officers still had a hard and often thankless task, but they had gained new respect from the majority of the population, and if many people still viewed them with dislike, it is possible that these malcontents had other things on their mind other than an honest life.

4

The Strange Affairs of Ann Crellin

One of the most romantic images in eighteenth- and nineteenth-century history is of an eloping couple fleeing to Gretna Green in Scotland. The image is usually the same: the laughing young people running from enraged parents, the carriage rattling through the night, lamps gleaming and horses straining, the glances behind to see if they are being pursued, the arrival at Gretna and the rushed ceremony at the anvil. It is a picture of daring and intrigue, laced with love and spiced with a dash of adventure, and strangely enough, there was a lot of truth in these images. The marriage laws in Scotland were easier than those in England, so if a young English couple shared a love of which their parents did not approve, they did have the option of galloping over the Border to tie the knot officially and then there was nothing that their parents could do to alter a *fait accompli*. However, there was also a strong streak of commercial cynicism inherent in even the most smiling of Gretna events.

Commercial reality

When the era of runaway marriages were at their height, the inns of Carlisle acted as agents between the lovers and the 'priests' of Gretna who performed the actual ceremony. These inns competed with each other to capture the runaways' money. They had post-chaises ready to carry the young couples to selected places and 'priests' in Gretna – with whom they had an arrangement – and the priests and Carlisle innkeepers shared the wedding fee. These same Carlisle inns would send people to waylay the pursuing parents and either slow them down or misdirect them, so the inn's clients and fees were safe. The marriage fees would vary, depending on the ability of the groom to pay, but could be as high as £100 if he was well-heeled and desperate. As much as 60 per cent of that fee could find its way back south to the Carlisle innkeeper. However, if the pursuers arrived at a rival inn, the post-chaise drivers from that inn would whip their horses after the runaways, all the faster to remove or discredit a rival. However, sometimes the situation was more complicated and the bride was not quite the nervous youngster escaping her parents.

A woman of property and substance

Miss Ann Crellin was no dove-eyed teenager eager to attain a handsome young groom, but a middle-aged woman of fifty-two, broad of features, with a high forehead and a roman nose. She habitually wore black satin, a black veil and a black bonnet, giving her quite a formidable appearance as she walked the streets of Liverpool. However, she was perhaps not the most moral woman in town and was not blessed with an abundance of intelligence, but she did have property and substance. It was this substance that made her a target for a number of hopeful suitors. One of these rapacious men was Samuel Martin Copeland.

If Miss Crellin's money was perhaps more attractive than Miss Crellin, neither was Copeland the most handsome of suitors, being pale faced, so thin as to be gaunt, unhealthily consumptive in appearance and with a look that all the cares of the world had descended on his shoulders. He was also married to somebody else, but hid that small inconvenience from his prospective wife by dropping his last name and calling himself Samuel Martin, and not mentioning his wife.

It was about in August 1840 when Copeland first arrived at Crellin's door. Crellin had posted a notice that her house in Seymour Street was to let and Copeland came to make enquiries. There was an instant spark between them and Copeland became a regular visitor after that, with Crellin a willing participant in the relationship. They met about twice a week, with Copeland sometimes alone and sometimes accompanied by a friend of his named Captain Tomkinson. Copeland made it obvious that he was interested in more than friendship with Crellin, and quickly proposed marriage, which she rebuffed in a friendly manner. He tried again and again, but was always met with a polite refusal or no answer at all.

In all events Copeland was not put off, and when Crellin caught the packet boat for the Isle of Man on 8 September that year, he booked a passage on the same vessel. They did not seem to travel together, but he manipulated a meeting on the island and when she returned to Liverpool in early November, Copeland seemed keen on continuing their relationship. He came to her new lodgings at Norton Street, this time with a man named Bulkeley, and again insisted that he wished to marry her. Copeland would not take no for an answer and as time passed, he became even more insistent. He called at Norton Street every day to push his case and ensure she did not have an opportunity to forget him. The two went out together, sometimes with others, and often they drank more than was sensible. Eventually, Copeland wore her down and she agreed to his demands. She accepted his proposal and no doubt he claimed to be the happiest man in the world.

'Now stick up for me and I will go and bring him.'

Once Crellin had agreed to be married, she and Copeland visited an attorney called John Nixon Thompson to arrange a marriage settlement. A friend of Copeland, Mrs Margaret Jones, also came along. Crellin had a private meeting with Thompson first, told him that her intended was surnamed Martin, which was the name she knew him by, and asked Thompson to ensure that all her property was in her own name. She added, 'Now stick up for me and I will go and bring him.'

Copeland and Jones came into Thompson's office, and Copeland complained that it was strange they had been 'acquainted nearly twelve months', but she had never insisted that she should have control of all her own property before. He thought it would be fairer that, as her husband-to-be, half of her possessions belonged to him and should be legally recorded as such.

'No,' Crellin said, 'I will have it all or I will not marry you or any other man.'

Copeland turned the argument around and said he would 'leave it to Thompson to say what was right and usual in such circumstances,' but if he thought that the solicitor would play it his way, he would be disappointed. Thompson told him that Crellin had a 'perfect right to exercise her own judgement and settle it as she thought fit.' Indeed, Thompson advised Crellin 'to have it so settled.'

Perhaps concerned about Copeland's preoccupation with Crellin's fortune, Thompson asked him privately how much he thought she had. Copeland replied 'about £50,000', so must have been disappointed when Thompson told him she had 'less than £15,000.' Copeland claimed it was 'not worth my while being troubled by it.' However, he still insisted that he should get half, but Crellin was unmoved and left with Mrs Jones. The marriage document was not made up and from then on their relationship was all downhill. On 26 February the couple broke up.

Crellin moved her lodgings again around that time, to move in with a Mrs Chamley. She still knew Copeland as Martin, and the situation became very confused for a while. Bulkeley, Copeland's friend and landlord, recommended a good lodging for Crellin in Lodge Lane.

The affair of McGill

It must have come as a shock to Crellin when a man named Duval informed her of Copeland's married state, but Duval was only the first of a whole queue of others who came to tell her, so it seemed that all of Liverpool had known. Crellin must have wondered why all these people kept so quiet when Copeland was courting her. Duval was all charm and smiles, and seemed genuine as he introduced Crellin to a thirty-year-old Irishman named John McGill, who was obviously eager to be friendly with her money and possibly also with her. They met on the same day Crellin waved farewell to her previous suitor, and McGill proposed marriage without delay. Having apparently learned nothing from her time with Copeland, Crellin became friendly with McGill very quickly, but in the meantime, Copeland had not finished with her, or rather with his designs on her money.

Although Crellin had dropped any plans for marriage, Copeland followed her on a visit to Mrs Jones' house and threatened legal action if she did not hold to her promise of marriage. The legal term was 'breach of promise' and it was not uncommon for courts to hear such cases. There were witnesses present, including Mr and Mrs Jones and a Mrs Parkinson but, strangely, nobody seemed to take into consideration the fact that an already married man could not claim a second wife.

Extortion

Copeland obviously wished to prove he was not completely heartless. He relented to the extent of saying that he would drop any legal action for the meagre sum of £250, or about four years' wages for a working man. With no desire to go to court, Crellin handed over the money. Unfortunately, that was not the end of the matter, for Richard Jones claimed he held some documents that negated Copeland's withdrawal, but if Crellin gave him £20, he would destroy them. When Crellin refused to hand over a single penny, Mrs Jones urged her husband to 'get £3 from her if you can!'

Jones continued to press his case, mentioning other documents that he and Parkinson allegedly had, which would also mean Crellin was forced to marry Copeland. He gave the same offer: he would destroy the papers for a few pounds. This time Crellin crumpled, agreed and handed over the money. Once she had got into the hands of Duval, McGill and their friends, Crellin could not escape as they pretended to befriend her but used her as a milch-cow and dupe.

Merry-go-round

They dragged her around Liverpool on fool's errands, always seeking to part her from her money. They took her to visit a Dr Dryden where they had a party with the drink flowing free; they visited a lighthouse and toasted it with more drink. Sometime about now McGill again proposed marriage, but Crellin laughed him off, saying it would 'want consideration'. He pulled back but kept company with her, smiling and laughing, always with one or more of his circle of friends around to ensure she did not slip away.

On one occasion, Thomas Rogerson, a friend of McGill's, gave her a glass of what Crellin described as 'dark liquid', but she was not quite as naïve as she appeared and she threw it away untouched. That same day the party took her to St Paul's Church and told her she was to be married to John McGill there and then.

'No,' Crellin said, 'not until my property is settled,' and this marriage ceremony also fell through. But still she did not learn, or perhaps she was playing both ends against the middle.

They visited various places in Liverpool, and the women of the party advised Crellin to try and get her £250 back from Copeland. They told her of various places that he could be, such as the White Bear in Dale Street. Jones hailed a cab and took Crellin there, to find that Copeland had just left. He had recently left the Vulture Inn too, when they tried there. They followed that damned elusive Copeland to Roby, to the Jones' house and to St James Walk, but each time he was elsewhere.

They wandered back to the Jones' and their friends invited Crellin to an apparently respectable house in central Liverpool. A twenty-nine-year-old woman called Mrs Jane Clayton was the host and handed her a full glass of a dark liquid she did not recognise, but this time, possibly already half drunk and certainly weary, she drank anyway. Jane Clayton was a 'woman of bad character' and possibly a full-blown prostitute.

The next thing Crellin admitted to remembering was waking up in bed beside John McGill, with the disreputable Jane Clayton making up the threesome. What was worse, they were no longer in Liverpool, but in Gretna Green in Scotland.

The journey north

She had no memory at all of her journey, but others had taken note of the strange party who had passed through their midst. Eliza Mawdsley, who helped run an inn in Oldham Street, remembered her. It was around four in the afternoon of St Patrick's Day that a coach rumbled up with Crellin sandwiched between Mr and Mrs Jones. While the Joneses ate and drank quite happily, Crellin slept soundly in the parlour. Mawdsley thought she was in 'a stupor' the whole time. She said that two other men came and all five left together, despite Crellin's protests. 'I won't go out,' she said, but she was too dazed to fight when Jones lifted her bodily and carried her into a cab. Mawdsley heard Jones tell the driver to go to Roby, a village to the north of Liverpool.

Evidence suggests that the other two men were John McGill and a man who called himself Doctor Quick, who was a druggist from Liverpool's Scotland Road.

John Hagan, a cigar dealer, had also noted the odd company on their rattling journey north. He had overheard some people talking in a pub. They had mentioned Crellin and spoke darkly of taking £200 from her or driving her to 'the mountains' and leaving her there if she refused to co-operate. They calculated Crellin's fortune at around £24,000, spread over two banks.

When they reached Roby, Crellin and her keepers caught a train, with Crellin apparently puffing happily at a pipe of tobacco. The railway gate keeper, John Rodgers, later identified all five: Crellin, Dr Quick, Mrs Clayton, McGill and Richard Jones. The latter two had to support Crellin into a carriage and Rodgers believed she was too drunk to stand. Quick tried to bribe him to say that he had not seen them carry Crellin away. Rodgers accepted the money but somehow forgot to pass on the false message. The train ran to Lancaster, where the party disembarked for the next stage of the journey.

There were other witnesses, and between them, they built up a picture of subsequent events. The people with Crellin took the *North Briton* coach from Lancaster to the small town of Shap, with Dr Quick smoking his pipe and paying for the tickets in the name of Thompson. Jones and Mrs Clayton kept Crellin company inside the coach while the other two sat on the cheaper seats outside. The coachman, James Baines, mentioned that he heard Crellin yelling and shouting as if she was drunk. Quick was not happy with Crellin's behaviour and told McGill to 'get inside and quieten the old bitch.'

John Wilson took over the driving after Shap and saw them feeding drink to Crellin when they stopped at Hackthorpe to change horses. The coach rattled on to Carlisle, changing horses at coaching inns to keep up the speed. They stopped at Carnforth and Burton, and still her companions poured spirits into Crellin, but rather than rendering her soporific, the alcohol animated her so she talked ever louder and gesticulated to everybody in the various inns. 'I want to go home!' Crellin yelled and pleaded, 'I want to go home.'

When passengers joined, Crellin's companions passed off her ravings by saying she was a rich lady, but insane, so they were taking her to a lunatic asylum in Scotland. Dr Quick claimed to be Crellin's private physician, adding that they were all army doctors on leave. There was more drink at Crookland when the doctor asked for the brandy bottle, but McGill answered 'she's drunk it all.' Eventually Crellin fell asleep, her head on Jones' shoulder. At one stop she left the coach for a few moments. Witnesses thought she looked bloated and swollen of face, and was far too drunk to walk.

They arrived at the Bush Inn at Carlisle on 18 March, where they spent the night. Wilson the coach driver thought that Crellin hated the men she was with. He said that she shouted at them when they escorted her from the coach to the inn. There was more brandy for Crellin and at half past eleven on the Saturday morning, they took a post-chaise to Gretna. When they stopped at the Sark Bar, the first public house, Quick said his companions were a 'lot of damned drunken devils.' At the toll bar for Gretna, Quick asked about weddings, to be told they were rare, and about the cost, which varied from a gill of whisky to an incredible £100. They came to Gretna Hall, one of only three places remaining in Gretna where impromptu wedding services were held, ordered supper and asked Mr Linton, the innkeeper, to join them.

'What's all this?'

Linton was also the 'priest', the man who would perform the wedding ceremony, and although he declined the offer to eat, he did help them to drink a bottle of whisky later that evening. McGill had introduced Crellin as his 'future wife' and Linton had no notion that she was unwilling. With Crellin more than half stupefied with drink and perhaps drugs, and the priest misled and well watered, a marriage ceremony was performed and Crellin was taken away. She was too drunk to know what happened and afterward had no recollection of events. The whole event had been organised, but so casually that neither Crellin nor McGill had bothered to purchase a ring. Thomas Rogerson had bought the ring on 1 March from a shop in Oldhall Street. He walked in, said 'I want a wedding ring' and was out in less than a minute.

It was not surprising that Crellin was confused the next morning. She woke up with a start and jumped out of bed. 'What's all this? What have you been doing with me?'

'You're married now,' McGill told her in his Dublin accent, and indicated the ring on her finger.

Crellin stared at the circle of gold. 'Married? Take this ring off. How is this?' She screamed aloud in horror and Dr John Quick arrived and tried to calm things down, but not in the way that Crellin would have preferred.

'Madam,' Quick told her sternly, 'you have deceived many, now you are deceived yourself.' As Crellin stared at him in incomprehension, Quick gave her his advice. 'You are now under the power of Mr McGill, and it's in his power to take all your fortune from you, so mind and behave yourself. There's nothing but the workhouse for you if you do not.'

Crellin was distraught. She pleaded with McGill to remove the ring, but it was so tightly jammed on her finger that he needed to saw through the metal. Even although she was confused and distressed, Crellin refused to believe that she was legally married, partly because of the presence of Jane Clayton in the same bed. However, when she complained to the daughter of the house what had happened, she was only given sympathy and not a way out. It seemed that the abduction had been successful and Crellin was a legally married woman.

According to Crellin, Dr Quick once again drugged her drink and she was hazy about much on the journey back. Other witnesses again filled in the gaps. They did not stay long in Gretna; not long after Crellin woke, they bundled back into a coach for the journey back to Liverpool. They stayed the night of 20 March at the Crown and Mitre Inn in Carlisle, where Crellin was seen to drink about six glasses of brandy. According to the chambermaid, Elizabeth Armstrong, Crellin said, loudly, 'I've just got married and I'm going to have a damned good spree.'

Crellin gave Armstrong a shilling tip, but was too drunk to get undressed. Armstrong had to help undress her. In that same inn, a waiter named John Macfarlane said that Quick told him the lady was 'a damned old hag with a deal of money and they had filled her drunk, and ran away and married her.'

Macfarlane thought that Crellin was either very tired or very drunk, with her bonnet crushed at one side and her clothes all 'open at the back.' He was not impressed with her appearance or her behaviour.

At two in the afternoon of the 21 March, they were at the Kings Arms in Kendal. They hit the bottle again and the waiter, John Hawkes, said that Crellin was 'in a state bordering on stupefaction.' She did not eat much but drank a lot of sherry.

Make the best of it

At last they reached Liverpool and Crellin came to her senses, back in the house of Thomas Rogerson. She protested that she did not want to be married but was again informed that she was now Mrs McGill, and had to make the best of it. The couple shared a bed, much to Crellin's stated dismay, but she had been assured it was now all legal and above board. After a while she managed to escape and find a lawyer to check her legal position.

Crellin did have a marriage certificate of sorts, but denied that the signature on it was her own. Dr Quick had been the witness, and McGill had signed his name distinctly, but Crellin's signature was a mere scribble, quite unlike her usual neat hand. On 23 March she marched into the office of a solicitor named Eden and told him she was 'married against her will.' Eden may have wondered what sort of person he was dealing with, but he made enquiries and summoned Quick and McGill to a meeting at his office. Eden's initial advice was that Crellin and McGill try to work something out between them, but that idea failed. McGill had landed his rich wife and wanted to keep her, while Crellin wanted her freedom, please.

Either Eden suggested that they call the police or Crellin decided that enough was enough, but the confused case was put in the hands of the professionals. Inspector Campbell arrested Copeland at 90 Vine Street. The police also arrested John Orr McGill, John Osborne Quick, Thomas Wormand Rogerson, Richard Jones, Margaret Jones and Jane Clayton. They had made a clean sweep of the principal actors in the great deception play.

The trial

At the trial in August, Crellin was termed 'a lady of great credulity, of unsteadiness of purpose and of great weakness of judgement'. The *Liverpool Mercury* called her a 'person of indifferent education.'

The defence claimed that McGill was an 'accepted lover', but conceded that he had acted 'in a sordid and mean manner.' It pointed out that just 'because a man married a woman of fortune, he was not, therefore, to be set down as being guilty of felony.' The defence also attacked Crellin, saying she was guilty of falsehood and had been a willing party to the wedding. There was no doubt that she 'was always loitering after men.' They said she drank too much and there was no evidence that she was drugged, as she had claimed.

The defendants tried to blacken Crellin's already chequered

character. For example, Richard Jones claimed that Crellin had once suggested that he should rape her seventeen-year-old maid servant, but Crellin's lawyers were equally aggressive. They pointed out that Copeland, an assistant to a quack doctor, was also a married man. The mud-slinging continued as the court heard that both Copeland and Crellin had been guilty of the 'grossest indecency' on several occasions. They had been thrown out of theatres and pubs for their conduct and had also been found in bed together, although they were not married.

After a complex and long trial, the jury found Margaret Jones and Rogerson not guilty of any crime but McGill, Richard Jones, Mrs Clayton and Quick guilty. They also said that Crellin was highly culpable in the business. Samuel Martin Copeland was found guilty of obtaining £250 by false pretences and was given twelve months with hard labour. McGill was given eighteen months with hard labour. Quick was sent to jail for fifteen months while Clayton and Jones were jailed for a year apiece.

It was a fitting ending to a strange affair.

5
Packet Rats

There were many categories of seamen in the nineteenth century, from the hardy Greenlandmen who braved the bitter Arctic ice in the quest for whales, to the South Spainer who faced the horrors of Cape Horn and the vast rollers of the Southern Ocean. However, of them all, perhaps the toughest was the Liverpool Packet Rat. These men were often of Irish extraction, hard men who lived in the dockland area and who rolled on board their ships with a minimum of seagoing clothes and a maximum attitude of unrelenting truculence. These men were not to be trifled with. For example, in November 1862 the packet ship *Robert L. Lane* was the scene of a violent encounter between the master, Captain Bryer, and two seamen named Patsey and Matthew Moore. The seamen drew their knives and stabbed Bryer to death. The first officer, Mr Leonard, also got involved and crashed a hand spike over Patsey's head, killing him. Patsey was buried at sea and a detachment of the 4th US Cavalry boarded the ship, and aided the New York police in establishing complete control.

A packet ship was originally one that sailed between two fixed destinations and also carried official documents, known as 'the Packet'.

In time, the term 'packet boat' or 'packet ship' became generic for any vessel that sailed regularly between two fixed ports.

The Black Ball line

In the early decades of the nineteenth century, Liverpool was one end of a major packet route across the Atlantic, with New York being the western destination. There were a number of shipping lines that crossed and recrossed the Atlantic, but the Black Ball line was arguably the most famous. This shipping line owned sailing vessels of between 300 and 500 tons, and left New York on the 1st and 16th of the month. They were sturdy ships that could hoist a cloud of canvas that withstood the worst of the Atlantic weather for day after stormy day. They were also fast ships. In an age when speed had replaced Poseidon as monarch of the ocean, the packet ships were known for fast and regular passages. Indeed, in 1818 the Black Ball line's *James Monroe* was arguably the first ever vessel to make the double Atlantic crossing six times within a single year.

In common with most sail-powered vessels, these packet ships were beautiful to watch: graceful and powerful with their three towering masts and vast spread of canvas. But the onlookers saw the outside only; life on board these vessels did not always match the picture-perfect exterior.

Blood boats

British ships were not always beds of roses in which to sail, but any mistreatment on board paled into insignificance when compared to life on the average United States sailing ship. British seamen often called them blood boats, but, paradoxically, there was an element of prestige in having served on board an American ship and some British seamen adopted American accents and slang to prove they had survived that rite of passage. The American shipmasters were superb seamen, but they ruled by the belaying pin, knuckleduster and revolver. Fear was their aim and violence their weapon. When the hard case American shipmasters met the equally aggressive Liverpool packet rats, the results were bound to be explosive.

> There's a saucy wild packet, a packet of fame,
> She belongs to New York, and the Dreadnought's her name
> She's bound to the westward where the wide waters flow,
> Bound away to the westward in the Dreadnought we'll go!

Dreadnought was one of the most famous of the packet ships, and she carried the red cross of her house flag with pride, as she proved that the United States merchant marine dominated the North Atlantic Ocean, despite all the bravado of Britannia ruling the waves. In 1837 a British parliamentary enquiry concluded that United States packet ships and masters were 'generally considered [...] more competent as seamen and navigators, and more uniformly persons of education than the commanders and officers of British ships of similar size and class.'

These competent masters were hard case Down East Yankees; there were legends that some sealed shut the fo'c'sle door as soon as they passed Sandy Hook on their voyage to Liverpool, so ensuring the crew, the packet rats, were always on deck or aloft. Some ships relied on the bully mates who used brass knuckledusters and the six-shot revolver. These bullies boasted they could 'whip their weight in wild cats' and proved it on the battered bodies of the hands. Others, such as Captain Samuel Samuels of Dreadnought, were opposed by the Bloody Forty.

The Bloody Forty

The Bloody Forty were perhaps the toughest of all the Packet Rats, an organisation, perhaps best described as a gang, based in the dockland area of Liverpool who went to sea in the packet ships. They signed on en masse and often terrorised the ship, despite all the skill and fisticuffs of the master and mates. They brought their own brand of terror.

According to the maritime historian Basil Lubbock, in July 1859, thirty of this gang signed articles on Captain Samuels' *Dreadnought*. Samuels thought that some of the Bloody Forty had already sailed with him and planned to take control of the ship and turn pirate. Although pirates were certainly not unknown in the nineteenth century, that seems unlikely. It was more likely that the Bloody Forty merely wanted to cause trouble for Samuels, or perhaps even kill him. Certainly Mr Mansfield, a Liverpool magistrate, thought so, for one of his informers had heard dark whispers in the den of Mrs Riley, a crimp of the old, evil school.

Samuels versus the Forty

When *Dreadnought* left Waterloo Dock with a full contingent of mainly German emigrants for the United States, the Bloody Forty were on board, but Samuels believed he was ready for whatever trouble they intended to cause. As the voyage began, he gathered the men aft and ordered that they muster at the carpenter's to have the points broken from their knives. This was normal practise on a ship where the master expected trouble from the crew. Three of the leaders of the Forty, Sweeney, Casey and Finnegan, were reluctant, but only Sweeney questioned the order and even he eventually went along with the others. When they were with the carpenter, Samuels sent the mate to scour the fo'c'sle for any other weapons, which was a common ploy with the packet captains. Any knives, knuckle dusters, or anything else that might be termed offensive were promptly tossed overboard.

Samuel's next encounter was with a recalcitrant helmsman and a difference of opinion about the course they were steering. When the helmsman reached for his knife, Samuels punched him to the deck and left Wallace, his Newfoundland dog, to stand guard until the helmsman was dragged away and locked up. Samuels called a council of war with his officers. There were six officers and forty hands; uneven odds, but Samuels was a hard man and expected his officers to back him up. Not all did: only the mate, a man named Whitehorn, agreed to stand alongside Samuels while the others gave their excuses for not getting involved.

Knowing he could not rely on his officers and certainly not on his crew, Samuels would have been very wary as he walked the deck of his own ship. The next time he gave the order to haul taut the weather brace, Finnegan, the apparent leader of the Bloody Forty refused, until the helmsman was released from irons. There was a standoff on the deck, as Samuels and Whitehorn faced the massed Forty. The emigrants watched as Samuels stood at the break of the poop with a revolver in each hand. In front of him, the Forty scrambled up the ladders, desperate to control this ship.

But Samuels was equally determined: 'Move an inch, one of you and we'll have the burial service in short order.'

The Forty stopped, staring at the determined face of their captain.

Finnegan pulled his knife, bared his chest and called Samuels' bluff. Samuels aimed a revolver at the seaman, but Finnegan did not flinch. He began to climb the ladder, one courageous rung at a time. Still Samuels did not shoot. He was a hard man, but no murderer; he could not shoot a man in cold blood. The two sides faced each other: the pair of officers and the forty men of the crew. One by one the Forty withdrew until only the three ringleaders, Casey, Sweeney and Finnegan faced Samuels, and then they also turned away. In the game of bluff and counter-bluff, Samuels had come out on top.

But that was only one round; the Forty prepared for a long war. They withdrew to the fo'c'sle and refused Samuels' orders to 'take in the royals' with a simple: 'go to hell.'

As the wind rose to a gale, Samuels needed the crew to take in sail or the ship would be in danger. Again the Forty refused, but this time they demanded food in return for their labour.

'You shall work before you eat,' Samuels roared.

The Forty swore back at him and began to leave the fo'c'sle. They wanted fed; Samuels refused food until the work was done. It was a mid-Atlantic stalemate, with the wind rising, howling through the rigging and straining the canvas against the spars. As the noise of creaking wood augmented the hiss and crash of the waves, the passengers began to worry. They asked Samuels to feed the hands and when he refused, the spokesman for the passengers said he would do it himself. He changed his mind when Samuels wrestled him to the deck and put him in irons.

When the storm eventually abated, Samuels offered the bulk of the Forty an amnesty: if they threw away their weapons and returned to work all would be forgiven and they would be fed. Only the three ringleaders, Casey, Sweeney and Finnegan were excluded. Time passed; hour after hungry hour and still the Forty refused to give up; twenty hours; forty; fifty; Samuels expected an explosion of frustrated violence. He told the second mate, Whitehorn, to wait with loaded revolver and fire if any of the Forty came toward the poop.

Reinforcements

It was still two against forty, so to equalise the odds, Samuels recruited seventeen of the German emigrants. He armed them with iron bars and had them as a mobile reserve. In the dark of the night, Samuels was on watch in the poop when Wallace growled and Samuels noticed two men crawling toward him. He shouted a challenge and both stood up and surrendered. They told Samuels that the Forty had sworn to kill him if he went forward, and they were going to charge forward to raid the galley. But there was mutiny in the ranks of the Forty, with some more keen to fight and others ready to surrender.

Samuels got ready for the final showdown. He brought the Germans into play, blocked the ladders to the poop, so the Forty could not gain access and closed the hatches. The Forty were now confined to the forward deck, while Samuels checked his pistol, patted Wallace and waited. He slipped down to the main deck and began a patrol, when Sweeney and Casey attacked with raised knives.

Despite his precautions, Samuels was taken by surprise and beat a hurried retreat, but Wallace was true to his name and launched himself on Sweeney. There was an instant scuffle and as Sweeney went down before the weight of the huge dog, he called on his followers to attack Samuels and Whitehorn.

Whitehorn led the Germans in a counter attack and the deck was filled with struggling bodies as the emigrants with their iron bars crashed into the pugnacious rats. When Samuels brought his revolver into play, the Forty began to withdraw. Finnegan remained as defiant as ever but his followers began to toss their knives into the long swells of the Atlantic. Even Casey and Sweeney discarded their weapons and finally, reluctantly, Finnegan did the same.

Samuels confronted Finnegan face to face; they argued and Samuels punched Finnegan down the fo'c'sle ladder to the deck. That was a signal for the Forty to attack again, with Sweeney and Casey reaching for hidden knives. However, the captain still had his revolver, which proved an excellent persuader. Next time Samuels gave an order, the Forty hurried to obey.

Samuels ordered Finnegan to apologise, but the Forty's ringleader refused, so he was locked up in irons. When he was released, Finnegan was a broken man and nearly ran to do the captain's bidding. That was the end of the mutiny. For the remainder of that voyage, the Bloody Forty were model seamen. At least according to Samuels, on whose published account all the above was based.

Other incidents on the packet ships were recorded by more than one witness.

Riot on *Fidelia*

On Tuesday, 14 June 1853 the Black Ball packet ship *Fidelia* was lying quietly in the Mersey. She was a 1,000-ton vessel and according to an advertisement in the *Liverpool Mercury*, she was 'first class, coppered and copper-fastened, and commanded by men of character and experience.'

Unfortunately, the advertisement did not stipulate what sort of character the commanders had, or of what their experience consisted.

Captain Thomas Dixon had her safely off the Egremont Ferry, near to the Cheshire side of the Mersey as she loaded her emigrants for the passage across the Atlantic. But that day *Fidelia* was rocked by a ferocious riot that saw the intervention of the Liverpool police and the arrest of thirteen of her crew. There were two different versions of events: Captain Dixon's, and that of the passengers who witnessed the scene.

Dixon saw the turmoil through a captain's eyes: the crew had signed articles (a contract of employment) for the voyage from Liverpool to New York, with *Fidelia* having over 300 emigrants on board. On the afternoon of Monday, 13 June one of the crew named Martin Madden took issue with an order the second officer had given him. The first officer, Mr Bragg, backed the second officer. The row escalated and became heated, with others of the crew joining in until there were thirteen men clustered around the officers. They decided that, despite having legally signed articles, they strongly wished to leave the ship, but Captain Dixon refused to allow them to go on shore. Dixon said he would treat them like men with 'watch and watch', meaning twelve hours on and twelve hours off duty in every day.

A man named John Lynach acted as the spokesman for the crew

and when Dixon asked what the complaint was, and if they had enough to eat and drink, he replied 'Tight enough, sir.'

Dixon replied that he had not been aboard the ship much but when he was, the men 'should have plenty to eat and plenty to drink,' but added that if they had come aboard to cause trouble they would be punished. American ships were known for having decent food, unlike the starvation diets served out on many British vessels.

When Lynach said he had worked 'long enough for nothing,' Dixon ordered the second officer to feed the men who worked, but not the others. Dixon then ordered them on duty until next day, when he would find out whether or not they could legally leave the ship.

Discontent and mutiny

On the next day the men were mustered to be passed fit for duty. According to the captain, the first rat called was the intriguingly named Benjamin Franklin, but he refused to move, saying he was 'not going in the ship.' However, the government emigration officer, Captain Higgins, ordered him forward and he came, reluctantly. The next dozen or so men were equally loath to step forward but were less vocal. Lynach was not scared to let his opinion be known and said openly that he was 'not going to sea in this ship.' Higgins again told them that they had signed articles, so were bound to sail, and the men grumbled their discontent.

Ignoring the protests, the mate ordered them to the topgallant fo'c'sle. Captain Dixon left them to it, as he mustered the steerage passengers on the larboard side of the ship for some purpose of his own. He did not see what happened next, but about ten minutes later he heard an explosion of sound and somebody shouted: 'I'm stabbed!'

In the captain's absence, the trouble between the seamen and the officers had continued. They had completely ignored the agent's orders to knuckle down to work and had congregated on the foredeck, with all three officers trying to cajole them to do their duty.

Not even the captain was sure who threw the first punch, but within minutes the men and officers were engaged in a wild stramash, with handsaws, fists, boots, chain hooks and chairs being freely used. In the confusion, some of the men thought that second officer De Costa smashed a man named Madden with an iron bar.

The chief mate Bragg was beside the windlass and Lynach pulled out his seaman's knife, and made a wild slash at his stomach. Bragg ducked back and fell to one knee, yelling, but Lynach altered his grip on the knife and stabbed him in the thigh.

That was enough for Dixon. He pulled out the revolver that shipmasters seemed to carry as a matter of course, shouted, 'Look out Bragg' and fired a single shot in the air.

Either that shot frightened the crew or they were working to a predetermined plan, but they charged forward to the topgallant forecastle. Dixon heard another pistol shot and shouted: 'Who is cut?'

'I am cut,' Bragg said at once.

Lynach also lay prone on the deck, apparently dead.

Higgins stepped in now, ordering Dixon to disarm the seamen. The captain called the rats forward one at a time to take away their knives. Surprisingly, the men obeyed: perhaps they had not expected the stabbing or the gunshot had temporarily subdued them. Once he had disarmed them, Dixon ordered them to the larboard side of the foc'sle. Once they were there, some of the men decided they had no desire to sail on this ship, so they simply jumped overboard and swam ashore.

The passengers' viewpoints

A passenger named James Hodson gave a slightly different version of events that does not show much credit to the ship's officers. He said that the discontented members of the crew had been closing a hatch cover when Madden had accidentally missed one of the ropes, which upset the rhythm of the work. Immediately after he did so, the second mate had run up to him and kicked him in the face. After that the men retaliated and the mutiny began: such occurrences were not uncommon on board United States blood boats. Hodson also said he saw Lynach fall to the deck, after which the second mate immediately began to thump him with a belaying pin.

'I'll murder him, by God!' the second mate roared, 'damn the bloody bugger, I will!'

That was enough for the chief mate, who hustled the second mate out of the way. 'I will not stand such work,' the chief mate told him. He stood over Madden, who lay on the deck. 'My dear fellow, you are down,' the chief mate said, 'and it will be a damned smart fellow that will pick you up. I am going to leave the ship.'

William Pritchard, another of the passengers, said that the conduct of the officers was truly revolting and he and his family often prayed to get back home. Pritchard claimed that the officers had a 'course of systematic cruelty and barbarity toward the steerage passengers.' He mentioned the previous Tuesday when there was a deal of confusion on the poop and he asked the captain what was happening.

'Mind your own business,' the captain told him brusquely and later added: 'how dare you speak to me in such an authoritative manner.' He ended with a threat to shoot Pritchard if he ever spoke to him like that again.

There was a hearing in Liverpool to decide what had happened on board, but the officers, passengers and crew all gave such totally different accounts of events that the magistrates could make nothing of it. The captain asked the magistrate to order the men back on board, but he said that was not in his power.

However, there is another side to the packet ships that is not always presented. Above all else, they were manned by superb seamen. In June 1841, the British government awarded gold medals to the captains of four American packet ships in recognition of their saving the crews of four wrecked British vessels. James Buchanan, the British consul at New York also presented a telescope to James Neish, an officer of the packet ship *Columbus*, for saving twenty-nine men and boys of the Belfast ship *Leonidas* on 25 November 1840.

Life was never easy on the packet ships, but the Liverpool packet rats always walked with a swagger, spat in the eye of the world and accepted the worst that the sea could offer.

6

The Leveson Street Murders

In 1848, the Hinrichsons, husband and wife, bought their family home at No. 20 Leveson Street. The house was only a few doors down from Great George Street in one of the better parts of Liverpool, inhabited by very respectable families of which the Hinrichsons were one. In May of that year Mrs Ann Hinrichson was heavily pregnant with her third child, while her first two, Henry George, was five years old and John Alfred was three. Captain John Hinrichson was at sea in his ship *Duncan* en route home from Calcutta. He was not expected back for some months, but the thirty-year-old maid Mary Parr was a good help to the family.

Although the master of a deep water ship was a man of considerable standing, Mrs Hinrichson came from an even higher social strata, so in the eyes of her family, she had married beneath her. She was from the Hull Fenwicks, a very well thought of family and a name that is still prominent in the area. Ann Hinrichson had been educated in all the skills considered essential for a woman of rank. She was particularly expert in music and gave classes to earn some money when her husband was at sea. For the same reason, she also let rooms in her house.

John Gleeson Wilson arrives

On Tuesday, 27 March 1849 a man from Limerick in Ireland tapped at her door and asked about the room to let. He said his name was John Gleeson Wilson and he was an artisan, a carpenter employed at £2 10/- a week, which was an excellent wage for the period. Ann looked him up and down: Wilson was five foot seven tall and broad shouldered. He wore his hair short at the back but strangely long over the right side of his face, which gave him a distinctive appearance. His eyes were deep set above high cheek bones and he spoke with a soft Irish accent. He also said his sister ran the Tranmere Hotel.

Ann must have approved of his appearance for she accepted him as a guest. Wilson took an upper bedroom and back parlour and everybody seemed very satisfied with the arrangement. Not long after Ann had accepted Wilson, a close friend, Mr Parsons called and voiced his concern that she had taken in a lodger without any real references. Ann laughed it off, but the thought may have raised some worries in her mind.

Wilson ate his supper with the family that night, had a pint of beer at ten and slipped up to bed. So far everything was absolutely normal, but the next morning things began to go wrong. Nobody saw him rise, but by nine o'clock he was in Frederick Street talking to a young man named Edward McDermott. Wilson gave McDermott a letter and told him to deliver it to No. 20 Leveson Street; the letter was addressed to Mr John Wilson. As soon as he handed over the letter, Wilson dashed back into the house, and was there when the letter arrived. After writing to himself, Wilson was out of the house again by eleven, bought some potatoes and had them sent to the house, where again he was there to accept them. Mrs Hinrichson had been outside and returned just after the potatoes arrived.

Around this time, Mary Parr was cleaning the front parlour and sent the eldest son, Henry, out of her way. He ran into the back parlour, where Wilson lived. Nobody will ever know what happened next, but a few moments later, Henry came running out, with Wilson slapping at him. The maid intervened to save the child, saying that the 'mistress did not allow anyone to strike the children', but Wilson did not take kindly to her interference. Rather than stop, he lifted the fireside tongs and knocked her to the ground. As she lay there, and before she passed out, she saw Wilson hit Henry again, and heard John Alfred, the younger boy, scream.

The real John Wilson

Wilson was really called Maurice Gleeson, sometimes known as Morrison, and he had lived in lodgings in Sparling Street, Liverpool for some fifteen months, eventually marrying his landlady. He was born in Brurie, nine miles from Limerick, but left his home village with a reputation of idleness and theft. He went first to Portsmouth, and might have been there when his sister was transported for ten years. From there he travelled to London and then to Liverpool. Soon after he seduced and married his landlady, he began to beat her, and not just the odd casual slap. She became so frightened that she sold her house and moved in with her father in Tranmere.

Before Mary and the boys saw the ugly side of Wilson, Mrs Hinrichson had been shopping. She had bought two jugs, but rather than carry them through the streets herself, she asked them to be delivered. Then she walked briskly home.

Through the keyhole

The delivery boy, William Bradshaw, collected the jugs and raced to No. 20. He came to the door and hammered away, but got no answer. When he thought he heard a noise like somebody in pain, he peered through the keyhole and thought he saw a pair of legs lying on the lobby floor. Alarmed, he looked in the window and was even more surprised when he saw a boy and young woman face down on the floor. That was enough for Bradshaw and he ran to get help.

Even before Bradshaw returned with a policeman, one of Mrs Hinrichson's music pupils had tried to get in, but nobody answered the door. She made a fuss and a bricklayer named John Hughes came to help. He also looked in the window and saw the servant and one of the young boys lying on the ground. The servant's head was a mass of blood and the young boy was partly beneath her with his arms around her waist. Unwilling to wait for the police, Hughes smashed a window pane, lifted the catch and climbed in. A number of other people followed to see what had happened. They were already in the house when Constable Henry Hough arrived on the scene.

They found Mrs Hinrichson stretched on the floor, while her eldest son, Henry, was near her, battered and bloody and with his hoop around him. Mary Parr was also prone and bloodied. She looked up when the men entered, but her words were hardly coherent. All the injured were alive, but only just, so an ambulance took them to the Southern Hospital. The second son, John, was in the back cellar, nearly decapitated, with a bloody knife lying on the ground at his side.

Mary Parr's statement

Mrs Hinrichson and Henry died shortly after they arrived in the hospital, but Mary Parr held on long enough to give a statement. She said that as soon as Mrs Hinrichson entered the house Wilson attacked her with tongs, a poker and a shovel. The poker was bent and the tongs broken and matted with hair, blood and what Constable Hough thought might be human brains.

The police searched the house and found a bloody towel in Wilson's room. They also found that Mrs Hinrichson's bedroom had been ransacked and jewellery had been stolen. Obviously, Wilson was the prime suspect and the police traced his movements. He had been seen in Toxteth Park, washing his boots and trousers, and had tried to sell a gold watch to Alfred Tunstall, a London Road pawnbroker. The pawnbroker's assistant had not trusted Wilson and examined him.

'What are you staring at?' Wilson asked.

'Handsome men are always admired,' the assistant replied.

The pawnbroker offered a much lower price for the watch than Wilson wanted, and he later told the police about the incident, as he did not think that such a man could afford an expensive watch. The beat policeman scanned the street but did not see Wilson. Later the police found a bloody handkerchief where Wilson had got washed, and a letter addressed to 'John Wilson, 2 Leveson Street, Liverpool.' The writing was later matched with that of Wilson.

As the police made enquiries, they instigated a search, but Wilson slipped away up to Washington Street. He was sweating so much that he attracted attention and witnesses could describe his clothes very well: dark blue coat, light cord trousers and boots. The police followed the trail to Thomas Finn's pawnbroker, where Wilson bought a new pair of dark trousers and a pair of boots, both of which he donned there and then. He handed his trousers over to a man he met in the street and hurried to 44 Porter Street, where he also had lodgings. His landlady very kindly found a clean shirt for him. Smartly dressed in new trousers and crisp shirt, Wilson's next stop was Jacob Samuels, a Great Howard Street barber, who trimmed his hair and shaved him smooth. Wilson said he was going bald and asked about a wig, which would have altered his appearance. Samuels noticed he had blood on his wrist and was not quite sure about Wilson's explanation of having cut his wrist on a nail.

Samuels took him to the bottom of Oil Street to find out about a wig, and Wilson asked if he had heard about the recent murders. Samuels had heard nothing and showed no interest. Wilson also enquired about taking a ship to America, and a number of crimp's runners – the men who found possible seamen to supply to short-handed shipmasters – appeared, asking £3 10s for the passage. Wilson said he was only willing to pay £3, and they turned him down and ran away.

Selling a watch

Rather than a packet across the Atlantic, Wilson took the ferry across the Mersey and stayed in Tranmere with his wife and father-in-law, whom he had hardly seen in months. For all his many faults, Wilson must have kissed the Blarney Stone, for he charmed his much-abused wife into bed that night. Early next morning he chanced the watchful police eyes and returned to Liverpool, hoping to raise hard cash for his passage to America, by selling his gold watch to a grocer named Samuel. The grocer promised to speak to him later at his lodgings in Porter Street.

For a while Wilson seemed at a loss what to do. He spent time on a river ferry before returning to his lodgings. Samuel the grocer was there, and they negotiated the sale of the watch, during which time Wilson's landlord arrived with a poster that mentioned the murder and described the murderer. It was Wilson to a tee, except for his change of clothing.

At half past eight that evening, Wilson returned to Samuel's shop to finally settle the sale of the watch. He had agreed to take £6 for it. When Wilson refused to sign a receipt, Samuel finally realised he was not to be trusted. He spoke in Hebrew to his son, telling the younger man to take Wilson to the police office.

The son changed to English and said he would take Wilson to a shop in Dale Street for the receipt. Wilson was either desperate or naïve for he agreed. As they passed the police station, the grocer's son thrust him inside and that was the end of Wilson's freedom.

Strangely, Wilson still had not realised what was happening. The younger Samuel told the policeman on duty, Constable Toole, that Wilson needed a receipt for a watch he was selling. Toole said that he had better have a stamped receipt and went through the back of the office for one. He returned with Superintendent Clough, who first questioned and then arrested Wilson. Toole searched Wilson and found some money, while there was still blood on one of the three white shirts that, for some reason, he wore.

'I am happy to stand my trial'

Clough charged him with murder there and then.

'I am happy to stand my trial for it,' Wilson said, in a nonchalant manner.

'Where did you get the trousers from?' Clough began the questioning. Wilson threw the question back at him, 'That is for you to find out.' He smiled around the police station. 'You should be sure of a man before you apprehend him on suspicion,' he said.

On the 30th of the month the police put handcuffs on Wilson and took him to where Mary Parr lay in hospital. They organised an identity parade, put Wilson in the middle, and Parr pointed to him without hesitation.

'That is the man with the hat on.'

When the police escorted the sweating Wilson out of the hospital, a crowd had gathered to jeer, hoot and insult the man accused of multiple murders. The police had to call up reinforcements before they considered it safe to take him back to the station.

The police cast their net wide. They brought Mrs Hinrichson's mother from Hull to identify the watch Wilson had tried to pawn. There seemed no doubt that Wilson was responsible for the deaths of Mrs Hinrichson and her two sons. On 5 April, Mary Parr died, so Wilson had killed four people.

At his initial court hearing, Wilson was quite relaxed, saying that he was hungry and 'You're not going to frighten me!'

He spoke in Gaelic to one of his guards, read the Bible and alternated between a seeming nonchalance to shaking fear. At one stage, he claimed that his wife and child would provide an alibi, but around the same time he said he was 'tired of my life' and 'I'll say nothing now but I'll tell all when I get on to the platform.' He mentioned another couple of people who would give him an alibi, but they said they had not seen him that day. He wrote a letter to his wife, but she did not come to see him.

There was no real need for a trial as there was so much evidence against Wilson, or Gleeson. As it became evident he would be found guilty, his confidence slipped and he became emotionless, standing in the dock without any expression on his face. Samuel the grocer identified the watch, the barber mentioned that Gleeson had blood spattered over his sleeve when he came for a shave and there was Parr's statement. The jury did not bother to retire to consider their verdict, but remained in their places. They pronounced Gleeson guilty and 50,000 people came to see him hanged in front of Kirkdale jail. There were even special trains put on for the event and George Howard, the hangman, made the trip worth the shilling fare by failing to calculate the correct drop so that Gleeson took quarter of an hour to die. When the death cap also fell off, the crowd had the edifying spectacle of seeing him slowly choke to death, with his eyes bulging and his face turning purple. Not all in the crowd enjoyed the sight. It was much worse for Captain Hinrichson, who arrived home in Liverpool to find himself a widower with no surviving family. In the days before radios and telephones, there was no sure way to send him the news.

After the murder, the name of the street was changed from Leveson Street to Grenville Street South, but the memory of that fateful day still lingers in the shadowed recesses of Liverpool's collective memory.

7
Blue and Red

Before uniformed police became the norm in the streets of British cities, the army was often called upon when there was riot or other civil unrest. Most cities had some sort of military presence, although soldiers were often lodged with the general public in inns and other establishments, rather than in barracks. Liverpool was no different in this respect.

In the early decades of the nineteenth century there was great discontent in many parts of the country and even fear of civil war and uprising, because of unemployment and general distress. There was also agitation about electoral reform that peaked in the 1830s, with talk of discontented men making pikes and planning bloody revolution. The government was in fear and quite capable of using force to repress any show of political dissent. Perhaps that was why there was some consternation in Liverpool in November 1831 when the garrison of redcoats were drawn up near the Exchange and live cartridges issued to each man. The people of the town must have wondered if the army was to be turned loose on them. In the end nothing happened, but the fear was genuine.

'Down with the blues'

Sometimes it was the army themselves who caused the trouble. On Tuesday, 1 July 1851, the 91st Regiment, the Argyllshire Regiment, were on duty in Liverpool but that night a number of them rioted and caused all sorts of trouble in the town.

The outbreak started in the Dale Street and North Street area, when a party of about fifteen to twenty of the 91st slipped off their belts, grabbed sticks and shouted 'down with the blues [the police]'. A soldier's belt was a formidable weapon of thick leather with a heavy brass buckle. When swung through the air to gather speed, it could be lethal. Using belts for fighting was common in the century. As Kipling put it:

For it was: 'Belts, belts, belts, an' that's one for you!'

In this case, there were also civilians handing out weapons, short, heavy sticks with knobs at the end, to the disaffected men.

The men continued to Fontenoy Street, shouting the odds at the police and obviously spoiling for a fight. Walking three abreast, they swaggered up Dale Street and saw a lone policeman, Constable John Duggan, outside the Earl Grey pub.

'Here's one of the buggers,' one soldier, Private McGill said, 'let's kill him.'

The soldiers made a rush at Duggan, swinging their weapons. McGill had a short cane and struck the first blow, but others followed, with Privates John Wraith and Thomas Powers prominent. Duggan had no chance to defend himself against so many; the buckle of a belt staggered him and he went down in a flurry of blows. McGill promptly jumped on top of his prone body. Duggan rose and ran into a clothes shop where he sheltered until somebody cried out, 'Picket!'

That was a warning that the army had sent out a patrol to quell the trouble and the redcoats immediately ran up Shaw's Brow, shouting 'down with the blues!' As soon as they had gone, people moved to help the injured policeman. Powers met Constable Nelson Lees in Richmond Row and at once reached for his bayonet, but Lees was quicker and struck his arm so he pushed the weapon back into its scabbard. Lees took the bayonet away and arrested Powers.

'We have it in for you'

As the redcoats roared along Shaw's Brow there was more trouble. According to the police version of events, Private Robert McFendries was first to see another lone policeman, Constable William Desseau, and immediately started a barrage of insults:

'You bloody blue-coated bastard; you damn thief, we have it in for you.'

If Desseau's words are to be believed, he turned around and asked, very mildly, 'What do you mean, my man?'

'I was in the picket last night,' McFendries obligingly explained, 'and there was a row between us and your men and we are determined to have revenge.' He said that McFendries punched the officer in the face, but Desseau was not intimidated; he thumped McFendries with his official staff and tried to arrest him. Naturally McFendries fought back. A draper named Samuel Lloyd ran to fetch Constable Lees and the two policemen arrested the soldier. They laid McFendries on his back, but he continued to fight, yelling and kicking at them with his boots. However, they got him under control and escorted him, still struggling, to the bridewell, but had not got past Fontenoy Street when McFendries started again, sliding to the ground and kicking at them.

Different point of view

There was another version of the events concerning McFendries. An upholsterer named Robert Weston said that McFendries had been walking quietly when a policeman had grabbed him by the collar and shook him roughly. McFendries had asked to be released, so he could return to barracks, but the policeman had held on. When McFendries tried to escape, the policeman had thumped him on the head and shoulders with his stick. McFendries had retaliated and knocked off the officer's hat, after which another policeman arrived and joined in. It was then that a picket of six soldiers under Sergeant Weber appeared.

Weber's picket

The picket was not pleased to see one of their comrades under arrest. The police later claimed that Weber drew his bayonet even although one of the privates advised him to return it to the scabbard. Weber grabbed hold of Constable Lees' shoulder. 'Clear out of this,' he ordered, and held the bayonet to the policeman's throat. Another version of the story had one of the privates draw a bayonet and Weber ordering: 'I will have none of your drawn bayonets', which seems more possible, given the rank and responsibilities of a sergeant. Either way, the picket released McFendries, who immediately began kicking and punching Lees as the sergeant watched but did nothing. The picket took the prisoner him back to the barracks, with the police joining them in vocal protest.

Even when they reached the safety of the barracks, the police had not given up. They informed the commanding officer of the 91st why they had arrested McFendries, who was handed back to their custody the next day.

More trouble

As the police argued with Sergeant Weber, there was more trouble in Scotland Road and Hunter Street when a number of soldiers met the police head on. The soldiers prepared for combat with belts and boots, but the police kept their batons under control, lifted their hands in the air to prove their peaceful intentions and bravely walked into the mass of trained and truculent redcoats. With a minimum of fuss and no violence, the police divided the soldiers into two groups and ordered them back to their barracks. That particular incident ended peacefully, but there were other groups of redcoats and discontent seethed beneath the surface.

There was further trouble in Byrom Street and Richmond Row. At about nine in the evening, a handful of the 91st were in Byrom Street when they saw half a dozen police walking purposefully toward them. 'Here they are,' an unidentified soldier shouted, 'go at them.' The skirmish was not major, but there was worse elsewhere.

In Richmond Street, there was much more serious trouble as police and soldiers met in a confused stramash that spread across the width of the street. Constable Rimmer was trying to arrest one unidentified soldier when Private McAddin swung his belt and cracked Rimmer on the back of the head. As Rimmer turned to defend himself with his staff, Private Higgens hit him with a stone wrapped in a handkerchief, a simple but effective weapon at close quarters. Constable Owen Fagan grappled with McAddin and arrested him, while Private Goodwin thumped Police Sergeant Halliday with his belt. Lunging in to help, Constable Samuel Lowe tried to reach Goodwin, but the press of bodies was too tight and he could not grab his collar. However he did manage to arrest Private McHugh, who was also actively kicking and punching at any policeman in his reach. Private Campbell also had a go at Halliday, kicking out with his heavy boots as Private Benson unfastened his belt, doubled it and flailed it around his head before aiming it at Constable Crane. The two grappled and Crane came out on top, throwing Benson to the ground and fastening handcuffs around his wrists.

As civilians either watched or scattered from the riot on Richmond Street, there were a number of minor and not so minor scuffles elsewhere in central Liverpool, as the police sought to arrest the soldiers and the soldiers actively looked for policemen to beat up.

And more

Sergeant McDonald of Rosehill Police Station led a section of five men toward Richmond Street to help control the situation and at the corner of Fox Street met eight soldiers. Rather than go on the offensive, McDonald acted calmly and simply requested that the soldiers return to barracks. Although that approach worked with most, one unhappy man, Private Connelly, tried to attack McDonald with a rock. He was quickly arrested.

In Richmond Row, six prowling privates attacked two police officers in a sudden frenzy of boots and belts. Private Donald McDonald swung his belt at Constable John Williams, while Private Joseph Dale struck him a number of times with his cane, and then kicked him viciously with his heavy army boots. Others had a go at Constable Probas, while further up the same street, soldiers felled Constable Laycock. Sergeant McDonald's six men arrived to help, and Constable Swarbrick subdued Donald McDonald. He was taking him into custody when another bunch of soldiers swarmed out of a public house and attacked him. The struggle in Richmond Row continued; the blue of the police outnumbered by the red of the army as blows and abuse were freely exchanged.

Constable Reed was off-duty and in his house when he heard what he called the 'row in Shaw's Brow', grabbed his hat and staff and rushed out to help his colleagues. He hurried toward the noise, still fastening the buttons of his uniform as he walked. It was not long before he saw the police and soldiers engaged in a furious struggle and identified Private Andrews, who was threatening Constable John Thompson with a heavy stick. Thompson had other things on his mind as he tried to arrest Private Burns.

'Let him go,' Andrews roared, 'or I will knock your brains out.'

Reed dived in, snatched the stick from Andrews and arrested him. All around him, the fighting continued as the guardians of the country battled with the forces of law and order.

'The soldiers are licking the police'

The public were interested in the spectacle of the two bodies of uniformed men, both intended to keep the country secure and orderly, engaged in a furious fight. Crowds gathered to watch the fun and a cry of: 'The soldiers are licking the police' ran around. Some of the civilians were caught up in the general excitement and joined in, generally on the side of the army. One man named Barnes was encouraging the soldiers to attack the police. 'Use your bayonets,' he yelled, 'stick them!' Thankfully the soldiers ignored his shouts, more inclined to fight than murder. Another civilian named Goodison attacked Constable Richard Rauthorne and tried to stop him arresting a redcoat, while youths threw stones at every policeman they saw.

According to the police, Private McGill, fresh from his escapades with Duggan, now used a life-preserver, a short, heavy and often lead-weighted club, as he thumped Constable Moore on the wrist to try and make him drop his staff. Not only private soldiers were involved; a Sergeant named Keely also joined in the general attack on the police. According to later police evidence, he had tried to rescue one of his privates in Richmond Row and threatened one of the constables that he would 'put six inches of steel into your guts.'

A confused court

The riot was so confused and involved so many bodies of soldiers spread over so many different streets that when the perpetrators eventually came to court, the judge and jury, to say nothing about the police, had had a difficult time deciding exactly which soldier had been responsible for which particular outrage. The police believed that the soldiers who had been involved in the original trouble in Dale Street had not continued their escapades elsewhere, while sundry other parties of redcoats had been involved in a series of scuffles throughout the town. The court asked Major Gordon of the 91st to give evidence, but he refused, saying only that the police had meted out 'brutal treatment' to his men. Gordon also added that the soldiers involved in the riots had disgraced the regiment and the army and should hang their heads in shame.

As the members of the court nodded agreement, Gordon told them that the police were in the habit of treating the men badly, and several civilians had come to his quarters to inform him of the savage way the police treated soldiers, some of whom were not in the same regiment and had not been involved in the trouble.

The trial was delayed and put off a number of times because the evidence gathered by the police was scattered and contradictory. The accused soldiers were returned to Major Gordon's command until the police could sort out their charges. Gordon said his men would be 'closely confined to barracks' and added that: 'some of them are blackguards but when put on their honour they would not forfeit their bail. Coming from these horrid cells without being cleaned might operate against them but if liberated on bail they would appear clean and orderly as becoming Queen's soldiers.'

Eventually, the case was heard in the Crown Court. The first men to be tried were Privates Trussler and Carey for assaulting a civilian named William Yates and attacking Constable Dodd. Mr Snowball, in defence, said that Yates was drunk and had struck the first blow, while the crowd had provoked the soldiers by jeering 'red coats' at them. He added that the police were prone to be aggressive toward private soldiers. The prosecution denied this of course but Ensign Sweeney of the 91st gave evidence that the crowd had been shouting 'bloody red ruffians.' At one time, the mob had Trussler and Carey backed against the wall and surrounded them with threats of extreme violence. The two soldiers had only defended themselves, Ensign Sweeney claimed.

Although the court would be reluctant to believe the word of an ordinary redcoat, a 'Tommy', they could not disbelieve an officer and a gentleman, however junior. Although Sweeney suggested that the police had beaten up Carey after he had been taken to the station, and Surgeon Richard Peel of the 91st was ready to give proof, the magistrates did not want to hear anything against the police. They seem to have already decided that the army were to blame for any trouble. They fined Trussler sixty shillings, with an alternative of six weeks in jail, and Carey forty shillings or four weeks in jail. As a soldier's pay, after stoppages, was around two shillings a week, these were huge fines.

McFendries was next and Snowball claimed that he was arrested merely because he had insulted the police: 'We all know that police officers are dignified persons and cannot submit to observations being made against them.' Snowball claimed that the arrest was illegal, but it was hard evidence that the magistrates were more concerned with. They heard a number of wildly differing accounts and decided they could not find out the truth, so discharged McFendries.

Snowball tried to cast doubt as to the identity of several of the soldiers who were in custody, pointing out that Power had been on guard duty until ten to nine and claiming he had been quietly walking along Richmond Row, minding his own business, when the police pounced on him. Snowball, who seemed to have been a very able defence solicitor, also produced three steady sergeants of different regiments who claimed they had seen McGill being attacked by the police and not the other way round.

The magistrates listened but did not always believe. They discharged Power for lack of evidence, but McGill and two others, Wraith and Cronin, were fined £5 each with the option of two months in jail. Other soldiers were discharged through lack of hard evidence after the testimony of the Rev J. R. Connor, chaplain to the 91st, that the police were 'running about in all directions, breaking the soldiers' heads wherever they could find them.'

With officers and the chaplain fighting hard to defend the honour of their men, the magistrates decided that sufficient of the soldiers had been prosecuted to 'satisfy the ends of justice.' Mr Dowling, who had been prosecuting, said he 'trusted that neither the soldiers nor the police would thereafter manifest any spirit of revenge or ill-feeling.' As the motto of the 91st was *Ne Obliviscaris* – do not forget – that may have been a forlorn hope.

However, Colonel Campbell, the commander in chief of the 91st, said he had always 'cautioned his men against getting into quarrels' and 'he had so much confidence in his men that he had no fear of a repetition taking place.' Perhaps fortunately, the loyal colonel's faith was not put to the test as the 91st left Liverpool very shortly afterward. Elements of the regiment were involved in severe fighting in South Africa shortly afterward, and they served with honour during the Indian Mutiny of 1857.

'We will call out the guard and sack the place'

That was not the only riot involving the military in Liverpool. On 11 September 1871 there was another case, but not on anything like the same scale. Again there was conflicting evidence, as the army and the police gave different sides of the same encounter.

One version claims that a brassfounder named Thomas Stanley was walking along Everton Road at half past midnight. He was sober as a sheriff and had been called from his house and asked to escort Mary Anne Williams, his landlord's daughter, home from her work. Her sister, Elizabeth, had tagged along and the three were innocently chatting when Stanley noticed a group of soldiers of the 4th Dragoon Guards coming toward them, arm in arm and noisy. Stanley and his female companions stepped onto the road to let the dragoons pass, but the soldiers came to confront them. One, Private Thomas Clarke, put his hand around Mary's waist. 'Polly,' he said, 'are you my wife?'

Mary said nothing, but when Stanley pulled Clarke's hand from her waist, the dragoon punched him on the head. Stanley retaliated by thumping Clarke with a sunshade. Clarke ran away, but Stanley chased him, shouting for the police. The two men fought in the middle of the street, with Clarke getting the better of it by nearly strangling Stanley. Another soldier, Corporal Jackson of the same regiment gave Clarke a hand, and both turned on the police when they arrived to clear things up.

Fists flew, but when more police arrived Jackson and Clarke were dragged to a nearby garden, overpowered and handcuffed. That should have been the end of the matter, but an officer of the regiment, Captain John Bates, had observed the scene. Regimental loyalty proved stronger than the concept of law and order and he yelled out:

'People of Liverpool, will you stand this? Will you have one of our men taken by these bloody police?' He raised his voice further. 'If they take him to the bridewell, we will call out the guard and sack the place.'

'Keep your eye on him,' one constable advised the others, and a moment later he fell as Bates threw a brick that crashed into his forehead. As he tried to get up, Bates leaped down, 'Bloody flunkies!' he shouted and grabbed the policeman by the collar.

As usual, a crowd had gathered, some baying their discontent and dislike of the police and others just there to watch this free entertainment. The police gave the crowd as 300 people.

Other versions

The police versions of the story were all slightly different, which was natural as they were all busy with their own affairs and would be only vaguely aware what happened at the periphery of their vision. One policeman thought he heard Captain Bates say, 'Kill the bloody sergeant: he is drunk!' Another said that the crowd had tried to rescue Clarke, and that may be true as in that period the crowd often intervened to rescue people from police custody. Yet, another thought the crowd were on the side of the police.

Another version of the incident denied that Bates had thrown a brick, but said that the crowd had stoned the police. Henry Buckley, a cotton salesman, claimed that rather than trying to incite the crowd to violence, Bates had offered to fetch a picket from the barracks to take Jackson away. Buckley claimed that the police had rejected the offer and arrested Bates instead. Joseph Byrne, another of the witnesses, put the crowd at around 150 rather than 200. He thought he saw a police officer run up behind Jackson and smack him on the back of the neck with his staff before dragging him into a garden. Byrne claimed that he ran to the barracks and told them the police were attacking the soldiers and asked for help. That was why Captain Bates had arrived. Byrne also said that the police had attacked Bates and not vice versa.

A number of soldiers, officers, privates and NCOs, mentioned that when Jackson and Clarke were taken into the bridewell, the police treated them with great brutality and refused to send for a doctor. Clarke was found guilty but Jackson and Bates were not prosecuted. When Clarke apologised, the charge against him was withdrawn and he walked free.

Overall, Liverpool had an ambivalent attitude to the military. The soldiers were treated much as any other group of people. They were part of the community and in the nineteenth century were possibly more accepted than the police, but they had a chequered past of riot and disorder.

8
Contrast: Criminal and Lawman

There are two sides to the law: the right side and the wrong side. Sometimes it is interesting to look at the rivals and see which had the more success.

The life and times of a career pickpocket

It is unlikely that anybody in the English-speaking world has not heard of Charles Dickens. He was undoubtedly one of the most talented novelists and social commentators of his time. Most people will be aware of, and may even have read, the book *Oliver Twist* with the infamous Fagin and his youthful gang. Dickens was very much in tune with his period, for pickpockets were a curse to the respectable and unwary who braved the crowded streets and public spaces of every British town and city.

The Industrial Revolution and the rapid expansion of trade, as well as the growth of cities, meant that there were more wealthy people in Britain than ever before. Merchants and their ladies, mill owners and their wives, landed gentry and the associated professionals of solicitors, engineers and accountants all promenaded the streets in numbers never dreamed of before. Nineteenth-century Liverpool was a city of amazing contrasts between the wealthy and the desperately poor, but sliding from one side to the other were the pickpockets who aimed at a redistribution of wealth from the pockets of the rich to those of themselves.

It was a good time to be a thief, for as well as an expanding number of possible targets, there were also more places for a pickpocket to operate. As well as a plethora of streets with denser crowds for cover, there were railway stations and coach stops, inns and markets, sporting events and public hangings, plus the docks where emigrants and immigrants shuffled shoulder to shoulder in their confused thousands. Through the crowds sidled the pickpockets.

There was a definite hierarchy of pickpockets, from tiny children hardly old enough to walk, through the gonophs, or street urchins, to what were known as mobsmen. These were the elite of the profession who walked among the respectable dressed like one of their own, tipped their stovepipe hat to the ladies as they relieved their husbands of the burden of excess gold. It is possible to trace the careers of some of these people by the breadcrumb trail of court records they left as they were caught and convicted, but these are incomplete for a variety of reasons. For a start, court records do not reveal the successes, only the failures, and many criminals changed their name with alarming frequency, so may have been convicted under two or more aliases.

Very few of the thousands of pickpockets left anything like a record of their lives, but in late 1850 the chaplain of the Preston House of Correction took down the slightly rambling memoirs of a man named John Flanagan, who was also known as Thomas Morris. Flanagan was a professional pickpocket with a Liverpool connection and his life story was one of constant theft, with no thought or prick of conscience for his many victims. There was no code of honour among thieves, no hint of Robin Hood. His life was sordid, pointless and, in a way, sad.

John Flanagan's story

Flanagan first graced this world in Chester sometime in 1822, his mother and father were both hawkers, people who travelled the country selling small items as a means of making a living. They must have been better than average parents for they taught their son to read and write, but at the age of fourteen he ran away from home. As so often, Flanagan started with small things and moved up the scale. He began as a petty pilferer, and then at some point he became embroiled with a number of older men, who taught him the gentle art of pickpocketing. Silk handkerchiefs were an easy first target as they were often ostentatiously displayed in the coat tails outside the wearer's clothes, hence the name of 'tailing' for that type of theft. Once Flanagan mastered that art, he graduated on to 'dipping' into pockets of gentlemen and then of ladies.

Liverpool was a tremendous place for a thief, with so much through-traffic who may not even miss their belongings until they were either at sea on a packet ship, or miles away in a train. One of Flanagan's favoured hunting grounds was the docks, where passengers were arriving or leaving on the packet boats to Ireland and Scotland.

The detective police

According to Flanagan, his older companions dressed him as a gentleman's son, so he was hardly challenged as he thrust through the crowded landing stages and the packed decks, dipping into the pockets of the unwary for any valuables that he could find. He worked the German packets at Hull as well, but preferred the pickings in Liverpool, because getting on board foreign vessels was not always easy. The detective police were also more vigilant around the German vessels and as Flanagan said, 'it was only them we dreaded when we went to work.' He also said that the presence of detectives forced him to change his clothes more than once, presumably so he was not as easily recognised. The fact that he made these admissions proved that the police were effective.

Bribery

If Flanagan or his companions witnessed a man who they knew had a heavy purse, they would follow him from the ship into the railway station and dip his pocket there. Sometimes that meant bribing a cab driver or even a policeman to turn the other way, but Flanagan knew who could be bribed and who could not. In a good week, he could make as much as £8 from pickpocketing, but it was dangerous work, for there were a number of men at the same game, and the majority of police were vigilant. He knew of at least eight other pickpocketing 'mobs' who worked the landing stage at Hull, but the police did not catch him because he was careful.

The penalty for being caught could be severe and sometimes it was better to be arrested than to have the victim become suddenly aware. There was one such occasion at the statute fair at Brigg, a small market town in north Lincolnshire, when he entered the local inn for refreshment. When a farm labourer saw him trying to pick the pocket of the landlady, he gave the alarm. A group of labourers, hard-muscled men of the soil, jumped Flanagan and, in his own words, 'kicked me like a football. I should have been killed but for a young farmer who came up.' Despite the farmer's intervention, Flanagan was badly injured and out of commission for some weeks after that incident.

By that stage Flanagan was a tall, broad-shouldered young man, but also a skilled thief; there was no looking back. But why should there be? He had a much easier life as a pickpocket, and made much more money than he would as a mill hand or working in service, on a farm or, God help him, at sea. His memoirs were confused as to time and sequence, and there were few names mentioned, for obvious reasons, but the anecdotes ring true enough.

An itinerant life

After the incident at Brigg, an unnamed man and woman befriended Flanagan and taught him more of the arts of the thief, but they also took most of the proceeds of his enterprises. The older couple exploited their young protégé and lived in style while Flanagan did the hard work, but they were eventually caught and transported. Frustratingly, Flanagan gave no details of their capture. He now joined, or was picked up by, a company of itinerant travellers who kept him in clothes and food, while his thieving supplied them with purses, silk handkerchiefs, watches and pocket books.

Eventually, Flanagan began to resent handing over the proceeds of his hard work, and he left the company to make money for himself. However, he was a successful thief but a poor businessman, for he had picked up bad personal habits in his disreputable life. As well as a thief, he was a gambler and lost most of his money at tossing coins or the turn of the cards. He based himself in Manchester, but worked much of the time in Liverpool.

Hunting grounds

As always, there were various places where the pickings were easiest: the docks where the packet boats came in were always teeming with excited, wealthy men and in such a crowd as gathered there, nobody noticed one more young man who momentarily pressed against them and withdrew again. Railway stations or even railway trains were also favoured, for here were more crowds, more distractions and more bulging pocket books and chinking purses. A third and even more lucrative area were the banks, for men taking money to, or withdrawing money from, were not always as careful as they should have been. Crowds attracted pickpockets, so Flanagan haunted theatres and concerts at opening and closing times, when people milled around in an excited throng; he robbed on trains and threw the empty purses and pocket books out of the window, or dropped them in the pocket of some unsuspecting naïve fool. Life was good for a successful thief.

A tax on thieving

In that period, large denomination bank notes were not as common as they became later, so anybody who was not obviously a gentleman tendering a note in excess of a pound was liable to arouse suspicion. For that reason, Flanagan needed a fence – somebody to launder the stolen money. He found a crooked Liverpool publican, but the man had to make a profit and charged for his services, so a stolen £10 note would only raise £9, with higher amounts gaining roughly the same amount of commission. It was like a tax on thieving. Publicans had a privileged position as they were used to handling relatively large amounts of money and had custom from all walks of life. However, Flanagan's fence ran out of luck in 1848 and he was transported for his sins.

Around the same time the police also caught Flanagan. He had stolen £20 in gold from a lady, but the Liverpool police pounced and he ended behind the cold walls of Kirkdale Jail for twelve long months. He emerged to a reception committee that comprised his old companions in theft, as well as his mother. Flanagan had a stark choice. He could return to his old life of thieving, but now as a man known to the police and therefore in danger of longer and tougher sentences if he was caught, or he could bid farewell to the left-hand road and allow his mother to guide him on the path of righteousness.

After so long on the wrong side of the law, and knowing the choice between poverty and comparative affluence, Flanagan chose the thief's way and only two days later, he was sniffing around a company of the 8th Foot, the King's Regiment. The ordinary redcoats were not worth robbing: their pay of a shilling a day less stoppages hardly left enough for themselves, yet alone surplus for a thief, but the officers were men of means, gentlemen who usually had independent fortunes to supplement their army pay. Flanagan watched an officer produce a heavy pocket book, look around and put it back in his pocket. That was surely an invitation to rob and the pocket book was soon in Flanagan's possession, with the £10 inside. Officers were good targets for a pickpocket. On one occasion Flanagan stole a Highland officer's wallet and found himself over £200 richer – four years' wages for an average labourer.

The criminal circuit

Now that he was committed to a life of crime, Flanagan worked a circuit, travelling through the English Midlands and North with a group of like-minded individuals. Travelling by coach or rail, they wandered as far south as Cambridge and as far north as Yorkshire. They once crossed the Irish Sea to take their plundering depravations to Dublin and the fairs and racecourses of the horse-loving community. He made good money but lost it again, quickly and foolishly.

In common with many of his kind, Flanagan liked fine clothes and good food, and that cost much of the money he stole. The rest he gambled away. Quality clothes enabled him to appear like a gentleman, and it was from the upper echelons of society that he got the best pickings. Pocket books, purses and gold watches supplemented the income he occasionally made when the cards turned in his favour. One lucky evening at the green baize table earned him £200; such wealth helped him avoid the scrutiny of the police, who expected thieves to inhabit the poorer areas of towns and cities and not the more upmarket public houses and inns. Flanagan enjoyed his success when it came, for he knew that a downturn in his luck could see him on a transport ship to hell.

Diversification

Nevertheless, Flanagan's lifestyle caught up with him. He developed a liking for drink, so he drank away much of his gains and had less to spend on fine clothes. He diversified his crime, going into partnership with a man and woman as street robbers, but found the three-way split was less lucrative than simple pocket-dipping. Street robbery was as old as creation; the woman would entice a naïve or drunk man into a dark place, where her two companions would pounce and either half-strangle him or just punch him into semi-consciousness, so the woman could go through his pockets for whatever he happened to have. There was neither finesse nor skill, but brutality and a lack of conscience.

Flanagan tried burglary but there was more danger than reward: he gained only £5, which for a man of his expensive tastes was hardly worth getting out of bed for. Once again, Flanagan found pickpocketing paid better than any of the rest. It was around this time, with maddeningly sparse dates or names to back up his story, that he mentioned George Wombwell's circus as another lucrative arena. Wombwell's Travelling Menagerie was well known in early Victorian Britain. From a humble beginning in 1810, by 1840 it was fifteen wagons strong and announced its arrival with a raucous brass band. Wombwell died in 1850, but the circus survived.

Flanagan said that if the thief made 'all right' with one of Wombwell's keepers, it was easy to pick the pockets of the circus users. The keeper would take the entrance fee, take note in which pocket the visitor put his money and tell the pickpocket. If the thief was seen or suspected, the keeper would give a false description of a non-existent person to 'shade off' or draw attention from the real culprit. People who acted like this were known as 'stallsmen for the dip' and they got their 'whack' of the proceeds. However, even with such help, the thieves could be caught. Flanagan claimed that James Dowlan, one of the most noted of the Wombwell dippers, ended his career on a transport ship to Australia. A search of the transportation records, however, did not find anybody of that name, although a James Doran was transported for fifteen years in 1840.

Flanagan's luck runs out

Flanagan also ran out of luck during a robbery at Burnley. At that time he was working with five companions. Three escaped but Flanagan together with William Thompson and somebody with the name of Bohanna were caught and arrested. There was a Maria Bohanna who was sentenced to be transported for seven years at the Quarter Sessions in January 1837, which seems slightly too early. Either her sentence was revoked or she sailed under a different name, for she does not appear in the transportation registers.

A window into crime

Flanagan was not inclined to be silent while in police custody and gave the name William Buckley and a description of one of the men who got away. Flanagan said that Buckley was a street robber and used 'picking up women' to draw in his victims. As seemed normal, Buckley operated in a mob. Flanagan gave particulars of his methods. He 'put the damper' on his targets, which meant he attacked from behind and put his arm around the victim's throat and mouth, so he was half-strangled and could not shout out for help. While in this position, two others of the mob, a man and a woman, would go through the victim's pockets for plunder. It is possible that Buckley was the man with whom Flanagan was earlier associated and the two had a disagreement, hence his willingness to inform the police.

Buckley used a cart drawn by three dogs. The woman travelled in the carts, which, under dog power, could travel as far as forty miles in a day. He worked with a man who used the name of Shawe, which was an alias for his real name of Lynham. Unlike many other criminals, Buckley did not gamble and did not drink to excess. At one time he had been part of an extensive gang that operated with two dogcarts, plus hawkers' licences to give the impression that they were respectable.

Flanagan also mentioned a man named Henry Kilty who trained youngsters to become pickpockets, and he mentioned a Liverpool woman who trained up her own three children in the gentle art of thieving. Dickens' Fagan was only one of a whole host of child-thief mentors and more true to life than fiction readers may suppose. Crime fact is more unbelievable and often more sordid and chilling than crime fiction.

Flanagan also said that there were around sixty men who drove their dogcarts around the markets, fairs and race courses of England. They set up stalls with cheap china and crockery, but their real business was in dipping. They provided the base and headquarters from where their sons, all trained pickpockets, would go hunting in the various places that the stalls were set up. In such a close community, the mothers of the boys also ran stalls, so if the boys were suspected of theft, the mother would be there to immediately take away suspicion and provide a safe haven. The women were as crooked as the men, for they had a stock of forged coins that they gave as change to their customers. Flanagan did not mention if the mothers and fathers of the thieves were married or not, or if they stayed together.

Flanagan spoke of a woman named Margaret Ridgeway who was part of a family of thieves and forgers. When her husband died, she carried on the family business, again using her sons as dips. He claimed that Ridgeway's daughter was transported for seven years for robbing a Cambridge farmer's wife, while Ridgeway and her sons had all seen the inside of a prison. Unfortunately, yet again, a search did not find a record of any female named Ridgeway being transported.

Flanagan gave the Chaplain an account of his thieving, but only the larger amounts were recorded. He was a prolific thief from 1838 until late 1849, and haunted concert halls, theatres, coach offices, packet boats, the race course and the zoological garden in Liverpool. He robbed in a whole host of towns, from Manchester to Chesterfield, Horncastle to Spalding and carried his depredations over the sea to Ireland.

In a career that lasted most of his youth and adult life, Flanagan was seventeen times in prison before his eventual transportation to Australia. Once more his name does not appear in transportation lists, so possibly he sailed under an alias. That only adds to the mystery of his confessions. In its confusion, total lack of scruples and roller-coaster ride, Flanagan's life story could be used as a microcosm of the underbelly of mid-Victorian life.

While the career criminal could have a varied life when he was out of prison, his nemesis the criminal officer or detective, also had an interesting career.

A mid-century detective

Joseph Storey was never to rise to public fame or become a literary figure. He was never to be a hero or a wealthy man. Instead, he was to work hard and steadily in his task of keeping the streets of Liverpool safer for the decent people of the town. Storey was a detective officer in the 1840s and 1850s, a time when Britain was surviving the Hungry Forties and moving into the Fighting Fifties.

These few pages give only a flavour of the day-to-day tasks of a typical Liverpool detective when Queen Victoria was on the throne. They cover only four years, 1848 to 1851, but reveal a lot about the methods a typical detective would use.

Phoney coins

In February 1848 Storey, then a uniformed constable, was working with Constable Marks in Myrtle Street, when they noticed a man and woman sidling furtively into a public house. The couple looked so suspicious in their movements that Storey and Marks followed a few moments later and watched them pass money over the counter to get some change. When Storey inspected the coins, he found them to be counterfeit and arrested the couple, Thomas and Mary Ford. Thomas immediately put his hand to his mouth, so Storey grabbed him and prised open his mouth. The man swallowed quickly, but Storey managed to extract a few fake shillings before the rest disappeared down his throat. The couple were eventually jailed.

Fencing

Toward the end of March that same year, a load of copper was stolen from a ship named *Haidee*, and an informant told Storey that Mary Smith's marine shop would be worth a visit. He searched the Challinor Street shop and found the copper in minutes, but being a thorough man he rummaged for anything else that could have been stolen. There was a bag of wool that weighed forty-four pounds that caught Storey's attention and he asked who had sold such a large volume of wool. Smith told him she had bought it from a warehouseman named Robert Kirkpatrick. Storey investigated further and discovered that two men, MacGregor and James Tyrer had carried the wool, with Tyrer accepting the money. More probing found that the wool had been in a warehouse run by a man named McKnight, who was the legal keeper, and Kirkpatrick worked there.

Tyrer and MacGregor were not charged, as they had not known that the wool was stolen, and Smith had bought it in good faith, and entered the purchase in her books with no guilt. Storey found her help invaluable in tracing Kirkpatrick and also William Ford, who was the shipkeeper of *Haidee* and had stolen the copper. Smith was reprimanded for accepting stolen goods and then released while Ford and Kirkpatrick were jailed.

Robberies

Storey had a quiet few months but came to public attention in December when there had been a spate of robberies in the St James Street area. A number of officers were stationed in St James Street and Simpson Street, and on the evening of Saturday, 9 December 1848, Storey saw a group of youths leave a house in a filthy court in Simpson Street. He watched closely as they slid into a narrow passage next to a flour dealer's shop run by Mr Hawksworth. They were there some time before they returned to the court, and while another officer watched the door of the house they had entered, Storey inspected the shop. The youths had been trying to cut through the brick wall at the side. Storey helped arrest John Kelly, John McGinn, Edward Valily, Ellen McCabe and Margaret Mansfield, who were charged with attempted robbery.

The following month Storey, now a sergeant, together with an officer named Povey, was investigating a number of robberies in shops and houses around the town. They suspected that a professional gang was involved rather than a number of isolated cases, and put out the word that they were on the hunt. As was so often the case, an informant whispered where the likely thieves may be, and on the last Friday in January, Storey and Povey raided a house in Primrose Street. They found stolen tobacco and tobacco pipes as well as a watch and various other articles that had been taken from different addresses. Three men and two women were arrested.

But things were not always so smooth.

The down-side of being a police officer

In May 1849, Sergeant Storey was on duty in Simpson Street with Constable Slack when a gang of men attacked them. Vastly outnumbered, the two officers fought back, but were knocked to the ground and kicked so badly that it was months before Slack totally recovered. Some of the attackers were arrested within a matter of hours, but two, Edward Digney and James Routledge, escaped and took ship to America, where the hid out for a few months. They returned to Liverpool in August and were promptly arrested, tried and thrown into jail.

A detective

Shortly after this event Storey was transferred to the detective branch, and continued with his often thankless task of cleansing the streets of crime. In June 1849, he was on plain-clothes duty, watching a gang of pickpockets. These men had an interesting method. They had teamed up with a group of black musicians and, when their songs attracted a crowd, the pickpockets would sidle around, lifting a purse here, a watch there and any loose money that might be available.

Storey watched until he was sure of his men and moved in. He arrested William Jones, Thomas Saxon and John McAvoy, who were all sent to jail for three months. That same month Storey was also involved in locating a quantity of stolen textiles from a cellar in Henderson Street. In common with every detective in Liverpool, Storey relied on informants to bring him information.

Coiners again

Forged coins were a major concern in the period, and Sergeant Storey was on the ball in October 1849 when an informant told him there was a gang of coiners operating in Tatlock Street. Together with detectives Povey and Ockleshaw, he slipped into the street and watched what was happening. When a man came out of No. 12 court, emptied some cinders on the ground, raked them and took away something, Storey thought he had his man.

Waiting for a few moments, Storey burst in the house and found three people, Patrick and Eliza Hackett and Mary McCormack, all watching a pot on a central fire. The police searched the room and found moulds for making false coins, as well as thirteen newly-created fake shillings. The three coiners were immediately arrested. Storey seemed to be on an anti-coining crusade that month, for he and officers Povey and Ockleshaw also raided a coiner's house in Peter's Lane and arrested David Brown for possessing a mould and a number of counterfeit shilling coins. When they entered the house they saw Brown slide something into his waistcoat pocket. He was searched and counterfeit coins were found in his possession and in the fireplace. Brown tried to claim that a 'man had called on him and left them there', but the police did not believe this, particularly when a local shopkeeper confirmed that Brown had paid for his purchases with a false shilling. He was arrested and charged.

That was a busy month for Storey, for he was also instrumental in investigating a break in at Great Homer Street, where four men were charged with stealing plate and jewellery.

An excellent officer, but ...

However, the next month Storey found himself in trouble as his methods were not entirely in line with the law. A man named Harrison came to the police office and said he suspected his servant, Harriet Jones, had stolen £10 from his desk. Storey followed Jones from Harrison's home to a house in Parliament Street, knocked at the door and told her of his suspicions. 'If you don't tell me about it,' he warned, 'I must search the house.'

As Jones proved reluctant to tell him anything, Storey carried out his threat and found a box with nine sovereigns and seven shillings. Only then did Jones admit that she had stolen the note and had exchanged it at a public house. Nonetheless, however successful Storey had been in his endeavour, the court was unhappy and told him that, although he was 'an excellent officer', he had 'no business to say "if you don't tell me about the note I will go and search the house".' Apparently the threat had excluded his evidence.

Observation and patience

That decade ended on a high as Storey used two of the detectives' most important tools to solve another crime: patience and informers. An informant had advised the police to watch a certain house in Mould Street, Scotland Road, where a man named William Barton was said to be hoarding stolen property. Storey brought a small team of officers to watch the house and for day after day that bleak December, they huddled in doorways and shivered under winter rain as they observed and took notes of all that happened. On 24 December, Storey saw Barton and two other men standing outside the house, obviously engaged in a deep discussion.

Storey decided that it was time to act, so, whistling up his men, he crossed the road and made his presence and function known. Barton looked up as soon as he saw the police.

'There is a large box in the lobby there,' he said at once. 'I don't know what's in it or where it came from.'

Storey led his team on a thorough search of the house and discovered that it was like an Aladdin's Cave of crime, with a sufficient haul to fill a pair of tradesmen's carts. The house was stuffed with stolen goods: scented soap, books, jars of sweets, garden seeds, cheese, even a pig all dressed for eating. Storey arrested two men and one woman, and asked more questions.

The thieves had a simple modus operandi that was neither particularly clever nor subtle. They watched shop doorways until goods were placed outside, then ran off with them. At a period when most shops were small and part of the stock was often displayed outside, they did not have far to go to find goods to steal.

A quiet year

After the adventures of 1849, 1850 was a much quieter year for Storey. He had only routine enquiries to deal with, such as the man and woman he arrested for loitering in Abercromby Square in November, and the four young boys he helped arrest for stealing shoes in Toxteth Park in December.

The following year, however, was entirely different.

A busy year

Storey had a successful third week in January 1851. At about midnight on Monday, 22 January, he was patrolling around a public house called St James Vaults, when he saw a face he recognised. In common with all the best policemen, Storey knew the most notorious criminals by sight, so when a face caught his attention, he mentally rifled through his filing cabinet of a mind to recall names and offences. This man was William Thomson, only twenty-six but already with a record of crime that could fill a medium-sized book. He had spent most of his youth and adult life in jail, with fifteen short and medium terms of imprisonment before being transported for seven years in 1846.

Storey took note of Thomson, but there was no reason to arrest him. On the following night, St James Vaults was burgled. The offices had been occupied by a man named Reeves, but he had gone bankrupt, and the Court of Bankruptcy had appointed two officers to check the figures and assets. Thomson was not concerned with the figures, but he certainly wanted as many of the assets as he could hold in his hands.

Thomson was a professional. He entered the house next door and chiselled a hole in the brickwork above the fireplace to gain access. He had crawled in, broken open the writing desk and till, and taken all he could find before leaving by the same route. However, Storey had warned the beat police that Thomson was on the prowl and he had only gone as far as Dale Street before the local policeman stopped him on suspicion. Despite Thomson's protests, the officer searched him and found a woman's brooch and a pocketful of silver and copper coins. The officer took Thomson to the police office and while he was there, the robbery was discovered. The barmaid claimed ownership of the brooch and Thomson's guilt was established.

He was tried at the Spring assizes and sent to Australia for the next twenty years.

More robberies

The same week, on Wednesday, 24 January 1851 Sergeant Storey was patrolling Scotland Road when he saw a pair of youths hanging around the pawnshop of Charles Roscoe. He watched them for a few moments and decided that they were acting suspiciously, so followed them at a distance. After a few moments they doubled-back to Roscoe's and tried to break the window, but failed, so Storey scooped them up. The two youths were searched and interrogated, along with another girl of around the same age, who was known to be a close friend. All three were arrested in different places.

It turned out that the three were all part of the same criminal gang who had been involved in an extensive robbery of jewellery, at a pawnbroker on Brownlow Hill the previous Saturday night. The three, Elizabeth and William Campbell, and Ann Duffy had carefully opened the shutters, cut a pane of glass from the window and removed £27 worth of wedding and other rings. Once finished, they had closed the shutters so nobody noticed the robbery until the Monday morning.

When Elizabeth Campbell was arrested, she was wearing one of the stolen rings, which pointed a very definite finger at her as a suspect. Storey did his usual rounds and located seven of the stolen rings at a number of different pawnbrokers in the area. He spoke to the pawnbrokers and their descriptions of the young women who pledged the rings matched the suspects exactly. There were other stolen items pledged as well, so Storey and his colleague Povey had broken quite a successful band of thieves.

The next month, Storey arrested a woman named Elizabeth Edwards, who was suspected of obtaining goods under false pretences. She had toured several shops in the Parliament Street area, bringing her two children with her and choosing items but not paying for them. She claimed that her husband was a sea captain and she would get the money from him. Of course, she never returned until Storey arrested her and brought her in to be identified.

A busy month

In March 1851, Storey was busy again with a couple of cases. The first time he only played a small part in the proceedings. This episode began on the night of Sunday, 8 March, when Peter Battersby, a night watchman, saw a light flickering through the window of Mr Troughton, who worked in the Harrington Lime Works. He knew that Troughton was not in his office at that time. Battersby was outside, so he stepped on some upended barrels to peer through the window.

There were three men in the office, their figures shadowy in the pooled yellow light of a candle as they flitted around the desk and cabinets, testing the drawers and speaking in hushed tones as they tried to unlock the safe. Battersby alerted the authorities and the police came thundering round, all heavy boots and rustling capes.

Naturally, the noise scared the thieves and they broke and fled, but one, William Napier, was slow and tried to hide in the yard. The police shone their lanterns, with the beams of yellow light flicking into the dark corners, until one gleamed on his face. He swore, turned and desperately clambered up the wall, leaped down and ran into the winter-black streets outside. But he had not gone far when a policeman grabbed him and held him tight.

In the meantime, the police examined Troughton's office. The door and a number of drawers gaped open, while there was a large bunch of keys left lying on the desk. The thieves had taken the keys from the lower to the upper office and were systematically trying each to see which opened the safe. Battersby's alarm had disturbed them before they stole anything important.

The police scanned the yard and found another bunch of skeleton keys, exactly where Napier had been standing; presumably that was how the burglars had gained access. They also scoured the area, searching for witnesses and spoke to a boy who had seen one of the other men running 'like a hare' along a narrow alley. His description was clear, despite the darkness of the night, and the police could identify a man named Peter Duff. Storey comes into the picture now, for he knew Duff as a professional thief, and arrested him the following day.

The second case that month was another robbery. On Saturday 14 March Storey was walking through Thompson Street when he saw Joseph Ormsby and Edward Richardson, two well-known thieves, leaving one of the houses. Naturally suspicious, Storey followed them at a distance as they walked through the dingy streets, but either the pair knew they were being tailed, or Storey was distracted, for he lost them.

Later that night, Storey learned that there had been a robbery in Thompson Street and he decided to have a word with Ormsby. He accompanied Inspector Locock to the beer shop Ormsby ran in

Richmond Row. This was not a large place, but a single room with a bad reputation of being a haven for thieves, ne'er-do-wells and assorted riff raff. Storey rapped on the door and shouted 'Police!'

There was no reply except the drawing shut of the bolt, so Storey booted the door open and rushed in. He arrested Ormsby and a man named John Lucas, who had an equally unsavoury reputation. However, there was no sign of any stolen property. Storey knew Ormsby's contacts and moved to a Leeds Street pub run by a known fence named William Mercer and admitted he had recently bought some small silver items from Ormsby. All three men were arrested.

Arrest of burglar gang

In the spring of 1851, the south-east of Liverpool and the surrounding suburbs seemed to be under siege by burglars. From March onward the residents of Catherine Street, Upper Parliament Street and the entire neighbourhood lived in nightly fear of robbery. They locked and checked their doors, bolted their shutters if they had them and tried to protect their valuables. However, their efforts were often in vain.

The burglars were interested in small, valuable but easily portable items such as watches, jewellery, silver pencil cases, teaspoons and other silverware. Items such as these could be easily transported and pawned in any of the many shady pawnbrokers in the back streets of Liverpool. The burglars had an interesting method of entering their selected properties: they would check to see that the lights in the house were out and approach the rear of the property. Then, quietly, they would cut a neat hole in the back door, thrust through a hand and withdraw the securing bolt.

After a spate of such robberies, the people of the district were very much on edge. Some householders began to arm themselves, so the district was filled with nervous men who had pokers, sticks and even guns handy. When a house in Edgehead was broken into, the owner heard a noise, lifted his revolver and rushed to investigate. He saw a gang of burglars, men and a woman, in his house, and fired three shots, but, either through inexperience or nervousness, or because revolvers were notoriously inaccurate weapons at the best of times, he missed each time. He stayed awake all night in case the gang returned and next morning he told Detective Officer Storey about the burglary and described the people he had shot at.

Storey recognised the description as a man he knew as Alfred Smith, but who called himself Mulvanny. Storey arrested Smith but there was not enough proof to hold him and he was released. The police, however, were still suspicious. They had Smith watched. He was seen often in Upper Parliament Street and eventually the local police arrested him and dragged him, protesting, to the police station. He was searched, but the police found only the stub of a candle and some matches. The police checked his address and released him. The burglaries continued. Mr Clough, head of the Liverpool detective department, put detectives Johnson and Storey on permanent duty in the area. Storey suspected that Smith was not all he seemed and asked the beat constable to arrest him if he looked even slightly suspicious.

Shortly afterwards, the constable arrested Smith for loitering in Parliament Street and when he was in custody, Storey searched his Park Street lodgings. The house was owned by a man named Michael Hickey, who ran the Cheshire Milk Company. The company used a number of milk carts to deliver locally and when Storey investigated further, he discovered that every house that had been robbed was also on the delivery list for the Cheshire Milk Company. Storey believed that Hickey and Smith worked together, with Hickey finding the best houses to be robbed and Smith performing the actual robbery.

When Storey interrogated Smith, he found that he wore a stolen hat, while he also found a stolen gold seal in Hickey's house and a large number of pawn tickets. They searched one of the servants as well and found a number of other items that had been stolen from a house in Huskisson Street. The woman claimed that she was innocent and Hickey had given them to her. Storey asked further questions and the woman gave the names of a number of other people who had been present with Hickey. The police searched the town for them.

One was a man named John McAlevey. The police arrested him and his wife as they sat in their house in Penrith Street. As a known criminal named James Burns was also in the house, the police arrested him as well. Mrs McAlevey had more pawn tickets hidden in her clothes and there was a soldier's scarlet tunic in the house, which led the police to believe that McAlevey might be a deserter from the army.

In total, the police arrested five people, including: Smith, otherwise known as Mulvanny, Catherine and John McAlevey, Burns and Hickey. They took the suspects to the Central Police Office in High Street and then to the Police Court. When various people identified the stolen goods as their own, evidence was collected but Burns was released. He had arrived from Ireland too recently to have been involved in any of the robberies. The others stood trial at the summer assizes. Hickey and Smith were given seven years transportation, John McAlevey got seven months in jail with hard labour and Catherine McAlevey was given a mere ten days with hard labour.

Sometimes Storey earned his pay by just recognising a criminal face. On Tuesday, 20 May 1851 Storey and Povey were patrolling Park Lane when they saw three known thieves, John Thomas, John Jones and Isaac Thomas coming from the direction of the docks. There had been a number of thefts from vessels recently and Storey stopped the trio and asked their business. When the men gave no satisfactory answer, the police brought them in for questioning.

A search found that both Thomases had a number of foreign coins in their pockets, so the police held all three men until they made enquiries. Storey found that the money had been stolen from a ship named *Madelina*, along with a watch. Storey did a tour of the pawn shops and found the watch in a Mill Street pawn shop. Margaret Bradley, the woman who pledged it, told him that Isaac Thomas had given her the watch, she had pledged a second stolen watch at the same pawnshop, but Storey could not trace the owner. However, Bradley had pawned a third watch at a different pawnshop. John Thomas had given her that one and it had been stolen from a Norwegian vessel.

Jones was released but the two Thomases were later jailed.

Inducements

Unfortunately, Storey was again in trouble that same month when he was accused of offering inducements to criminals. It was claimed that Storey had offered a criminal his freedom if he gave information about more crimes. When the man refused to co-operate, Storey had returned him abruptly to the cells. In this case, the inducements had failed and the case collapsed, with all three accused walking free.

However, Storey continued with his endless and often thankless task of trying to keep the streets safe. In July, he arrested two men for stealing a chair from a pub called the Crooked Billet, but that month he was involved in a noisier affair.

Orange march

The 12th of July was often a troublesome time in Liverpool, when the Orangemen paraded their colours through the town and their Roman Catholic rivals responded with jeers, name-calling and the occasional riot for good measure. It was no different in 1851, with the Orangemen gathering at London Road. They were collecting in the forenoon, but a number of men opposed to them marched in a body with staffs and sticks, and pelted the Orangemen with rocks. Never men to retire from a fight, the Orangemen replied with stones, used the staff of their banners, or anything else they could find, as weapons. Within a few moments, what had started as a peaceful march ended like Donnybrook, with boots, fists and sticks busy.

The police were called, which seemed to anger the Catholic side, and one officer, Constable Jackson, was badly hurt. Around that time Sergeant Storey and Officer Povey arrived to try and calm things down. Although he was more used to the painstaking work of detecting crime than the physical danger of mob control, Storey dived straight into the middle and grappled one of Jackson's attackers. He managed to subdue and arrest the man, while Povey and some uniformed officers grabbed others of the more violent.

Things could have turned very nasty, as some of the Orangemen drew revolvers and fired a number of shots. Witnesses reported seeing men with gunshot wounds and the Orangemen attacked at least one innocent man, William Duff, a Protestant French Polisher.

With the police in control of that riot, the march started in earnest. There were around 2,000 Orangemen complete with five bands, flapping banners and women riding in carts decorated with emblems and symbols. Unfortunately, the appearance of the procession was marred by a bunch of hangers-on who had nothing to do with the Lodge, but everything to do with trouble. These were the unemployed and probably unemployable dregs of the town, the layabouts, pickpockets and beggars. Many carried weapons and made threatening gestures to the audience who watched.

Storey and Povey dogged the procession, hoping there was no more trouble, but ready to jump in if there was. The procession marched to the Custom House, halted for a while, and then headed along Duke Street and Great George Street to Mill Street. Storey must have hoped the rest of the day would pass peacefully, but there was a huge crowd waiting around St James Market. By that time, there were large numbers of police accompanying the march and, despite hostile looks and name-calling, there was no violence.

The march continued until they reached Mansfield Street, where a group of men lunged out and attacked one of the marchers. The Orangemen retaliated and chased the attackers down Myrtle Street North. In the meantime, the rest of the march continued with the bands playing loudly and their sashes and banners battered by boisterous wind, until they reached Fox Street, where there was more trouble.

Not even Storey knew who started it, but all at once Orange and Green were hammer and tongs, boots, fists and sticks, but it blew over with only one serious casualty and the march resumed to the place where it had started. As the various Lodges scattered to their headquarters, the police were ready in force – a sober blue phalanx among the fluttering Orange banners and multi-hued colours of the crowd. There were more gunshots here and some of the riff-raff who had remained with the march the entire way tried to cause trouble, but Storey again jumped in and wrestled the worst of the offenders away.

There were riots in Scotland Road later that day, but Storey was not involved as the uniformed police dealt with the matter. To Storey, it was just another day at the office and probably a distraction from his usual job of tracing stolen goods and tracking offenders.

Back to routine

After the excitements of the Orange Lodge, it must have been a bit dull to return to tracing stolen goods. In August, Storey was involved in a much more typical case when a group of six people were arrested for breaking into a house, threatening the householder, stealing a collection of clothes and wrecking the place. After that there were a group of young pickpockets to bring in and then, in his last known case that year, Storey and Povey brought in two well-known thieves. George Woolrich and John Smith had broken into a house in Park Road.

Overall, Storey and his partner Povey had experienced an interesting few years. He was no angel and seemed quite capable of bending a few rules in the pursuit of what he thought was a positive goal, but he was effective, obviously hard working and dedicated. His methods are probably a microcosm of the techniques used by a mid-century detective and show the patience and thoroughness needed, the step-by-step approaches, and the use of informants backed by a steely ability to deal with some of the worst elements of Liverpool society.

9
Death in the Family

Most murders and other killings were very private affairs, between husband and wife, mother and child or other close relation. In an age when family values were highly regarded, such events were doubly sad.

The Jenner killings

Fifty-seven-year-old William Jenner was a cotton broker. He lived at No. 25 Portland Place, not far from Scotland Road and within a shout of Everton. Jenner was not a tall man, with a stout body and round shoulders, and a red face under his bald head, but somebody had found him attractive as he was married with two sons and was at least outwardly happy. So there seemed no reason for his actions on Tuesday, 28 April 1841 when he rose from his bed, armed himself with an impressive array of four double-barrelled pistols, and shot his wife.

Jenner had left his own room at about six in the morning, dressed and lifted his outdoor shoes, then walked downstairs to the kitchen. His wife, Mary, was drinking a cup of tea and probably looked up and smiled to him. They would have exchanged the usual pleasantries before Jenner told her that he would clean his shoes himself as the servant was out. He left the kitchen, but a few moments later he returned with the guns and calmly shot Mary through the head. However murderous his intentions, he must have been a terrible marksman, for even with a sitting target, at point-blank range and the element of surprise, he failed to kill her. At first Mary did not know what had happened. She felt the shock of the shot and heard the children screaming, 'Mamma! Mamma! Mamma!'

Mary fell to the ground, bleeding heavily. Still unaware that her husband had shot her, she yelled, 'For God's sake, William! Help me.'

Shooting the son

But Jenner walked away, leaving Mary lying, confused and bleeding on the floor. Jenner walked into the room where his two sons slept. They had seen what had happened to their mother and would be nearly paralysed with shock and fear. Young William Jenner scrambled out of bed and stood next to his father, unable to comprehend what had happened: dads did not do that kind of thing. Thirteen-year-old George saw his father present the pistol at William and grabbed his hand to try and stop him from firing. He was too late: he smelled burning as William fell.

'Murder!' George shouted out and managed to scramble away from his father. As he ran, he heard the sound of the gun again. George ran downstairs to the front door, but it was locked and he could not escape. He backed away and scuttled into the front parlour, but his father was already there, with a pistol in each hand.

George was obviously a very capable boy for he grappled with Jenner and disarmed him.

'What made you do this?' George asked, and Jenner told him that he had gone mad. Still holding the pistols, George asked where his mother was, although presumably he already knew, unless Mary had been mistaken when she thought she heard her sons crying for her.

'Upstairs,' Jenner told him and George asked if he could go and see her. Jenner refused and tried to retrieve the pistols, but George sensibly kept hold of them. He had a quick check in his mother's bedroom, but did not see her, and returned to the parlour.

Jenner was waiting there for him, with another pistol. As soon as George stepped in, Jenner grabbed hold of his head and pressed the trigger. There was the sound of a shot, but if there had been a ball in the barrel, it missed for George was uninjured. He grabbed the pistol from his father's hand and smacked him along the side of the head with it. Jenner must have staggered but was not knocked unconscious. George, very mature for his age, thought he heard his mother shout something and again asked Jenner where she was.

'She's lying downstairs,' Jenner admitted and once again tried to grab hold of George. The boy broke free and fled downstairs, where he saw his mother lying on the kitchen floor, bleeding from her head. Jenner followed him downstairs. George tried to help his mother up, but he could not do so with the pistols in his hand. He said he would throw the pistols away, but his father said 'Give them to me.' Sensibly, George kept hold of them, but Jenner lunged forward and as George recoiled, Jenner again tried to grab him.

George was terrified and, leaving his mother lying on the ground, he ran out of the house and into the yard. He glanced around, heard his father's footsteps and quickly threw the three pistols into the midden. Jenner pounded after him, but rather than demand the guns, he asked George for help to lift Mary. George refused, probably because he did not trust his father, and instead said that he was going to 'fetch a policeman.' He ran into the street and stopped the first passer-by he saw.

'What's to do?' the man asked and when the terrified boy told him what had happened, he immediately ran for the police. In the meantime,

George fled to Richard Ackerly, who was the local surgeon, to get help for his mother and brother.

The stranger was as good as his word. He ran into Great Homer Street and saw a number of police including John Thomas and Constable William Maddock, marching back to the police office after completing their shift. It was just twenty to six in the morning.

'You must go to 25 Portland Place,' the man said.

When the police arrived, they did not kick the door in, for it may have been a hoax, so instead Maddock knocked politely. It took a few hard knocks before Jenner shouted from within. 'Is that George?'

'Yes,' Maddock said and Jenner opened the door. Maddock pushed past and searched the house. He found Mary lying on the kitchen floor in a puddle of blood and, helped by Constable Thomas Wallace, lifted her from the floor onto a chair. The blood poured freely from a wound in her head.

'Who's that?' Mary cried.

'We are police officers putting you on a chair,' Maddock told her.

'Where is Mr Jenner?' Mary was obviously confused.

'He's upstairs,' Maddock told her, and looked up. Dr Ackerly, the surgeon, had arrived with Constable John Thomas. While Ackerly attended to Mary, Maddock and Thomas searched the yard and the midden, where they found three small double-barrelled pistols. In the meantime, Constable Wallace had continued the search of the house. He found young William lying on the bedroom floor beside the window. Ackerly lifted the boy, bandaged his head wound and put him to bed. William was alive, but only just. He could hardly breathe and seemed to be gasping out the last few moments of his life. Wallace stayed at the side of his bed and did all he could, but William died at twenty past ten that morning.

Constable George Harley took charge of Jenner as the others searched the house. Harley had asked 'What's to do?', but Jenner had not replied. When the police searched him, they found a fourth pistol in his pocket, fully loaded and with percussion caps in place ready to fire. Jenner had been reluctant to relinquish his hold but Harley was stronger and more used to physical encounters of that kind.

Inspector Jonathan Anders questioned Jenner about his motive for the shootings. 'We should all have come to poverty,' Jenner replied. He did not look up.

'Yes,' said George, who had come into the house, 'and you intended to shoot me too.'

'Yes, George,' Jenner agreed. He told Anders: 'I have been unfortunate in business and in a state of insanity for a length of time.' After that he wrung his hands in a very melodramatic fashion and added: 'Oh Mr Roberts, Mr Roberts, what have you done for my wife and family?' That was the first the police had heard of a man named Roberts, and they immediately probed further.

Dr Ackerly knew Jenner quite well. 'I never expected to see you under such circumstances,' Ackerly told him. The last time Ackerly had visited the house, Jenner had been suicidal and the doctor found a phial of prussic acid in the house. He had given Jenner an emetic, which seemed to work, and tested the acid on a cat, which died at once.

As the doctor examined his patients, Inspector Bryce Smith arrived and ordered a thorough search of the house. The police found powder flasks, powder, pistol balls and a phial of laudanum. When the police questioned Jenner, he told them darkly that it was 'all the fault of Mr Roberts', but did not explain who that gentleman might be or how he was involved. He added with sinister emphasis: 'If we had all four gone to the cemetery, it would have been all right.' Not long after, as the police escorted him to the bridewell, Jenner spoke of his wife and 'poor boys'. After trying to massacre his family, he now seemed genuinely concerned.

Mary Jenner died on 6 May 1841, so Jenner had killed two of his family. He was charged with wilful murder at the next assizes, but pleaded 'not guilty' as he stood in his neat black suit, staring anxious-eyed at the judge and jury. He appeared quite calm for a while, but broke down in tears when the details of the killings were given.

Dr Ackerly was called as a witness. He said that Jenner had been 'deranged' on his visit in September 1840 and thought he was 'in a dangerous state to be allowed to go at liberty.' In the perceived knowledge of the period, insanity was divided into classes: mania and monomania, with the latter meaning the victim was 'mad on one subject'. Ackerly believed that Jenner was monomaniac on the subject of his personal financial circumstances, which Ackerly said 'were not so bad as they appeared.' Ackerly quoted Jenner as saying it was 'better they should all be in heaven than starving.'

The judge, Lord Chief Justice Denman, wondered if that was madness or 'deliberate preference', in other words: did he deliberately kill his wife and son, or was his mind unhinged at the time? Ackerly answered that he believed it was madness and told a hushed court that last September, Jenner had wished his wife and children to drink prussic acid. All eyes in the jury swivelled to Jenner, who stood there with his head bowed.

More witnesses were called. A gunsmith named Thomas Blisset said that Jenner had purchased four double-barrelled pistols, apparently for an American customer, back at the beginning of March. This was many weeks before the actual shootings, which surely argued for a predetermined act rather than a sudden onset of insanity. Jenner bought the pistols fully loaded and returned on 23 April to have the charges drawn and replaced. Blisset stated that it was not uncommon for customers to buy loaded pistols, with many gentlemen retaining them in their houses in case of burglary. The defence pointed out that that Jenner was a cotton broker who worked closely with American clients, so it was quite possible he had bought English-manufactured pistols to export.

The Roberts link was also explored. He was a Manchester-based merchant and had worked closely together with Jenner. In 1824, both

Roberts and Jenners hit a bad patch and their businesses were in serious trouble, but Roberts was by far the worst. As the companies were tied together, Jenner agreed to commit 'fraud and perjury' to help clear Roberts. Although both men scraped clear of that particular episode, Jenner, according to the defence, had spent the last fifteen years worried about both his reputation and feeding his family. It was this twin stress that had gradually worn away his sanity. The defence argument swung the jury around and they took only fourteen minutes to find Jenner not guilty on grounds of insanity.

But bad although Jenner's crimes were, they pale beside what may be the most cold-blooded killers in Liverpool's history.

The Black Widows

Most cities had one high profile criminal in the nineteenth century, a person whose crimes still have the ability to make one shudder. Edinburgh had Burke and Hare, and London Jack the Ripper. Liverpool had the Black Widows: Catherine Flannagan, a fifty-five year old housekeeper and the forty-one-year-old charwoman, Margaret Higgins.

These two ladies were sisters, with the maiden name of Thompson, and had come over the Irish Sea to settle in Liverpool. They lived in Skirving Street, which was then a festering slum between Scotland Road and Great Homer Street, but soon after, they moved to Latimer Street and then Ascot Street.

The first suspicion was aroused when a forty-five-year-old man named Thomas Higgins, a healthy and fit robust bricklayer's labourer, died very suddenly on Tuesday, 2 October 1884. Higgins was a hod-carrier, so strong that his nickname was 'crack of the whip' and until this bout of suspected dysentery, he had never been ill in his life. He lived with Margaret, his wife of ten months, in lodgings in a cellar of No. 27 Ascot Street. His brother Patrick was immediately suspicious, especially when he knew that Dr William Whitford, the district medical officer for the parish, had been attending Thomas and thought him cured. When Patrick learned that the funeral was rushed, he recollected a number of ugly rumours he had heard about Margaret Flannagan and checked around the insurance companies and burial clubs. He told the police and Dr Whitford, who advised him to go the coroner.

The coroner thought there was enough evidence for suspicion, and he stopped the funeral until the body could be properly examined. Two doctors, William Whitford and John Limerick hurried to the house, arriving at exactly the same time as the horse drawn hearse. Both groups entered together, to see a woman already arranging the shroud around the corpse. Whitford said that there were 'a great number of women there, most of them drunk.'

There were a few moments of confusion as the undertakers strove to take away the coffin and the doctors insisted that they could not. The less-than-grieving relatives looked on, but one, Catherine Flannagan, who was the sister-in-law of the so recently deceased man, decided that she was better elsewhere and hurriedly left the house by the back door.

Insurance

She had disappeared by the time the police arrived and the body was taken away for a post mortem. The doctors found arsenic in the stomach of Thomas Higgins, while the police discovered that Flannagan had insured his life with a number of societies throughout Liverpool. The coincidence was a bit much to ignore and the police began a search for Flannagan. In the meantime, they arrested her sister, Thomas' wife Margaret, on suspicion of helping in the supposed murder. Margaret had only been married to Thomas for ten months, after lodging with him and his daughter for many years.

The police were even more suspicious when they discovered that Thomas Higgins was not the first person that Flannagan had insured. There were others, and the companies had all paid out when they had died. The case reached the Home Secretary, who ordered that the bodies of at least one other possible victim should be exhumed and examined. In the meantime, the police made their usual routine and exhaustive enquiries, interviewed relatives, neighbours and the representatives of insurance companies as they strove to build up an accurate picture of the suspects and the deceased. One of the neighbours told the police that Margaret Higgins had recently said that she had not poisoned her husband and if he had been poisoned, her sister Catherine was the poisoner.

When the police searched Margaret Higgins, they found traces of arsenic on her clothing, while there was a bottle in her house that held liquid laced with arsenic. The suspicions grew as the enquiries deepened.

On the night before the death, 1 October, Margaret Higgins was in her house with her thirteen-year-old daughter Ellen, Mrs Flannagan and two neighbours, Ellen Lawton and Elizabeth Manville. Thomas Higgins was lying in bed and in obvious pain, groaning and tearing at the wall with his fingers. Flannagan spoke to Margaret Higgins, 'You had better go home and take Nellie [Ellen] with you.' When Margaret Higgins left the room, Thomas Higgins asked for a drink of water. Flannagan fetched a mug of water but Lawton and Manville were surprised that, rather than just hand it over, she spoon-fed the sick man.

'Take it away,' Thomas said, trying to push Flannagan away from him, 'take it away, I will not have it.'

Flannagan poured the contents of the spoon back into the mug and emptied the mug on top of the fire. Manville and Lawton thought that rather strange, but not until they heard the rumours of poison did they wonder if Flannagan was disposing of the evidence.

It was not long afterwards that Thomas Higgins died, still groaning in agony.

On the run

As the police uncovered the events of the night, Catherine Flannagan was still on the run. She may have been an alleged murderer, but she seemed to be a woman with little imagination, for she remained within the confines of Liverpool. Even so, she managed to evade the police for two weeks, despite leaving a trail of clues and guilt behind her. Calling herself Mrs McCormick, she stayed for a while with a Maria Mckenzie in Rockingham Street, saying she was 'in a little trouble.' Mckenzie ran a shop and whenever a customer appeared, Flannagan hid in the pantry. Flannagan also confessed to Mckenzie's sister, Margaret Parkhouse, that she could not sleep because she 'could see it all' before her. These words could mean anything, but, in the circumstances, were twisted until they became a virtual admission of guilt. Parkhouse also heard Ellen mention that her aunt had been taken to the 'coalhole' (bridewell) and her father had been poisoned. Ellen also mentioned that Flannagan had said that she had 'nothing to do with it', but had sent her to the house to 'destroy my winter medicine' and that there was a 'likeness' (picture) of her on the wall. Ellen had been told to take her picture out of the frame and replace it with a picture of her cousin, no doubt so the police would look for the wrong person. Flannagan also told the girl to fetch her shawl as they were going to Scotland.

James Mckenzie, Maria's husband, was a seaman and he guessed that Flannagan was the alleged murderess whom the police were hunting. He confronted her in the house and told her she had 'disgraced them' and took her to a public house, where he later accused her of poisoning 'the man Higgins.'

'Nonsense,' Flannagan said, 'what are you talking about?' But she made no defence and did not stay long with the Mckenzies.

When she left Rockingham Street, Flannagan lodged with Margaret Burns in Lydia Ann Street. She still called herself McCormack and claimed to have just 'come off the Irish boat.' She never left the house, but when Mrs Burns read about the poisoning in a newspaper she commented, 'A wholesale poisoner! She is still at large I see. I would not hurt a worm, but I could find it in my heart to string her up myself, the walking bitch.'

'Oh she's a bad one,' Flannagan agreed.

When the Burnses seemed to be suspicious of her behaviour, Flannagan left hurriedly. She may have spent a night walking the streets or sleeping rough before lodging with Mr and Mrs Booth at No. 3 Mount Vernon. Unable to read and write, Flannagan was unable to follow the news of her own pursuit unless somebody else told her, so on the Sunday, she asked Booth to read her pieces from the newspaper.

Flannagan listened intently when he chose the poisoning story. 'Do you think Mrs Flannagan will be caught?' she asked. When Booth said he did, she asked, 'do you think she will be hung?' and he replied:

'Yes, I think it will be another job for Marwood's successor.' Marwood had been the public hangman for many years. The news must have been a cold shock for Flannagan, hearing her execution discussed as a near inevitability. She left Mount Vernon the next day, claiming she was collecting her niece from the Workhouse.

No doubt terrified and desperate, Flannagan scurried to the house of Mary McGovern at One Street in Wavertree, south of the city, where she asked the time of the Blackburn train, but she had no money to pay for her keep. Now her story changed again. She said she had a difference with her son over some furniture and there was a warrant out against her. As soon as McGovern heard the word 'warrant', she looked for the police, but by the time she arrived home, Inspector Keighley had already put Flannagan under arrest.

Charged with murder

Flannagan was taken to the county police station at Wavertree and then to the central police station, where she was charged with the murder of Thomas Higgins. 'I never knew anything about it,' she said, 'I never did it and I know nobody else who did.'

Margaret Higgins said something similar: 'I know nothing at all about it. I went for his medicine at Burlington Street Dispensary and I gave it to him as I got it. He was suffering from diarrhoea; he was ill three weeks and lay eight days in bed.'

The police investigation was complicated, when a number of the insurance documents that were to be used in evidence disappeared. In the meantime, the police had the unpleasant task of searching through the rubbish heap behind the Flannagan and Higgins houses, to find a bottle that may have held arsenic. As enquiries continued and newspapers published lurid and imaginative speculation, public interest mounted, ballad singers created songs about the case and the two suspects languished in their cells, eating little as their coughs echoed from the grim walls.

'She'll never live to comb grey hairs'

The body of an eighteen-year-old woman named Margaret Jennings was exhumed from the Ford Cemetery, while Chief Constable Captain Nott-Bower offered a reward of £100 for information that would lead to the conviction of Thomas Higgins' murderer. When Jennings was examined, traces of arsenic were found in her body. Jennings and her father, Patrick, had lodged with Flannagan, before she was married. Patrick told the police that Flannagan shared a room with his daughter when young Margaret had taken sick, and she had died a few days later. Her symptoms had mirrored those of Thomas Higgins.

'She's been sick before,' Flannagan told Patrick callously, 'and she'll never live to comb grey hairs.' In common with Thomas, Jennings' life had been insured and payment came to Flannagan.

The police interviewed a number of insurance collectors and managers, each of whom knew Higgins and Flannagan. Samuel Finnegan of the Prudential said that Higgins also spoke about insuring Partick Higgins, which suggests he was next on the danger list, but Finnegan also mentioned that the shadowy Bridget Stanton was also involved in paying the premiums. Stanton tried to claim the premium, but failed.

The plot thickened when Francis Bowles of the Pearl Life agreed to insure Thomas Higgins for £40. The company had every intention of paying the agreed sum, until Bowles viewed the deceased. The man he had interviewed in Mrs Flannagan's house in Latimer Street was not the same as the man who had died, so the money was not paid out. Representatives from the Wesleyan General, the Prudential and the Royal Liver insurance companies were also interviewed. Richard Jones of the Royal Liver actually interviewed Thomas Higgins, who seemed less than pleased at the idea of life assurance.

'To hell with the clubs,' Higgins told him. 'You won't get any club money from me.'

William Cartwright of the Scottish Legal Life Assurance paid out £7 17/6 to Flannagan, who had posed as Higgins' wife. She was crying like a soul demented, saying she had 'lost the best husband in the world.'

Other victims

As the people of Liverpool were mentally digesting the presumed murder of Thomas Higgins and Margaret Jennings, the police produced yet more mysterious deaths for them. One was Mary Higgins, the eight-year-old daughter of Thomas Higgins. The modus operandi was exactly the same. She had died on 29 November 1882, about three months after Patrick had married Margaret and after a week of intense suffering. The Home Secretary ordered her body exhumed, so it could be examined. Margaret Higgins had insured her for £22-10s, and was with her as she sickened and died, with Flannagan on hand to assist. The post mortem discovered arsenic inside the body.

Finally there was John Flannagan, the twenty-two-year-old son of Flannagan. He had died in 7 December 1880, after being insured by his mother for around £70. Flannagan had set the scene by telling everybody that her son was unwell, so the world was prepared for his demise. His corpse was dug up and examined and once more the doctors surmised that he had died from arsenic poisoning.

In court

When the case came to court, the two sisters provided a complete contrast. At fifty-four years old, Flannagan was plump-faced, pale and shaking with fear, while Higgins, ten years younger, was much leaner of features and was described as 'haggard'. Higgins was the younger, but both had the low foreheads that the Victorians delighted in assuming were a mark of lesser intelligence or even criminal intent. She looked more composed, but stood in the dock giving darting glances around the court at the judge, jury and audience.

Both pleaded 'not guilty'.

The police were there in force, surrounding the court to keep back the crowds, who had hoped to hear all the juicy details of the murders. Those who got in saw two of the most calculating killers that Liverpool ever knew.

As well as evidence of the death of Thomas Higgins, the court heard about Margaret Jennings. Margaret and her father, Patrick, had lodged with Flannagan for twelve years. He said that Flannagan had nursed Margaret when she was sick and had sometimes refused him entry to his daughter's room. When a doctor came, he called Flannagan 'Mrs

Jennings' which made Patrick Jennings wonder and he asked how this had happened 'unbeknown' to him. She had made a joke of it. She passed herself off as Margaret's mother to the doctor, but acted as her aunt with the insurance companies. Dr John Rafter said he had been surprised at Margaret's death and Flannagan, whom he had believed to be the mother, had appeared very upset at the time.

After promptings from Flannagan, Patrick Jennings had insured his daughter with the Scottish Insurance Company, but it was Flannagan who paid in most of the money and who gained most when Margaret died. Patrick got ten shillings and Flannagan £8 10s – the value of an eighteen-year-old's life. Patrick had not known that Flannagan also paid into the Liver Insurance. Flannagan gained a further £32 there, Patrick £17 and Flannagan's daughter a pound for herself. Strangely, rather than complain of this uneven split, Patrick felt guilty about keeping £17 and was apprehensive in case Flannagan's son attacked him to get the money.

Despite their initial nervous appearance, both sisters appeared confident that the jury would find them not guilty. Flannagan was unmoved even when the evidence was rolled out against them, but that changed when Ellen was called up to tell the court what she knew. Flannagan cried openly when her daughter gave evidence against her.

As the case moved on, Flannagan became more emotional and with reason. They had simply soaked fly paper in water, which they then fed to their victims. Flannagan tried to wriggle free of the impending noose by offering to turn Queen's evidence against her sister. She mentioned a number of other people they had been involved in poisoning and offered a list of another five female accomplices, including the shadowy woman named Bridget Stanton, as well as a Bridget Begley and Margaret Evans, with Margaret Potter and Mrs Fallon. Apparently a Catherine Ryan bought the arsenic. Flannagan also hinted strongly that three of the insurance agents were also involved to some extent.

However, the authorities decided that there was not enough evidence to make a successful prosecution. On 3 March 1884, the Black Widows were hanged at Kirkdale jail. The full extent of their poisoning career will probably never be known, but they remain amongst Liverpool's most notorious and cold-blooded murderers.

They were not alone in using poison.

The case of the contaminated cup

Poisoning was the Victorian crime par excellence. It was subtle, often clever, cruel and usually secret. It will never be known how many successful poisoners got away with murder, as the victims are long since buried along with the evidence, but sufficient were discovered and convicted to reveal a fairly wide spread practice throughout Victorian Britain. Most poisonings were domestic, as husbands and wives had access to their spouse's food and drink. The opportunity to add noxious substances to them was easy and frequently the motive was domestic tension, which rose over weeks or months of petty disputes and sometimes abuse.

In November 1855, Ann Merchant was thirty-seven years old. She had been married to Frederick Merchant, oil and colour merchant for the last eighteen years, and they lived at No. 32 Scotland Road. About late October that year Ann had become sick and took to her bed, where a woman by the name of Amelia Greer came to nurse her. Dr Joseph Ingham had seen Ann and left careful instructions about doses of medicine, which Amelia obeyed punctiliously. Amelia was a good choice: she was a very responsible person, steadily married and employed as a teacher. She was careful to follow the doctor's orders as to the best care and medicine for Ann.

Because of Amelia's care, by November Ann was well on her way to recovery and Dr Ingham rarely visited, leaving her care all in the hands of Amelia. However, in the last week of November, Ann took a turn for the worse. She had terrible pains in her stomach and side, with associated sickness and diarrhoea. Amelia called the doctor, and asked Ann's daughter, Hannah, to come as well.

Amelia asked Ann if she had taken anything that might have made her so bad. After a few moments thought, Ann said that she had taken nothing different except some porter that Frederick had given her. The porter had been warm, Ann said, but she had also thought that it had tasted strange, as if Frederick had put something extra in it. Ann explained what had happened.

On the Sunday night, Ann's family had bread and cheese for their supper, but Frederick had pea soup, and put a bottle of porter on the table. Ann poured out a cupful, added sugar and nutmeg and drank it, and Hannah also had a small amount, but Frederick did not have any as he was teetotal. After her first cupful, Ann had gone to see her neighbour and placed the porter on the hob to keep it warm. Hannah saw her father stir the porter while Ann was out, but did not see him add anything to it, but he did put a saucer on top, possibly to help retain the heat.

As soon as Ann came back, Ann had another cup of porter, but only after a few swallows she said that it tasted foul

'That's queer looking stuff at the bottom of the cup,' she said.

'That's nonsense,' Frederick replied, but Ann took the cup to one of her friends and neighbours, Jane Dickinson. Jane also noticed that there was some strange sediment at the bottom. Jane had seen Ann's sudden decline at the same time and associated the two in her mind. She knew quite a bit about the Merchants and said that although they appeared a happy couple to the outside world, during the preceding eighteen months, there had been quite a bit of tension within the marriage. It seemed that the couple had a maid servant of whom Ann was very jealous as she suspected that Frederick had taken a fancy to her. According to Jane, Ann had often joked that when she died, Frederick would soon replace her with another woman.

Another neighbour, Harriet Horne, ran a hatter's shop in the cellar beneath the Merchants' house and Ann had shown her the residue in the cup. Harriet said that Ann had been 'in a great fright' and thought she had been poisoned. Harriet accompanied Ann to Dr Whittle of Crosshall Street to have the cup examined, but Whittle thought there was nothing to worry about. Ann was not so sure, and told her daughter Hannah that if she died, it was her father's fault. Ann died at quarter to one the following day, quietly and without much fuss.

Dr Ingham performed a post mortem and thought the cause of death was an ulcerated stomach, with the ulcers created by 'some metallic irritant.' Mrs Merchant's stomach and liver were sent to Professor Brett of Liverpool Infirmary to be analysed. Professor Brett found that the ulcers were of long standing but there was also evidence of arsenic in both the liver and the stomach. When the case came to court the verdict was that Ann had died from arsenic poisoning but whether by accident or design was not known. Merchant walked free.

Other family murders were just as brutal.

The Murder of Mary Corrigan

Murder was not uncommon in Victorian Britain. Some murders have been remembered, but most just vanished into the murk of history. Then there are those in between, not quite famous but well-known locally for some aspect or other. The murder of Mary Corrigan fits snugly into this category, for it was a brutal killing that was long remembered in Liverpool.

Chisenhale Street was in the centre of an ugly area, with the alternative name of the North End Slum. It was on the route between the docks and around two hundred brothels, so was well frequented by visiting sailors. The street had a reputation for violence, with seamen frequently being attacked by the local thugs and street corner men, with one garrotter, Martin Corrigan, being categorised as one of the 'terrors of the neighbourhood' in 1869. Yet, it was another Corrigan who made headlines a couple of years later.

In the early 1870s, Mary Corrigan and her husband kept a lodging house, living in the kitchen and the adjacent parlour of No. 36. Their twenty-three-year-old son Thomas also lived there along with his partner, Martha Knight, and there was a lodger named James Canavan. Completing the household was the Harris family: Richard, Johanna and their three children, so the house was as crowded and cramped as many in that locality. It was unfortunate that Mary was not on the best of terms with Martha, and did not approve of her son sleeping with her.

On Saturday, 1 November 1873 Mary hit the bottle. As with many people, alcohol made her melancholic and she reviewed her life and situation and, as usual, began to complain about Martha Knight. She was not quiet when in drink, and the noise she made woke up Thomas, who slept upstairs. Leaving Martha in the room, Thomas came down to confront his mother and ask her not to voice her opinion of his woman, but she was having none of it and continued her verbal assault.

Thomas altered his attack. 'Where's my supper?' He demanded.

Mary did not want to admit she had been drinking all day and nothing was ready. 'It's in the oven,' she temporised, but that only put Thomas off for a moment.

Thomas checked the oven and saw it was empty. He was already angry because of his mother's verbal attack on Martha, but now he lost his temper completely. He started by pulling back his fist and punching Mary full in the face, then, when she staggered back, he grabbed her by the hair and banged her head on the floor, again and again and again.

'I'll clear this house'

When his father appeared and tried to stop the attack, Thomas yelled, 'I'll clear this house' and jumped at him as well. His father did not wait to check on the condition of his wife but ran out of the house. Not yet finished, Thomas had a go at Harris, but soon stopped and turned on Canavan instead, knocking him to the ground. Canavan proved no braver than Mr Corrigan. He staggered up and fled outside. In the meantime, Harris had run upstairs to his wife and family.

Having nearly cleared the house as he had promised, Thomas locked the door so there were no interruptions and continued where he had left off. His mother lay on the ground, bleeding but conscious, and Thomas made sure of her. Holding the table with both hands, he leaped onto his mother, crashing down on her again and again with his heavy boots. He continued until she was unconscious, and then relented slightly and shouted to Martha, who had remained upstairs through the commotion, to bring him some water.

When Martha obeyed, Thomas dashed the water in his mother's face to wake her, and had Martha and Mrs Harris strip her and put her into her bed in the parlour. Thomas watched while the women worked, but the moment his mother was in bed, he altered his anger to Martha and began to attack her. In the meantime, Mary, now petrified, slid out of her bed and crawled slowly and painfully upstairs to what she hoped was the sanctuary of the Harris' room.

When Thomas had enough of slapping his partner around, he realised that someone was missing and shouted for his mother. There was no answer, so he searched the house for her. She was still in the Harris' room, huddled in terror at the foot of their bed. The Harris family were mute spectators. Without any delay, Thomas recommenced his assault. He took off his belt and beat her with the buckle end before kicking her about the room and throwing her downstairs, where he used his belt again and placed a knife across her throat.

By that time Mary Corrigan was unconscious again. Either Thomas or the other women put her back in her bed, but she had taken enough and died a short time later. When Thomas heard the news, he told the women to say Mary had been drinking and had fallen and hurt herself, then he left the house, apparently unconcerned that he had murdered his mother.

The police were not fooled for a second and began their hunt. It did not take them long to trace and arrest Thomas, who had not had the sense to leave Chisenhale Street. When he was picked up, he told Constable Thomas McDonald that his mother had died suddenly and he was looking for a doctor. For some reason, the police did not believe him.

Despite a spirited and imaginative defence that blamed the killing on a fit of the 'horrors' brought about by excess drink, the jury found Michael Corrigan guilty of murder.

On the morning of Monday, 5 January 1874, he was taken from his cell in Kirkdale jail to a store room near to the yard where he would be hanged. As the prison bell clanged its doleful message of judicial death, a handful of spectators, including prison wardens and the press, watched Michael Corrigan leave the store room for the short walk to the black-draped gallows. With his arms tied, Corrigan climbed the steps to the gallows, where Anderson-Owen was the hangman for the day. Corrigan looked composed, except that he prayed constantly. He stopped under the hanging beam and prayed as Anderson-Owen arranged the noose around his neck and the customary white hood over his face and head.

Michael Corrigan died quickly, far quicker than his mother had, and the prison hoisted a black flag to show that there had been an execution. Corrigan was buried inside the prison beside the other murderers that had been executed there. It had been a pointless and brutal murder, and a quick and efficient execution. Murder was usually more sordid than exciting.

10
Prostitution

As a seaport, Liverpool had a high number of prostitutes. Some were professionals who spent years in the trade, others were women in desperate and temporary need of money to pay the bills, and many were inveigled or forced into prostitution by false promises or violence. In the latter years of the 1820s, there was a sharp increase in the number of people who seduced women into prostitution. At that time there were an unknown number of brothels in the town, some of them well established and fairly substantial. Some even had agents in the town, who were always on the look-out for new girls. These agents would pose as respectable women and offer positions as servants to innocent girls who were new to Liverpool. Once the girls accepted, they were slowly broken in to prostitution.

It was the normal practice to hand the girl over to a man who posed as a gentleman, but who in reality was nothing of the sort. At first he would act with kindness towards her, but after a while he would seduce her and then she was introduced to the other members of the stable; with her reputation gone, she could never again be part of respectable society and had little choice but to continue with her new career. In the meantime, one of the longer-serving women would be discarded, to take her place among the unfortunate street walkers who drifted among the lowest in alleyways and dockside pubs until violence, disease or destitution ended their lives.

The proprietors of the largest of these brothels were not always easy to distinguish from their less disreputable neighbours. There was one brothel which was reputed to have a turnover of £20,000 and another whose owner was a solid family man with an excellent reputation. As the police system was much less efficient at that time than it became later, the prostitutes and pimps were able to run wild in the town.

Fighting vice

Mary Ann Gilchrist ran a brothel in Bengal Street, off Hall Lane. In September 1827, a number of her neighbours complained of the constant passage of men, loud noises and degraded women, day and night. Chief Constable Greig ordered Inspector Bainbridge to do something about it. Bainbridge made several house calls and on each occasion the house was busy with men and women. However, when the case came to court Gilchrist defended herself vigorously. She said that each time the inspector called, he had 'frightened her and her children', while the people he had seen were her lodgers. She told the court that she had recently changed her lodgers and they were very respectable – a claim that caused a ripple of laughter to run around the room. However, despite her tenacity, the judge, Mr Raffles, ordered her to quit the house.

The problem continued. After a night of drinking in August 1842, a blacksmith called Thomas Watts called at a Liverpool brothel and spent the night there. He woke in the morning to find he was short of a sovereign and eighteen shillings, a lot of money for a working man. Watts challenged his woman of the night, Mary Ann White, with the theft but she denied it. Watts immediately ran to the window and shouted out 'Watch!' – a shout for the night watch to come and help, but instead he succeeded only in summoning one of the other women of the establishment who raced up the stairs and told him to 'hold his noise or she would send somebody who would break his head.'

Knowing of the brutality of some of the men who looked after the girls in Liverpool's brothels, Watts quietened down. He got dressed quickly and left as if he had no more to say, but once outside he told Constable Lawton what had happened.

Lawton came into the brothel and arrested White as she dressed. He searched the room and the woman but found no money, so when the case came to court, it was dismissed.

Maggie May and friends

Some of the names of the most colourful of Liverpool's prostitutes have been retained as the city has a form of inverted pride in its chequered past. For example Maggie May, a name famous in song, Tich Maguire, Harriet Lane and 'The Battleship', with the slightly scary 'Jumping Jenny' and 'Cast Iron Kitty'. These good ladies frequented Lime Street and Paradise Street, both haunts of prostitutes and places best to avoid after dark.

Sometimes it was the customers who were troublesome.

Murder of a brothel keeper

In 1841, William Crummer and his wife Bridget had been brothel keepers for three years, happily serving the male population of Liverpool. William was aged thirty-one and Bridget was a few years younger; she had married him when she was just sixteen and they had a growing family.

The Crummers lived in Christian Court, Preston Street where William had once been a cooper, but there was not much money in that during the Depression, so the couple lived by the profits of the brothel. It was strange that even in the worst of times there seemed to be money available for drink and sex, but the Crummers, at least, did not complain and survived the bad times better than most. They did not seem to have any resident girls, but rented out bed space to women of the streets.

On Saturday, 12 June 1841, the brothel was doing its usual business. Men and women entered, rented an upstairs room for an hour or a night, slaked their lust and left, with the men hopefully satisfied and definitely lighter in pocket and the women having made a few pennies towards their rent. About ten o' clock that night a forty-one-year-old foundry worker named James White brought a woman into the house and they slipped up the outside stairs to one of the bedrooms. They were left alone behind a closed door, with the Crummers downstairs, when after a while the shout 'Murder!' was heard.

Bridget Crummer immediately dashed upstairs but rather than burst into the room, she respected her customer's privacy. She stood outside the closed door and politely asked White to leave. 'If you please, sir, will you come down?'

White did not reply but as the room became silent Bridget returned to the kitchen. After a few more minutes she again heard the woman shout 'murder' and demand to leave the room. Bridget took a candle and climbed the stairs again.

'What's to do in there?' Bridget asked, hoping for a peaceful resolution to whatever the trouble was, but instead, she heard the woman.

'I'll return your sixpence if you let me go!'

Bridget stood outside the room with the candle in her hand, the yellow flame flickering and casting a weak pool of light around her. She asked White to come down again, Bridget returned to the kitchen and a few moments later White followed. By then, Bridget and William were talking to a woman named Anne Gallacher. William was in his shirt and prepared for bed. When the woman came down a minute later, she was angry and upset. She did not stay in the kitchen long but soon stormed out the door and away.

William glanced up as White arrived, but he was not unduly concerned as minor arguments were quite normal in the brothel. Anyway, he seemed to leave much of the work to Bridget. His attitude altered when White asked, 'Who hurried me down?'

'I did, sir,' said Bridget.

White made a lunge at Bridget but did not hit her. There were hard glares and tension as William said, mildly, 'It's no manly act to strike a woman.'

'I'll either hit her or you,' White retorted.

William still did not retaliate. 'My good man,' he said, 'go home about your business; I've nothing to say to you.'

White took that as provocation and punched William in the face.

What happened next is unclear. Bridget said that William returned the punch and then guided White out of the house with a hand on his shoulder, while White later claimed that William had punched him and was much more aggressive. Either way, what had begun as a run-of-the-mill dispute escalated into something a lot more serious. White left the house but did not go far. He remained in the dark passage between the door and the street, fuming. It was about ten minutes later that he banged back inside, with his right hand deep in his pocket. Immediately after he entered, he swung a left-handed punch at William, only for William's loose nightshirt to ensnare his fist.

Swearing, White pulled William closer by the tangled folds of his nightshirt, whipped something from his right pocket and before William could speak, plunged it into William's stomach and ripped it downward into his belly.

The result was terrible. White had torn a great wound in William, whose bowels began to slither out.

William yelled: 'Murder! I'm killed!'

Bridget, who seemed to be a very calm, even docile woman, later claimed that she said: 'It's a pity you had to be killed, and him,' she pointed to White, 'to have his liberty.'

After the stabbing, White fled. Bridget now lost her composure and chased him, screaming 'murder' at the top of her voice. She was not going to allow her husband's assailant off easily. She pursued him into Preston street, still shouting 'murder,' grabbed the tail of his coat and held fast despite his desperate struggles, until Constable John Gristenthwaite arrived and put him under arrest.

As soon as White was in custody, Bridget ran to find a doctor. However, William's wound proved fatal and despite the attentions of Frederick Cripps the surgeon, he died on the Sunday afternoon. When White was told the news, he said, 'Then I am an unfortunate man.'

He was found guilty of manslaughter and transported for twelve years. The original cause of the argument in the brothel was never disclosed.

The social evil

By the middle of the century, prostitution was known as 'the social evil' and was taken very seriously by the borough magistrates. They spoke of the number of respectable young men who were waylaid on their way home after work and 'very often ruined' by prostitutes. The men, of course, were entirely innocent in these matters. Other, equally naïve men had been 'lured to singing saloons' to be ruined. The magistrates considered heavily fining the establishments where prostitutes gathered, which were often misnamed as 'supper rooms'. At that time the Lime Street area, now the site of Liverpool's main railway station, was notorious for brothels and supper rooms.

At the end of the 1850s, the police knew of 714 brothels in Liverpool, with 430 in the South division alone and a prostitute population estimated at 2,318. There were also 1,445 public houses and 896 beer houses to service both the locals and the transient seamen. The brothels were in groups in various red light areas of the town, with the most popular being in Copperas Hill with nearby Skelhorne and Pellew Streets, and Albion Street in Everton. By that time the police claimed to have cleaned up Spittalfield and have made progress in Peter Street. Genuinely worried about the morals and reputation of Liverpool, one of the town magistrates, Mr Anderson, visited a supper room and declared he 'did not see a single female that had any signs of modesty' in their 'appearance, boldness, dress and demeanour.' But he claimed that he saw nothing immoral either.

In the late 1850s, the pubs and coffee shops of Lime Street were known haunts of prostitutes. In 1858 a coffee shop run by Mr Baxter was renowned for having as many as thirty-five prostitutes at any one time. Inspectors William Wilson and Tobin tried to keep prostitution down in the area. When they found thirty-five prostitutes and forty men in Baxter's coffee shop, they warned the manager, Mr Allen, that unless the prostitutes were cleared, the place would be shut down. The police visited the premises several times on 19 May 1858 and each time found a number of prostitutes with their clients. The police said that the men and women were 'larking' and 'pulling' with each other, and there was foul language and laughter. A second coffee shop was kept by Joseph Bendino and had even more prostitutes. Both these cases came to court but were dismissed as the women had not been disorderly or riotous. As the police continued their campaign against the prostitutes of Lime Street, others were less fortunate.

Women of evil name and fame

Mrs Ann Harrison Wickham was one such. She ran an 'ill governed and disorderly house' in Lime Street, where men and women of 'evil name and fame' gathered. In the 1850s, Lime Street was improved with many fine buildings erected there, so that not only locals but also visitors passed through. Unfortunately it remained a haunt of prostitutes, their bullies and the low kind of men who used such establishments, with known thieves and returned convicts, a fact that shamed the town. Buildings that had been intended for respectable businesses had been taken over as supper houses. Wickham's was also a public house and did not close until four in the morning, until which time the noise was constant, with the inhabitants spilling outside to argue and fight. The women also stopped passers-by and invited then to sample the wares.

Inspector Smith said that there were thieves and returned convicts in Wickham's house, with prostitutes, bullies and betting men as well as some elderly respectable men who prostitutes had 'dragged in.' The neighbours, including the Queen's Hotel, complained about constant brawling and noise.

William Derry's Lime Street supper house was open from nine at night until four in the morning. The rooms were divided into a number of small compartments with wooden walls and doors that could be locked. When the prostitutes took their clients into a room, they put out an 'engaged' notice on the door. The principal clients were clerks and young men who worked in shops, and the waiter locked and unlocked the door for the prostitutes.

Inspector Morgan O'Brien said that two years before, Lime Street had been very quiet, but prostitutes had virtually taken over and the street was now noisy and dangerous.

The police cracked down on brothels, not so much for the exchange of money for sex, but for the disturbance and criminal activities that went hand in glove with the sex trade. Often the prostitutes were criminals, but sometimes they were the victims.

The killing of Sally Drummond

Sally Drummond did not have an easy life. By the time she was in her mid-twenties she was a prostitute with a reputation of vice and immorality. Before she reached twenty-nine she was dead, murdered by a man whose reputation was even worse than her own. For four years Sally had lived with a man named John Thomas; they had a brace of children but both died in infancy. Sally and Thomas fell out shortly afterward, and she shifted her affections to a distant relation named John Ferguson, a man she had known all her life. Unfortunately, although Ferguson was a younger man, he was even more dissolute than Thomas.

John Ferguson was only twenty-eight, but his companions called him 'Old Falk' and kept a wary eye open whenever he was near. He was a little over five foot in height, with a permanent frown on his face and battered, tattered old clothes on his body. He lived amongst the worst elements of Liverpool, passed his time in burglary, theft and drinking, and by early 1856 he was known to the police as well as to the people who infested the lowest alleyways of the worst slums in the town. He had been friendly with Sally as a youth and welcomed her back to his fold when she separated from Thomas.

The pair moved in with Ferguson's aged mother, Maria Williams, in Prince William Street. There was also Maria's second husband and a lodger named Mary Anne Loftus in the house. Sally was soon once more a mother and fell pregnant yet again. On Sunday, 20 January 1856, Sally and Mary were walking along Woolfe Street when they met Thomas face to face. There was no animosity and the women asked Thomas to buy them a drink. At some time in the evening Ferguson joined them. Thomas took his coat off and Sally grabbed it and gave it to Ferguson to pawn; that simple act was the beginning of the final tragedy in Sally's tragic life.

All four walked to their local, a pub named The Ruthin Castle at the corner of Woolfe and Warwick Street, and Sally shared half a gallon of ale with a female friend of hers. Not long after, Ferguson and Sally argued about the coat. The ill feeling continued throughout Sunday, when Ferguson wandered into his mother's house from time to time, slept fully dressed on the kitchen floor, got up at four on the Monday morning and vanished into the stews of Liverpool. He claimed he was going to the Brunswick Police Station to see a friend who was being sent to jail. Instead he met Sally in the street and returned home with her. Sally was very drunk after a night on the town.

With two drunk and tired people staggering around in the dark, it was almost inevitable that they should quarrel, and when they had been out the previous night with an old sweetheart, there was no need to search for an excuse. They began to argue once more about the jacket, and Ferguson told her to 'ask her husband about it' – presumably referring to Thomas. Maria Williams woke with the noise, and left her husband in bed to find out what the fuss was about. She entered the room, but in the darkness she could see nothing and judged only by sound.

Sally replied to Ferguson's jibe with a volley of what Maria Williams termed 'great heavy oaths'. She moved quickly to a cupboard, grabbed a heavy basin and threatened to 'split his skull'. Words escalated to blows when Ferguson punched Sally in the face.

She recoiled, holding her face and shouted, 'Oh, oh, my face!'

'Sally! Are you hurted?' Maria tried to help and separate the battling couple up, but both were intent on the fight now.

Ferguson pulled Sally to the floor, where they struggled for mastery. There should not have been any contest between the heavily pregnant woman and her stronger, fitter boyfriend, but Sally must have been holding her own as Ferguson had to resort to more extreme measures. Pulling out a clasp knife, Ferguson slashed Sally across the throat.

Sometime around that point, Maria lit a candle and the yellow light bounced around the room.

Sally looked at the blood pulsing from her throat, glanced at Maria and said 'God bless you.'

Maria, who was obviously a caring woman, asked Sally if she would go to the Southern Hospital. Sally nodded quickly.

Ferguson said he would take her there himself. He supported her out of the house, only for Sally to die in nearby Woolfe Street. Ferguson ran to tell his mother, threw the knife into an ashpit and asked for twopence half-penny. 'This is the last tin I will ever get from you,' he said. He shook hands with Maria's three children from her second marriage, held his mother for an agonising moment, said 'God bless you' and ran from the house.

Rather than flee as far as he could, Ferguson walked to the Rathin Castle and immediately told John Thomas, 'I've killed your wife, and cut her head half off.'

Thomas was a bit doubtful. 'Is that a fact?' he asked.

'If it's not true,' Ferguson said, 'I wish my two eyes may drop out.'

There was a friend of Sally's named Ann Hughes in the pub and when she looked around Ferguson told her 'I would think very little of doing the same to you.'

Word spread and Constable John Pharoe began to search for Ferguson. He was in Prince William Street when Ferguson came out of a cellar only a few yards away. 'Here I am,' Ferguson said. 'I am the man who did the deed.'

While in the bridewell, Ferguson's apparent nonchalance left him and he had to be prevented from committing suicide.

When the inquest was held, Ferguson's mother was in deep distress. 'Oh my son,' she said, 'Lord have mercy upon him.'

Until that moment, Ferguson had been as expressionless as a Liverpool sphinx, but now he also burst into tears. He was less emotional when the evidence was presented, except when Detective Samuel Povey gave evidence against him and claimed to have heard him swear to cut Sally's head off. Ferguson denied saying that and stated that Povey would 'swear anything against' him because he had refused to divulge information about robberies on a previous occasion.

'He has a spite against me,' complained the man who had slit Sally's throat. The trial judge was not impressed to hear the detectives had been in the habit of listening at Ferguson's door, but did not discard the evidence thus collected. He advised the jury toward manslaughter rather than murder because of the verbal provocation, and sentenced Ferguson to transportation for life when he was found guilty.

The death of one prostitute was a personal tragedy, but it did nothing to alter the overall picture. They continued to swarm over Liverpool, causing and getting into trouble.

More problems for the police

In February 1866, Mrs Jane Gallacher, who was one of the most notorious and experienced brothel keepers in Liverpool, was fined a massive £50 for disturbing the public peace. This, her third brothel, was in Lord Nelson Street. Despite her infamy, Gallacher put up a defence that her establishment was not nearly as bad as that of Mary Lovesay in the same street. The authorities appeared to agree, for Lovesay was jailed for nine months. However, the judge did not let Gallacher walk free, for she was imprisoned until the fine was paid, with the imprisonment not to exceed a year.

Brothels were often the scene of robberies, but sometimes there were serious assaults carried out there as well and not always by people from the lower end of society. John Harrison was a respected tradesman who ran an extensive drapery business at No. 800 Great Homer Street. He was a well-educated man with excellent diction and bearing, but he was also a man who frequented brothels.

On the night of Sunday, September 23 1867, Harrison came to the brothel at No. 36 Gloucester Street. He was not a regular there but soon slipped off to an upstairs room with twenty-two-year-old Elizabeth Scott. It was about half past one on the Sunday morning that Rose Maxwell, who was in the bedroom immediately below

Harrison, heard a loud cry of 'murder!' from his room. Rose was used to disturbances in the house, so rose quickly and ran upstairs. There was a crack of light under Harrison's door, but as soon as Rose burst into the room, Harrison blew out the candle and put his hat on top. However, there had been sufficient light for her to see that he was thumping Scott, perhaps stabbing her with something as the young woman continued to scream for help.

'Murder!' Rose shouted, 'Don't kill the girl!' She tried to interfere but in the dark could do nothing. Something sharp sliced across her hand and she lifted the skirts of her night clothes above her ankles, ran back downstairs, and fumbled for a candle. She lit it at the embers of the kitchen fire and returned, shielding the flame with one hand and accompanied by another woman named Sarah Ridgeway. Sarah had heard Scott say: 'give me half a crown and you can go', just before the screaming started. The two women thrust into the room and allowed the candle to pool its yellow light around.

Scott was crumpled on the floor with blood spreading around her and Harrison standing at her side. Scott was making small noises but did not respond to Rose's anxious questions.

'You've murdered her,' Rose accused and thought she heard Harrison say: 'I'll murder her a thousand times.'

Sarah worked in the brothel and thought she also saw Harrison standing over Scott, striking at her prone body with a broken jug.

Rose called the police and had Scott taken to the infirmary, where they pronounced her badly injured.

Naturally, Harrison's account of the incident was completely different. He claimed that when he walked into the house there had been five or six women who had surrounded him and he feared for his life or at least his wallet. He tried to get out again but the women would not let him. He said that he was 'desperate' and tried to rush for the door, and in the struggle the woman Scott was knocked or fell down and landed on a pottery jug. Her injuries came when the jug smashed and the shards cut her; Harrison was adamant that he had no intention of injuring anybody but only wanted to get out of the house and save himself.

Lying in her hospital bed, Scott told Detective Inspector Carlisle that she had 'improper sex' with Harrison but when she asked for payment he had refused her a half crown. The case came before the Police Court in October, but when Scott did not appear to press her charges, Harrison walked free.

That was one case of many.

In 1867, William Crankshaw worked as a tallow boiler. He lived in Preston but often caught the Liverpool train. He had been working in Liverpool on Wednesday 9 October and was waiting in Lime Street for his train, when two women approached him. Crankshaw recognised them as prostitutes but he was a respectable man and turned down their kind offers. While one of the women held him in conversation, the other snatched at his watch and chain, and the pair made off at speed.

Crankshaw was not having that and he followed. 'You've got my watch,' he told them, loudly. As he said that a muscular man, who had been walking behind the women, ran to Crankshaw and punched him in the face. The blow knocked Crankshaw to the ground. He lay there for a moment, temporarily stunned, and saw the women running away, but his attacker was slower on his feet.

Crankshaw rose and chased after the man, all the time yelling for the police. He was relieved when the beat policeman arrived and grabbed the attacker: his name was William Stoker and he was the 'bully' or enforcer, in a local brothel. He was also an ex-policeman, but was found not suitable for the job and had been thrown out. Stoker was jailed.

There were many more incidents as Liverpool prostitutes lived on the edge of legality, daily coping with the desperate, the despicable, the down-at-heel and the defeated. They were a hardy bunch of women who fulfilled a need but who were looked down on by a society that found it hard to reconcile respectability with reality. Some broke the law, others were victims but they were always there for those that required them, and that is something that cannot be said for other, better regarded members of society.

11
Cracksmen and Thieves

Theft was the most prolific of crimes, and Liverpool had a fine variety of differing types, from the clever to the naïve. There was also the highly unusual . . .

Stealing a carriage

In 1855, Britain and France were at war with Russia. As most of the action took place in the Crimea Peninsula in the Black Sea, the combat became known as the Crimean War. The opening battle between the allies and Russia was at the River Alma, where the British and French Armies faced very strong Russian positions. The Russians had been so confident of the power of their position that they had invited a number of dignitaries and their ladies who have a ringside seat and watch the inevitable destruction of the allied armies.

In the event, a frontal attack by the British completely broke the Russians and they fled in something like panic, leaving a great deal of spoil including the carriage of Prince Menschikoff, who had commanded the Russian army. The carriage was loaded onto a ship named *Mohawk*, commanded by Captain Barclay, and taken to Great Britain. By 1855, this carriage had arrived in Liverpool and was on display at the Queen's Hall in Bold Street as the centrepiece in an exhibition about the ongoing war.

In August 1855, while the owner of the exhibition, Mr Hough, was still in the process of setting it up, a mob of about thirty-five people came rushing into the hall, seemingly intent on doing as much damage as possible. The four ringleaders at least were Irish: Henry Cassidy, Nicholas Flaherty, William Rafferty and Lawrence Dornan.

The mob crashed into the room, knocked down the cashier and a couple of the other officials and spread around the exhibits. They attacked some of the other people at the exhibition and congregated around the carriage of Prince Menschikoff. They unbolted its wheels and carried them to a wagon they had waiting in the street outside, and then dragged the body of the carriage downstairs. The motive seemed unclear, for unless they carried the carriage away bodily, or refitted the wheels once outside the building, they could not transport it very far. But that was exactly what they did. They intended to steal the carriage of Prince Menschikoff.

Mr Partridge, Hough's father-in-law, ran past the men as they struggled down the stairs, and intended to slam and lock the front door so they could not get the carriage away, but a few of the intruders grabbed hold of him. However, before the mob carried the carriage away, the police arrived and stopped the proceedings dead.

Rafferty, one of the foremost men of the mob, argued his case. He said he had a contract with Captain Barclay for the carriage, but the captain had reneged on his agreement and sold the carriage to Hough instead. It seemed that Rafferty had already tried to negotiate ownership of the carriage from Hough, but the exhibition owner was having none of it, so Rafferty tried more direct, if illegal, action.

When the case came to court, Partridge handed over the document with which Rafferty had originally tried to lay claim to the carriage. It read:

To Mr N. Partridge

Sir – I do hereby demand from you the immediate delivery of the undermentioned articles:
One carriage styled [that is known as] Menschikoff's carriage; two headstones which were lettered in a foreign language; a quantity of foreign vestments; one barrel of a gun, two pairs of Turkish slippers, and one brass helmet.

31 July 1855

Although the captain had known about the purchase of the carriage, as soon as *Mohawk* docked in Liverpool he had travelled to Scotland, leaving the mate in charge of the ship. The mate had promptly sold the carriage to Hough, although he knew all about the arrangement with Rafferty.

After the magistrate had heard the facts, he decided that there was no larceny as Rafferty believed that the goods were his. He did say that there was a case for a charge of assault, but that would be in a later court. Rafferty walked free that day after what was surely one of the strangest cases heard in Liverpool.

The Liverpool bank robbery

The vast majority of nineteenth-century crime was petty, from sneak theft and drunken disagreements to domestic disputes. However, there was occasionally a robbery that caught the public's attention and achieved national notoriety. The Liverpool bank robbery of 1878 was one of the latter. The image of a bank robbery is often of armed men bursting through the door, of brandished shotguns and screaming customers, of shoot-outs with the police and mad car chases through crowded streets, but few were like that in Britain.

The Liverpool bank robbery was the exact opposite of the popular image. The chief perpetrator was a bank clerk named William Ohlman Stafford, a twenty-seven-year-old married man who lived with his wife and children at the Esplanade, Rock Ferry, New Brighton. He sported a fashionable moustache and was very careful of his appearance, so he always looked presentable as he dealt with his customers. As so often with white collar crime, Stafford was well connected, with an uncle who had been a cabinet minister. Stafford had been employed by the Bank of England for eight years, four of them in London, and was transferred to the Liverpool branch in Castle Street in 1874. Either the pressures of bringing up a family were too severe for him, or he just succumbed to temptation, but on 3 October 1878 he altered career from bank clerk to bank robber.

His modus operandi was very simple. On that day there was the usual number of customers in the branch, but two handed over unusually large sums of money. One customer deposited £10,000 in notes and Great Eastern Stock bonds, and the other £5,000, mainly in Bank of England notes. These were huge amounts for the time, far more than enough to set up anybody for the rest of their life. When money was handed into the bank, a fellow clerk named Stamworth Adey placed it in a drawer behind the counter, and Stafford had the responsibility of taking the money out of the drawer, recording the amount in a ledger with a record of the notes' numbers, and placing the bundles in a locked box for security. The box was placed in the strong room, safe from thieves and robbers.

Stafford performed two thirds of this duty: he removed the notes from the drawer and he entered the numbers in the ledger, but the third and crucial part he neglected. Rather than putting the notes in the secure box, he seemed to have concealed them somewhere in the bank, or perhaps slid the bundles into his pocket. The latter seems unlikely, given the bulkiness of a wad of notes of that value. That night the accounts seemed to balance: the ledger and the money taken over the counter were both the same.

The next morning Stafford thought it prudent not to come to work, and at the same time the manager realised that his bank was £15,000 short. The coincidence of both events was obvious.

On 3 October, Stafford had teamed up with an old school friend named Malcolm MacBeth, a twenty-seven-year-old financial and commercial agent. MacBeth was in trouble with the police for the minor offence of refusing to pay a cab fare. Rather than advising him to pay the fare and whatever fine was issued, Stafford recommended that he leave Liverpool, and invited him to the Paris Exhibition. When MacBeth wondered about money, Stafford said that one of his wife's relatives had recently died and left him enough money to pay for the trip. They met at the Grove Hotel at nine that night and took a cab to the bank where Stafford worked. Stafford went inside for a moment, possibly to pick up the money he had secreted, and then the cab took MacBeth home. MacBeth later joined the twenty past eleven train to London and met Stafford on the train. There was a young woman with Stafford, who he introduced to MacBeth as his wife.

The fact that Stafford was so ready to leave for Paris, and he had a woman in tow, suggests that this operation was not spontaneous, but something he had thought about for some time. Perhaps he had been waiting for a substantial sum of money to be handed in, or knew in advance that the deposits were due. Possibly the woman was the lynch-pin, or at least the reason, for the whole operation.

The threesome travelled to London and got off at Chalk Farm Station then either walked or got a cab to Broad Street. They booked into the Terminus Hotel at London Bridge and took separate rooms. MacBeth must have thought it strange when Stafford and he were in one dressing room and his supposed wife in another: that was an unusual way for a married couple to act, even in Victorian Britain.

As MacBeth was getting washed and shaved, he saw the reflection of Stafford in the mirror, holding a bundle of bank notes. Stafford asked MacBeth to take £2,500 and change the notes for gold at the nearest bank. According to MacBeth's later statement, he knew nothing about the bank robbery at that time. He stared at the pile of notes on the mantelpiece and said:

'Oh my God, what a lot of money,' and added, 'they will want to know at the bank what I want such gold for.'

'You must say you come from Benas,' Stafford told him, referring to a well known firm of money changers in Liverpool. 'If they say they haven't seen you before, you must say you have just come up from the Liverpool house.'

When MacBeth asked why Stafford did not go himself, he was answered that 'some of the fellows might know me.'

By now MacBeth sensed that all was not well and he refused to go unless Stafford put his own name to the exchange documents. When Stafford would not do so, MacBeth pressed further, asking him why he would not go himself until Stafford said, 'Hush, they are the Bank of England's.'

Only then did MacBeth realise that Stafford had stolen the money. Or so he later claimed.

'I will not have anything to do with it,' he said at once, possibly shocked that he was in the middle of a major crime.

'Oh, it's all right,' Stafford said, 'don't be a fool! They won't know anything about it until eleven o'clock and if the directors are down, which I think they will be, they won't know for two or three days.'

There was some thought and persuading, with Stafford saying they could 'share the swag' and showing how much money there was. MacBeth eventually agreed he would do it. He took some £3,000 and then the two calmly had breakfast, with the young woman still alone in the next room. As they ate, Stafford produced a copy of the *Friend* magazine, and pointed to advertisements for yachts for charter, including one at Southampton. The woman may have joined them, but she was not part of the conversation; she was not Stafford's wife but a Miss McLean and her part in the proceedings remains a mystery. It is possible she was simply Stafford's lover.

However, despite having agreed, MacBeth did not take the notes to the bank. Either his conscience got the better of him, or he lacked the nerve to participate in a bank robbery. The three left the hotel and stood outside the London Bridge station. MacBeth was a bit self-conscious as he carried a thick wad of notes and a stout bag in which to put the gold. He said farewell to Stafford shortly after half past nine in the morning.

'You'll come back with it, won't you Mac?' Stafford asked, suddenly anxious. 'You're not going to bolt?'

'Oh no,' MacBeth replied, 'if you don't trust me you'd better take the money yourself.' He proffered the cash but Stafford shook his head.

MacBeth watched as Stafford returned to the hotel and then, rather than go to the bank, he ran to the Temple (one of the most important legal districts of central London) and sought advice from a barrister's clerk he knew. The interview was painful but honest, and the clerk introduced him to a solicitor named Jones for another open conversation. All this took time, but shortly after two in the afternoon, Jones accompanied MacBeth to the Bank of England, where he handed over all the notes he had. It was only then that the bank realised it had been robbed. The bank or the solicitor informed the police, but when they raided the hotel, Stafford had fled. He had only waited about twenty minutes for MacBeth and then had panicked, grabbed Miss McLean and run; perhaps he had seen his companion walk in a completely different direction to that of the bank. Stafford still had the bulk of the money, a beautiful young woman and four hours head start. But the authorities had a mass of experience and huge resources.

The first thing the Bank of England did was to offer a £500 reward 'for information that will lead to the apprehension of the clerk'.

There followed a manhunt as the police raked the country for Stafford and the missing £12,000. They telegraphed the main urban centres and followed MacBeth's advice that he may have gone as far as Southampton. They issued a photograph of Stafford and said he may 'try to leave the country in the guise of a gentleman.' However, despite their professionalism, it was a bit of blind luck that enabled the police to trace his movements to West Cowes in the Isle of Wight.

Once Stafford and McLean left London they had vanished. The police had only MacBeth's vague clue about Southampton to follow, but the police there drew a frustrating blank. Nevertheless, beneath the official channels there was an unofficial network of police contacts, and a Liverpool policeman sent a newspaper report of the robbery and disappearance to his brother who lived in West Cowes. That officer noticed a man who he thought suspicious looking at the local yachts and thought the sighting was worth following up. He telegraphed his brother and asked for a description, but by the time it arrived, Stafford and Miss McLean had hired a cutter yacht named *Surge*, saying it was for a cruise around the coast of France. At that time before formal extradition treaties, the authorities thought that Stafford might sail to Spain and disappear forever, but Stafford only sailed as far as St Helier in Jersey.

By that time the West Cowes policeman had spread the news and the London police had taken further precautions. They sent Detective Sergeant Henry Webb to visit Le Havre and Cherbourg in case Stafford landed there, and telegraphed the police in the Channel Islands.

Back on *Surge*, Stafford had been anxious to get to Spain and asked the captain of the yacht to go there directly, but the captain said he had been chartered for a cruise to the French coast and that was where he would go. He had his contract to fulfil. It is not hard to imagine

Stafford's worry when they sailed around the French coast, with the clock ticking and the knowledge that the British police would undoubtedly be searching for him. His worry was justified as they cruised around the Channel Islands. The authorities on these islands were alert; when his yacht passed Alderney a sharp-eyed official noticed the cutter and telegraphed to the other islands. When the police saw *Surge* come in to port, they already had their suspicions and sent a boarding party.

Stafford met them on board. Calling himself Henry Mitchell, he had altered his appearance by shaving off his moustache, cutting his hair short and wearing yachting clothes, but the police had guessed he might do that. They arrested him under his new name and escorted him to the island, where they held him until he could be taken to London. All the same, they had taken the precaution of asking one of Stafford's colleagues to go south. Sergeant Webb had this man with him when he came to collect the suspect and immediately Stafford was identified; Webb arrested him and charged him with the robbery.

Webb searched Stafford's pockets and found sealed letters of introduction and a great number of bank notes. Once faced with reality, Stafford did not deny his crime and admitted everything.

'It's all right,' Stafford said. 'I know you. It's quite correct. I took the money from the bank at Liverpool, from a desk.' When Webb questioned further, Stafford said: 'I'll tell you the reason I took it. I was in difficulty. An acceptance of mine was due the next day for £200 and if I had not been able to meet it, the bank authorities would have known it. I should have got into serious disgrace. The monies I took were monies paid in by Messrs Leyland.'

Stafford finished by saying, 'if MacBeth had been true to me I should have been in Spain.'

He handed over all the money he had – around £11,000, so altogether the bank had £14,000 of the £15,000 that Stafford stole.

On 18 October, Stafford appeared before Lord Mayor in the Justice

Room of the Mansion House in London. He was pale and tired; he still wore the yachting suit in which he was arrested and the room was crowded as people packed in to see the fun.

Stafford said 'I am certainly guilty', but now he began his defence. As so often with thieves, he attempted to shift the blame onto an accomplice and claimed that MacBeth had put him up to it. He said that MacBeth was a moneylender and had offered to exchange the money for him. The £1,000, he said, were in MacBeth's possession.

Whether that was true or not, he was sentenced to seven years penal servitude. There is a slight postscript to this unhappy robbery: the Bank of England gave a reward of £50 to the three policemen from Jersey who arrested Stafford. Miss McLean seems to have escaped scot-free; her part is as mysterious today as it was then.

Robbery through hunger

At twenty past ten in the morning of 24 January 1856, two gaunt young men walked into the offices of John Dorandu and company at No. 30 South Castle Street. They were brothers and their names were Henry and Robert Eyre. When one of the assistants, Francis Stoddart, asked their business, they asked if Mr Dorandu was available.

Before Stoddart had time to reply, the taller of the men, nineteen-year-old Robert Eyre, an unemployed clerk, grabbed him by the throat and slammed him against the wall. As he did so, sixteen-year-old unemployed shop boy Henry produced a revolver and said that if Stoddart made a single noise he would kill him.

Half throttled by Robert Eyre, Stoddart nodded quickly. As Dorandu was a bullion dealer he may have been half expecting a robbery at some time, but this attack in broad daylight must have come as a shock. Robert released Stoddart, who slid slowly down the wall but said nothing when the door of the office opened and the managing clerk walked in. He carried a heavy locked box in his hands, and took in the scene at once but the Eyre brothers were ready for him and held all the advantages. One smashed a poker over his head while the other dropped a life preserver from his sleeve to his hand and thumped Stoddart on the back of his neck. Stoddart dropped at once, but Hughes was older and stronger. Despite the blood that ran down from the wound in his head and nearly blinded him, he fought back as best as he could.

As Hughes struggled with the Eyre brothers, Bernard Levy in the jeweller's shop next door heard the noise. He came to investigate, saw the fight and shouted out: 'Murder!', which was the accepted cry for help at the time.

The people of Liverpool must have been ready to help each other, for a number of passers-by immediately rushed into the office. The Eyre brothers had been getting the better of the struggle but when a deluge of angry Liverpudlians arrived, the tables were completely turned. Within minutes both the Eyre brothers were at the centre of a struggling knot of men, with fists and boots flying. Only the arrival of a lone police constable ended the melee, and while the Liverpudlians glowered their distaste at the armed robbers, the constable handcuffed them and dragged them away to a comfortable cell.

Hughes had a two-inch long wound in his skull and spent some time in the infirmary before he recovered.

The Eyre brothers were unfortunate in their choice of father. Henry Eyre senior was a forty-eight-year-old commission agent who was in Australia serving a term of transportation for forgery. When the police came to arrest him he fled to Ireland with Robert Eyre, his eldest son. Henry was caught but Robert was left fatherless and soon after, jobless as well.

In their defence, Robert Eyre wrote a letter, in which he claimed that they were in a 'state of extreme want' and 'actual starvation', so that he 'scarcely knew what I did.' He catalogued his poverty and the steps he had taken to find a job or some food, but his erstwhile friends turned him away and the authorities told him he would be sent back to Ireland if he applied for relief. To his credit, Robert defended his younger brother, saying he had a good character and had just done as he had ordered. Finally, Robert Eyre said that as soon as he was at liberty he would join the army. However, that would not be an option as the judge ordered both transported for the 'term of their natural lives.'

Robbing a jewellery shop

To a professional thief, banks and jewellers' shops must have been a prime target. Both contained high value goods that were relatively easy to transport, and both were usually situated in the centre of towns, where there were customers. But a location there also meant there was a network of streets and alleyways down which the thief could escape. However, there were difficulties for the thief. These establishments were always well guarded with an array of locks and other security precautions, while the beat police were well aware of the temptation they gave to the more professional of the criminal community.

There were many types of criminal in Victorian Britain, but at the top of the tree were the 'cracksmen' who specialised in this type of theft. There were a limited number of such men and each had his own particular method of breaking into an establishment to rob it. In most cases of house or shop breaking, some thieves could remove a number of roof tiles and go in that way, while others could cut away the lock of a door or remove a pane of glass from a window or even break into the building next door and cut through the intervening wall. Locks could be forced, or a child could be inserted through a skylight, fanlight or even under the floorboards, but banks and jewellery shops were wise to such methods and took adequate precautions.

In the early morning of Wednesday, 12 August 1867, a cracksman targeted the jeweller's shop of Frederick Clarke at No. 77 Church Street. This was a busy street with good lighting and there were always people walking past, even during the night. Clarke also had his assistant sleep in the shop overnight. These facts helped make the shop harder to rob, so Clarke must have slept fairly quietly at night. However, difficulties were only challenges to the professional cracksman.

On Monday, 10 August 1867, the assistant had to leave his job for a few nights, so the shop was more vulnerable. The news must have spread to the criminal fraternity, and on the Tuesday night four thieves had arranged to meet in Church Street. They stood on the opposite side of the road from the jeweller's shop and quietly discussed the best method of breaking in. They were concerned about the number of people walking past and the cab stand only a few score yards away from the shop, but as the hours passed the street became quieter until only the odd drunken sailor passed, too under the weather to be of any danger. One by one the cabs drove away as well, either because their shift had ended or because they had a fare. When only one cab was left, and the street was empty of prospective clients, one of the thieves boarded and asked to be taken to the pier head.

With the cab out of the way the three remaining cracksmen set to business. They were not subtle about making an entry. Going straight to the front window, they ripped off the protecting iron bar. There were wooden shutters behind the bar, but there was a single weakness. The police had asked the owner to leave a small aperture in the shutter and a light burning, so the passing beat policeman could look in and check that nothing was amiss. The owner had covered the hole with a grating, but the thieves soon pulled that off and set to work on the window. They used a diamond glass cutter, made a neat hole, and one thrust his arm through to scoop up everything he could. In a very short time he stole about £100 worth of brooches, lockets, rings and other easily portable jewellery and they all made off before the beat policeman arrived.

Once the robbery was discovered, Clarke informed the police, and Mr Kehoe, the head of the detective department, ordered detectives Marsh and Allinson to look into the case. The detectives headed straight for the worst parts of Liverpool and began making their enquiries. They knew full well who the major players were in Liverpool's underworld, and who was most likely to have been involved in an operation of this type. One area they visited was Ben Jonson Street, then known as Upper Canada, and they began to look closely into houses they knew were frequented by professional thieves.

It was not long before they had their first success. They banged on doors in Comus Street, not far off Scotland Road and visited a dirty court that was a known haunt of thieves. In one of the cellars there they found a known bad man called James Keating, a nineteen-year-old stonemason. While Allinson questioned Keating, Marsh searched the room, and found seven gold rings inside a mattress.

When Allinson asked Keating to explain these rings, he said, 'A boy gave them to me at the bottom of the street. I don't know who he is.'

Strangely, the detectives doubted that version of events. They took him to the police office and continued to question him, but Keating was an old hand and said little, except a demand for 'the assistance of counsel.'

'Of course,' Allinson replied, 'if you can afford it. Have you any money?'

Keating said he had some money in Tom's beer shop in Bolton Street, off Copperas Hill. The detectives knew this beer shop well: it was run by a man named Thomas Summers and was notorious for its clientele – thieves, prostitutes and layabouts to a man and woman. The detectives brought a number of uniformed officers with them, which was wise for as soon as Marsh and Allinson announced their business there, the inhabitants began to get rowdy, with many clenching fists or reaching for whatever weapons they could find. Summers demanded to see a search warrant, while Marsh saw Keating's mother talking to a young lad named Madden outside the shop. He watched as Madden slipped inside and spoke to Summers' sixteen-year-old brother-in-law Richard Shacklady, who then ran upstairs.

While the uniformed police kept the people reasonably quiet, the detectives tore the place asunder and found two gold rings hidden in the soot of the fireplace. As the detectives searched, a party of the uniformed men thundered upstairs to look for Shacklady, who was a known thief. Summers shouted out for somebody to bring him a gun, but the police ignored the implied threat. They found Shacklady, searched him and discovered a woman's bracelet. The police immediately fastened on the handcuffs.

While Summers blustered and shouted, Detective Marsh noticed his wife was wearing a very fancy ring, and had attempted to pass a purse to another woman. The detectives seized the purse and found a brooch that looked brand new and far too expensive for the wife of a back street publican. Marsh pulled Mrs Summers aside and asked her hard questions, but Summers stepped forward to protect his wife. He took the blame for his wife's jewellery, admitting that he had given her the pieces. The police put handcuffs on him as well and both prisoners were escorted to the central police station, where they found James Keating already snug in a cell.

When Marsh continued the questioning, Keating altered his story. He said that he had been walking down Church Street when he met Summers, Shacklady and a third man, whose hand was bleeding and bandaged with a handkerchief. The men had dropped the rings by mistake and Keating picked them up. Summers, he said, had given him a sovereign and asked him not to mention meeting him.

Summers story was slightly different. He said that Keating and another man had visited him on Monday and Tuesday, and had invited him out on the Wednesday morning. Apparently Keating told him he had 'a little job to do' but 'there was a cabman in the way', so he gave Richard Shacklady two shillings to take the cab away. After that,

Summers claimed, he went innocently home, and later Keating handed him a parcel in which were the ring and brooch to which his wife had 'taken a fancy'. The other man was John Grassam, a sixteen-year-old errand boy, who had put his hand through the window.

Summers and Keating were given eighteen months in prison and the others only a few months. This was not the only shop to be robbed in Liverpool.

Robbing the watch shop

On the evening of Saturday, 4 January 1851 Mr Clarke locked the inner door of the cellar of his shop and ensured the bolt was firmly in place. Then he left the shop, closed the outer door, locked it securely and checked it with a firm hand. He looked at his premises, ensured everything was in order and walked home for his one-day weekend. He had reason to be cautious, for he knew that his premises, Clarke and Morris, would be a natural target for any thief.

Clarke and Morris made watches. Their shop was at the corner of Church Street and Tarlton Street, with offices above and a cellar below. It was as secure as any shop in the area, with a brick wall all around, topped by an iron railing. The cellar was also strong, with walls four bricks thick, giving eighteen inches of solid brick. Even that was not enough for Clarke, for he was aware that many burglaries were through the cellar, so he had added an iron plate around the walls.

Liverpool thieves however, were tenacious. They did cut through the eighteen inches of brick to get into the cellar, wriggled to the edge of the iron plate and unhitched the hinges, climbed the stairs, forced the door and robbed the place of £1,800 worth of watches and jewellery before vanishing into the night. They were never caught. But houses were targeted as well as businesses.

The Huskisson Street Robbery

Catherine Wilson lived at No. 77 Huskisson Street. She was a very respectable lady, married to John Wilson, a shipmaster and the mother of two well-behaved children. She kept tight but loving control over her family while a servant, Elizabeth Sparks, a rather large woman, helped her keep her house as trim as her husband kept his ship.

On 1 November 1855 Catherine took her children to visit a friend. They were away most of the day, and arrived back at ten at night. Catherine was surprised to find the front door locked, but rang the bell and knocked loudly to get entry. There was no reply. No doubt annoyed at the laziness of Elizabeth, Catherine trailed her children around the back of the house, to find both the back doors gaping open.

Catherine ran inside the house and immediately saw that the living room door was also open. Concerned as well as angry, she barged in and stopped in shock: Elizabeth lay prostrate on the sofa, with her face bruised and bloody, her hair a mess and her dress torn open. She was unconscious, so, not surprisingly, Catherine was immediately upset. She shook the servant awake and demanded to know what had happened.

'Leave me alone,' Elizabeth said, in a dazed voice, 'and I won't make a noise.'

When Elizabeth was able to speak coherently she told her story. She said that a woman had come to the door and begged a drink of water. When Elizabeth went for water, the woman had come into the house. Elizabeth challenged her, but the woman dragged her into the parlour, threw her face up on to the sofa and poured some liquid into her mouth. The liquid must have been a drug, for Elizabeth passed out and did not regain consciousness until Catherine returned to the house.

Catherine ordered Elizabeth to a chemist to see if there was some sort of antidote for whatever drug had been forced into her, but the chemist could find no trace of anything unusual. While Elizabeth was away, Mrs Wilson inspected her house. It had been robbed. Burglars had systematically gone through every room and every item of furniture. Everything that could be stolen had been stolen, from very valuable items, silverware, money and blankets to the best clothes and even Elizabeth's clothes. The thieves had stripped the house bare of anything that they could carry, and with Elizabeth unconscious, there had been nobody to stop them. The thieves got away with around £50 worth of household goods.

With nothing left in the house, Mrs Wilson was forced to spend the night with a neighbour while the police began their investigations. A reward of £5 was offered to anybody who could help trace the thieves.

The police listened to Elizabeth's statement once more, questioned her closely and wondered if she was speaking the exact truth. They asked about her background and family, and learned she had a sister named Mary who lived in Workington while her mother, Jane Sparks, lived at No. 4 Sawney Pope Street, a rat-ridden slum off Scotland Road. More significantly, her mother had recently been released after seven months in prison for stealing from St Anne's Church. The police decided that it might be a very good idea to question Mrs Sparks.

When Detective Officer Samuel Povey entered the house at Sawney-Pope Street, both Mrs Sparks and her daughter Mary were lying on a bed on the bare floorboards of the house. They looked up when the detective walked in, but did not rise as he told them about the robbery.

'Was the mistress in?' Mrs Sparks asked.

Povey asked a few questions but without getting any useful answers. Shortly after he left, Mrs Sparks and Mary hurriedly left the house. The police arrested them both two days later in Park Lane, on suspicion of being involved in the robbery. When the police searched them they found a pawn ticket, but it was not for any of the items stolen. However, Detective Laycock realised that Mary had something in her mouth and forced his fingers between the woman's teeth. He pulled out another pawn ticket for a flannel petticoat. There was no reason for an innocent person to hide a pawn ticket, so Laycock and Povey followed the trail. The petticoat had been pledged to a broker called Syers in Park Lane, and it had been stolen from the Wilsons' house.

Elizabeth was also arrested under suspicion of being part of the robbery and all three women were charged. In the meantime, the detectives followed the trail of the missing items from the Wilsons' house. They found the clothes in a house in Cazneau Street, and the other items in various places in Liverpool. Everything was recovered except two £5 notes.

At the borough sessions, Mary and Elizabeth Sparks were sentenced to twelve months in jail and June Sparks to four years penal servitude.

Theft continued, and still continues. It is highly unlikely that society will ever rid itself of those people who have a desire to help themselves to the possessions of others, but the Liverpool police will fight to prevent such incidents, as they always have.

12
Corner Men and High Rippers

There have probably always been groups of disaffected young men infesting urban areas. No doubt the ancient Greeks had their youthful gangs, and Babylon and Egypt would have had the equivalent, but some cities have become notorious for gang violence. With the Industrial Revolution altering the character of British cities and the authorities fretting about civic control, places such as Glasgow, Manchester and Liverpool gained an unenviable reputation for these gangs. They bred in the seething slums that surrounded factories and docklands, battled for territory with bottle, boot, belt and blade, and preyed on the unwary or the unaware who happened to stray into the streets they thought of as their own.

In Victorian Liverpool, the gangs were known as corner men and they haunted the dark streets of the city in the middle decades of the century. In the 1870s, the gangs did not seem to have any territorial or other name attached to them, but were just an assembly of young men who were prone to violence. Later, around the 1880s, gangs adopted names, with the High Rip of the 1880s one of the best known at the time.

In January 1875, at the quarter sessions of the peace for the borough, John Aspinall QC explained that a corner man was one 'whose business it had been to muster at the corners of streets and commit assaults with the view of robbing and plundering unfortunate persons who might happen to pass by.' He added that the corner men inhabited the lower quarters of the town and attacked people of the working classes, while if they gathered in Abercromby Square or Falkner Square, the more prosperous areas of town, there would be a larger police presence. His solution to ending this infestation was obvious: send more police to the 'parts of the town where they occurred.'

At that time Liverpool had been slated in the national papers for its gang troubles. The town council also debated the 'lawlessness in Liverpool' and indignantly referred to other towns and cities where there had also been violence. Mr Picton of the council said they had 'a hostile population to deal with in certain parts of the town' and unless some action was taken, 'no man would be safe in going through these districts without a revolver in his pocket' and 'if the police would not protect them they must protect themselves.' Picton stated that: 'it was said there was great difficulty' in dealing with corner men. He disagreed: 'All they had to do was have a sufficient body of policemen . . . to drive these men away.' He thought that an organised horse patrol would do the trick. A fellow councillor, Mr Balfour recommended a 'thorough inspection of public houses' which he called a 'canker.'

The worst parts of Liverpool for corner men were said to be around the docks, with the *Liverpool Mercury* of 8 March 1875 claiming that 'filth, ignorance, disorder [and] disease are rife in the area commencing at Tithebarn Street and extending to Scotland Road, Vauxhall Road and Boundary Street.' He had a good reason for selecting this area of the town, for that was where the Tithebarn murder took place, a killing that had given Liverpool the bad reputation the councillors were so eager to disprove.

The Tithebarn Murder

The Tithebarn murder is one of the best known incidents of nineteenth century Liverpool's crime, and one that echoed around the country as an example of the city's unruly state.

Bank holidays were rare days of pleasure in the hard lives of working people, when whole families could get together and for one full glorious day enjoy each other's company; there was a possibility that the weather might be good and the pressures of work were certainly eased. However, some people did not rest on those days: policemen, shopkeepers and publicans were among those who had to work, and of course the corner men were always on the prowl.

On 3 August 1874, Richard and Alice Morgan were making the best of their holiday. Richard was a twenty-six-year-old porter from Leeds Street and the couple had been at the New Ferry Druids Gala on the Wirral. They met Richard's brother, Samuel, at Liverpool Landing Stage. Samuel was a carter, so both Morgans were respectable men. As they passed Exchange Station and approached the corner of Lower Milk Street, a group of five men approached them. One was named John McGrave, a notorious corner man. He deliberately bumped into Richard.

'Give us sixpence for a quart of ale,' McGrave demanded.

Richard Morgan refused, and advised the speaker to get a job so he could pay for his own ale. That was not the reply McGrave wanted, and as Richard walked away, he thumped him from behind, sending him face first onto the ground. Samuel swung a punch at the nearest of the gang, but they called up their friends and McGrave, Patrick Campbell and Michael Mullen surrounded the Morgans, hunting like wild dogs. The boots were soon crunching into Richard as he lay helplessly on the ground.

Alice tried to shield her husband and threw herself on the attackers, but one of the corner men kicked her on the side of her head, and the mob continued their assault. Two were kicking and a third unfastened his belt and used the heavy buckle as a weapon, hammering it down on Richard's head and back. Helpless, Alice could do nothing but scream for help.

A crowd gathered, but instead of helping the Morgans, some joined in the attack, so there were as many as seven corner men hammering at Richard. They kicked him up and down the street, until about fifteen to twenty minutes later somebody saw a policemen approaching and gave the warning cry of 'Nix! Nix!' The gang scattered and ran down Lower Milk Street. Samuel, who had been doing his best to help his brother, chased after them but lost them. When he returned, Richard was already dying, with a stab wound to the neck and his body battered and bruised. Alice was also injured. Not only had she lost her husband; the blow to her head also deprived her of her hearing. Among the interested spectators was McGrave, who had doubled back to mingle with the crowd.

The police picked up McGrave, Campbell and Mullen. The jury found them guilty but recommended mercy for nineteen-year-old Campbell, who not only held a steady job, but who was engaged to marry McGrave's sister. The judge sentenced all three to death, but Campbell was in fact reprieved and sentenced to life imprisonment instead. McGrave and Mullen were hanged at Kirkdale Jail on 3 January 1875 with McGrave very afraid now that the tables were turned, but Mullen stoic as he stepped forward into oblivion.

Aftermath

After this pointless murder, the city gained a reputation as a den of corner men. The London papers in particular slated Liverpool, and without any recourse to evidence, said that the government would take control of the city if Liverpool town council did not clean up its act. There were various theories about the creation of such people as corner men but the Rev Nugent voiced the most popular when he said: 'corner men and corner women too are made by corner houses.' By that he meant public houses and other places where alcohol could be obtained. The Victorians linked much crime and vice to drink, and often the evidence proved them correct. Other theories included overcrowding, with Liverpool having a reported population density twice that of London.

Corner men in action

While the politicians debated and newspapers reported or gloated at this scandalous news that added to their circulation figures, criminal activity in Liverpool continued. In January 1875, there was a scuffle outside the Abercorn public house in Dryden Street when Ann Birchall attacked Elizabeth Underwood. The two had argued in the pub and Birchall followed Underwood outside and smacked her over the head with a brick, before stealing all her money. The magistrate echoed the Rev Nugent when he gave the wry comment that there were corner women as well as corner men.

Sometimes, however, the corner men found they had a tiger by the tail. About the middle of June that same year, a Scotsman happened to be walking along Great Crosshall Street late in the evening, when two corner men lunged out of the shadows and asked if he had any spare money to buy them drink. The Scotsman stopped and looked at them; he was aware of the glitter of his diamond breastpin and the weight of his wallet, and knew of the reputation of the local corner men.

'If it's drink you want,' he told them, 'but I want to get home. Come and I will take you to a pub nearby.'

However, instead of a pub, the supposed victim led the two corner men to the house of a friend of his, locked the door and challenged them to fight. 'Defend yourselves if you can.' The Scotsman was well built and on guard, not at all like the helpless drunkards the corner men preferred as victims. Once he had beaten both corner men helpless, he literally kicked them out into the street and warned them to try another line of business.

There were many other incidents with less favourable outcomes.

On 16 May 1875 a constable noticed a man named John Whalley 'behaving indecently' in Vauxhall Street and moved to quieten him down. Whalley resisted and was arrested, but he called on two lounging corner men to help him. Always ready for trouble, they rushed forward and one tripped the policeman up. Wriggling free, Whalley turned around and kicked the policeman in the face, splitting his lip open and damaging his teeth. When more police arrived, the corner men quickly disappeared but Whalley was taken into custody and received three months hard labour.

The reign of the corner men continued. On 22 June 1876, a corner man named John Nicholson visited Warrington, then about twenty miles east of Liverpool. He hit the pubs and soon began challenging people to fight. When the police came to arrest him, he continued to struggle and injured a constable badly enough for the officer to have to go off duty. Nicholson ended with two months with hard labour.

And there was more: on the evening of Monday, 21 July 1876 a barge captain named John Carter was crossing the railway bridge at Market Street in Birkenhead on his way home when somebody asked him for money for a drink. He looked up and saw three men sitting on an abutment of the bridge, but ignored them and walked on. When they began to swear at him, Carter stopped and bravely asked if they were addressing him. Twenty-one-year-old Michael Halligan, one of the three and a well known corner man, jumped off the wall and punched Carter in the face.

As the barge captain staggered, the other two men joined in. One was twenty-seven-year-old Patrick Halpin, also known to the police, but the third was unknown. All three began to punch and kick Carter, but he was a bargee, tough as they come and unwilling to give in without resistance. He beat a fighting retreat toward his house, two hundred yards away. By the time he got there, he had been battered stupid, with his shirt half ripped from his back and was bloodied and bruised from legs to forehead, but still standing and still trading punches.

John Coates, a friend of Carter, saw him knocked down six times, and struggle to his feet each time and fight on. Coates ran for the police and Detective Hodgson and the bridewell keeper, Glass, came to Carter's assistance, by which time the bargee was virtually unrecognisable. Halpin and Halligan were both imprisoned with hard labour.

The police fight back

After the Tithebarn murder, the police must have taken the councillors' advice to heart, for by 1879 they were harassing the corner men when they could. For instance, on 10 October 1879 they found John Keating and Michael Shea lounging on the corner of Athol Street and arrested them for loitering. The police had often had dealings with both men, who were fined forty shillings plus expenses, with a month's jail as an alternative. In June that same year two more corner men were fined five shillings each for loitering on the corner of Vauxhall Road. It seemed that the police were intent on keeping the corner men on the move rather than let them wait for victims.

Michael Gilligan might have thought that the police could have been more efficient in moving the corner men along. He was a dealer in sugar casks, so not rich, but a hard working man making his way in the world. On 14 December 1878 he was walking along Fontenoy Street minding his own business. He noticed a group of young men standing at the corner of Lacey Street but took no notice, no doubt hoping that he was not prosperous enough to matter, but corner men were prone to casual violence as much as profitable robbery. There were at least four of them, and one put out his leg to try and trip

Gilligan up. Gilligan staggered but recovered, only for one of the others in the gang to thump him to the ground from behind.

As Gilligan fell, the corner men jumped on him. One clasped a hand over his mouth to prevent him from shouting for help; another rifled through his pockets for his money and the rest just stuck the boot into the helpless man. When they had his purse, they landed a few more kicks and ran off: job done.

Unluckily for at least two of the corner men, a sharp-eyed policeman had seen a group of four known corner men together a short time before, and when he heard about the assault he put two and two together and had the lot rounded up. When they appeared in court, Gilligan recognised John Reed, alias Cunningham, and John McGee, alias Maloney and they were found guilty. The judge must have been determined to stamp out the corner men when he had the chance: he gave Reed eighteen months hard labour plus twenty lashes with a cat-o'-nine-tails, while McGee, a known offender who had been in jail, got seven years penal servitude plus twenty lashes. In the judge's eyes: job done.

Stabbing the police

The Great Howard Street area was a place to avoid in the early 1880s, with a known gang who attacked passers-by and caused mayhem whenever possible. There was one notorious occasion when a police constable grabbed a corner man named Michael McLean, but the man pulled a knife and stabbed him badly in the hand. McLean escaped justice and the constable had to go to the Northern Hospital.

Murder of a sailor

About twenty to eleven on the night of Saturday, 5 January 1884, the local beat constable Edwin Evans was passing along Blackstone Street, when he noticed a crowd gathered under the Lancashire and Yorkshire Railway Bridge. As he came closer the crowd scattered, leaving a slender man in the clothes of a sailor lying on the ground. Evans thought little of it, believing the sailor had been drinking, which was not unusual among seamen in that part of Liverpool. He sent for a wheelbarrow to trundle the seaman to a cell to dry out, but when he investigated further he saw the sailor was injured and bleeding from a number of wounds. The man was taken first to Saltney Street police station, from where the officer telegraphed the Northern Hospital for the ambulance wagon.

It was too late. The man bled to death from a stab wound to the neck before he reached the hospital, and the police began to piece together his last hours. Although they knew the victim was a foreign seaman by his clothes and appearance, the police had difficulty in identifying him. They thought he came from a vessel named *Leo XIII*, but when they checked, the seamen from that vessel did not recognise the corpse. A local man thought the body was a labourer named Michael Mullet, but when the police brought in Mullet's brother, they found that was also incorrect. Only after considerable trouble was the body identified as a Spanish seaman. The police questioned various witnesses to ascertain what had happened.

Attack in Blackstone Street

Two seamen, including Exequel Rodriguez Nuniez, a five foot five, slightly built Spaniard with a wispy beard and moustache, were unfortunate enough to meet the corner men. The seamen were from different vessels but both came from Malaga in Spain so had teamed up to tour the Liverpool high spots. Nuniez came from the ship *Sierra* and they were walking down Regent Road on the way back to their ship from a café in Pitt Street. As they reached the corner of Blackstone Street a group of corner men lurched out of the shadows. One, probably named Ballantyne, nicknamed Mooney, punched one of the seamen in the face and split his lip. A number of others jumped on Nuniez. Both seamen took to their heels and ran, but in different directions as the corner men followed. There were a number of youths in the gang, including seventeen-year-old Michael McLean, a labourer from Steel Street. He was the man who was accused of stabbing a police constable in an earlier incident. He was only five foot one inch, but well built, slightly chubby of face and did not at all appear like the predator he in fact was. The others included Patrick Duggan, Alexander Campbell, William Dempsey and Murdoch 'Mooney' Ballantyne.

One of the Spaniards, José Giminez, managed to escape the worst of the gang violence and fled toward the docks. He met a dock policeman, John Davies and tried to tell him his story, but he was scared, excited and nervous, and the constable found it difficult to understand his broken English. Nuniez was slower to get away and the pack hunted him down in Regent Road. Duggan swung his belt, which wrapped around the Spaniard's neck and stopped him dead; McLean hauled him to the ground; two of the corner men held him there while McLean rammed into his groin and belly with his heavy boots. Nuniez broke free and ran again, shouting for help, but the gang followed, baying for blood, with McLean and Duggan to the fore. Nuniez, terrified and in pain, ran into Fulton Street and hid in a narrow passage for a few moments until he thought the corner men were away.

While Nuniez hid away, Duggan approached a watching woman, Esther Ramsden, and asked if he could wipe his hands on her apron.

'No murderer shall wipe his hands on my apron,' Ramsden told him, but just then Nuniez cautiously emerged again and Duggan did not pursue the matter.

The gang were still alert and spotted him right away. Somebody, perhaps Campbell, yelled out: 'knives, boys, knives!' and chased him again, swinging their belts around their heads. By now there were others attached to the original pack, so there were children as well as youths chasing the unfortunate Spaniard. As he neared the Fulton Street Foundry the mob caught him again, and again the boots and belts rained in. Nuniez rolled away, staggered to his feet and tried to escape, but by now his injuries slowed him and the corner men were toying with him. They chased him under the railway arch at Blackstone Street and then there was no escape.

'Give me a knife,' somebody shouted, 'my belt's broke!'

The Spaniard turned at bay and the corner men surrounded him and hammered in with boots and fists, with Duggan swinging hard with his belt and McLean kicking Nuniez on his lower body. Then McLean and Duggan pulled out clasp knives and stabbed at him. Eventually, pleased with himself, McLean shouted out:

'Mooney, Mooney, I've done it.'

At that time Mooney Ballantyne was a few yards away and was not involved in the assault. He moved forward to join in the struggle but his sister, Georgina, at all of twelve years old, gave him sound advice, 'Mooney,' she said, 'come back: they are fighting with knives.'

'I've done him,' somebody shouted. Ten-year-old John Lodge, watching the fun, thought it was Campbell.

'Here's a bobby,' Mclean shouted and the gang immediately scattered and ran away, leaving the seaman lying on the ground. He managed to pull himself up, and that was when Constable Edwin Evans found him. The hospital examined Nuniez not long after; there were a number of stab wounds in his back and an ugly one in his neck. The wound on his neck proved fatal.

After the murder the corner men had split up, with Ballantyne taking Campbell and Dempsey to his house. Dempsey borrowed a brush from Ballantyne's mother to help clean the blood off his trousers and returned to his own house. The next day Dempsey's mother handed the stained trousers into a pawn shop. The police found them there, still damp and still stained. McLean and Duggan teamed up with a couple of girls and vanished in a completely different direction.

Inspector Pegler knew his local bad men and gathered information around the area. He asked the right questions and at eight the next morning, he entered the unfurnished house of No. 41 Fulton Street and arrested McLean as he hid behind a bedroom door. When the police picked him up he dropped a knife on the ground in an attempt to hide. He was searched and two more blood-stained knives were found in his possession. He also had a large and heavy belt buckle, sharpened to inflict maximum damage, but he denied any involvement in the killing.

When the police searched the house they found sixteen-year-old Mary Reardon hiding in a closet.

The police continued their enquiries. Joseph McCrabber had been in the Seven Stars public house on Regent Road and had seen Ballantyne, Campbell and Dempsey there; they had still been there at about half past nine. He saw Ballantyne with Duggan and McLean at the corner of Regent Road and Blackstone Street a few moments later, not long before the assault. However, in his opinion, Dempster and Campbell were quiet respectable young men. When Duggan and his girl, fourteen-year-old Mary Burke left the house in Fulton Street, they walked along Regent Road and right into the waiting arms of Inspector Pegler and a constable. They arrested him straight away, while Dempster was taken in a garret in Great Richmond Street.

The High Rip

The police picked up the others, at home or elsewhere, and charged them with murder. They all denied assaulting the Spanish seaman and in the time honoured way of passing the buck, each blamed the others. When Dempsey was arrested he said 'What I have to say, I will say at my trial.'

As always after any particularly brutal act by corner men, the papers condemned them roundly. In January 1884, the *Liverpool*

Mercury called them 'rough, brutal and lawless [...] and utterly degraded in their habits.' The paper thought that the north end of town was 'infested with them' and that they were the 'savage fringe of our civilisation.' The north-east saw attacks by corner men virtually every day with comparatively few arrests, and there had been a murder of a young boy in Commercial Street not long before. The press demanded that respectable people should be protected from these 'Bashi-Bazouks.'

On 8 January 1884, five corner men appeared before the Police Court charged with the murder of Exequel Nuniez. As well as McLean, there was eighteen-year-old Patrick Duggan, a twenty-year-old barber named Alexander Campbell, nineteen-year-old labourer William Dempsey, and twenty-year-old Murdoch Ballantyne, who was also a labourer.

Used to casual affrays and assaults by sundry corner men, the Liverpool public were nevertheless shocked when they read about this murder. Rather than an aimless collection of disaffected youths, the public learned that this group of murderers was a more organised gang and had a name. They were the High Rip: it was a label that travelled around England and carried undertones of menace that had never quite been heard before.

Except for the hardened seventeen-year-old McLean, the men were not quite so brash when faced with the consequences of their actions. Dempsey wrote an affidavit in which he admitted giving the Spaniard a 'slight wound' because he thought he was 'dealing with a madman.' He did not deny that he had been involved in the struggle, but claimed that one of the Spanish seamen had tried to slash him with a knife and he had retaliated by knocking the man down and kicking him. As so often in such cases, he blamed one of the others for the knife wounds and said he had been mistaken for Duggan. With no real evidence against him, the police released Dempsey, who scuttled off for San Francisco and oblivion.

McLean was a different case and a known bad man with a history of violence. He had been accused of stabbing a policeman in the hand, but wriggled free at the assizes. Previous to that he had half-blinded a respectable widow when he threw a handful of pepper in her face before running off with her money. Now that they had him, the police were reluctant to let him escape again and watched him very closely.

When he heard the statements of each corner man, the judge said 'the statement of each prisoner is absolutely valueless'. The defence mentioned that the murdered man had a knife inside his shirt and suggested that the cry of 'knives, boys!' might have been a warning that the Spanish were using knives. He said that Dempster had not been involved in the initial fight and may well have merely retaliated when Nuniez tried to slash him.

The jury found Dempsey, Ballantyne and Campbell 'not guilty' and they were free to go. The other two were found guilty but with a recommendation of mercy because of their youth. McLean immediately blamed Dempster for the murder. Duggan agreed, saying he was innocent and Dempster was the murderer.

When the judge passed the death sentence, Mclean and Duggan apparently 'walked jauntily' with a 'callous smile,' or so the reporter of the *Liverpool Mercury* claimed.

The drunken hangman

On 10 March 1884 Michael McLean was hanged at Kirkdale Prison, but there was still drama left in the man's short and brutal life. McLean's execution did not go exactly as planned. Bartholomew Binns, the executioner, was drunk when he arrived at the prison and fell asleep before he could make any arrangements. A warden woke him and Binns reacted violently and appeared ready to fight anybody and everybody who crossed his path. The wardens had to send for the police and an inspector and two constables hurried into Kirkdale just as the hangman calmed down. The assistant hangman, Samuel Heath, fresh from hanging the poisoners Higgins and Flannigan, came to the jail as a reserve, but Binns had sobered up sufficiently to perform the execution.

At the last moment, Duggan was given a reprieve but although McLean hoped for the same, the Home Secretary turned down all requests for leniency. McLean steadfastly announced his innocence, even to the Roman Catholic priest who attended him. As the prison bell tolled its doleful message of judicial death, Binns tied McLean's arms to his body and led him to the scaffold. McLean did not struggle or appear scared; he showed more courage than would be expected. Rather than climb the ladder with reluctance, he raced up, as nonchalant as if he was walking to the pub. However, he was not rushing to embrace death, but to make a statement to the gathered reporters before the white hood was placed over his head.

'Gentlemen,' he shouted, 'I consider it is a disgrace to the police force of Liverpool and the laws of the country that I am going to suffer death, and another boy is going to suffer imprisonment for life for a crime of which we are both innocent, as God is my judge.'

It seems a very eloquent speech for a seventeen-year-old boy on the verge of death, but perhaps he had been coached, or was reconciled to death and had decided to make his executioners uneasy once he was gone. Whatever the reason, once he had spoken, he stepped onto the trap and allowed Binns to tie his legs, put on the hood and noose and pull the lever. Although Binns looked very nervous, McLean lost consciousness immediately after he fell but his heart beat for another thirteen minutes before he finally died.

Even after the execution of McLean, the drama continued. Binns and Heath caught the same train for Dewsbury and Binns entertained his fellow passengers by showing them lengths of rope he used in his profession. People thought this was disgraceful behaviour by the government's professional killer; it was acceptable to hang somebody but not to show the rope afterwards.

Leaning on the gangs

After the murder, the police leaned heavily on corner men. For instance in the police court of 9 April 1884, no fewer than eighteen corner men were fined, with many paying costs as well. In most cases, the mother or sister represented the accused, with the corner men refusing to attend court.

The Blackstone Street murder did not signal the end of the corner men: such people under different names still infest Liverpool and most other towns, but the incident did spur the authorities to greater preventative methods. The name High Rip became notorious throughout the city and the press tended to use it at every opportunity. It is unlikely that the High Rip deserved the publicity they got, but no doubt the members of the gang enjoyed the fear factor.

The High Rip gang centred on the Scotland Road district and continued the violence of the corner men. They hunted in packs, attacked with boots and sharpened belt buckles and targeted the vulnerable and the unwary. The term High Rip may have been used to refer to a specific gang, or as a generic word for any loose organisation of youths who used violence, as corner men had been so used. Rather than use the term 'corner men' the press and no doubt the general public, now spoke of Rippers or High Rippers. The gang attacks continued, and the court cases.

Female in command

In February 1885 William McConnell and William Boylan, both seventeen-year-old labourers, were accused of assaulting a youth named John Grant, who himself was no angel, as he had a record that included attacking a policeman. The gang of which they were members frequented Back Portland Street, with McConnell as the reputed leader, although one witness at the trial claimed that a girl named Ellen Grant was the 'high leader' – an interesting example of female involvement or even leadership of a teenage urban gang. The local beat policeman said he knew of a 'heavy gang' that carried knives, swords 'or any weapon they can lay hold of.' In this instance there had been a confrontation where pokers and belts were freely used. There was no doubt about McConnell's and Boylan's guilt, and both were given six months with hard labour.

The attacks continue

In April that same year two more youths, Richard Duggan and Michael Madden, were in court, accused of being members of the High Rip gang and of attacking Michael Howard and Thomas Noon in Scotland Road; belts were freely used and Howard was slashed across the head with a knife. A few days later a carter, nineteen-year-old George Whitehead, was in court accused of being a Ripper and attacking Hugh Cunningham in Tichfield Street. Whitehead used a belt and a knife. The prosecution suggested that the Rippers were hunting Cunningham as he had previously given evidence against gang members. Whitehead denied that story and said that Cunningham had attacked him: the court preferred Cunningham's version and sent Whitehead to jail for five months with hard labour.

One member here or there did not seem to matter much to the High Rip gang, or gangs if there were more than one branch. They continued their lives in the same old manner, infesting Scotland Road and instigating a reign of terror on the inhabitants. Because of the fear they inspired, it was difficult to obtain prosecutions against them, but from time to time one member or another would appear in court and the judges moved against them with the full force of the law.

In August 1886, Hugh Donnelly appeared in court charged with being part of a group that assaulted a man named William Hignett in Scotland Road. Hignett was obviously a brave man. The gang had stopped him and demanded that he buy them spruce beer, but he refused, so they knocked him down and kicked him around the head and body. That same month the Rippers exported their violence to New Brighton, on the Cheshire side of the Mersey. Five members of the gang were in a pub there and two, William McConnell and John Shute, argued. They stepped outside to settle the dispute with fists and boots, when two more Rippers, James Burns and Thomas Crichton joined in on the side of McConnell. Somebody stabbed Shute in the chest, with the knife penetrating his lungs.

As their friend lay bleeding on the ground, the other Rippers walked calmly to the pie stall of William Bowker and began stealing his pork pies. Bowker grabbed one of them, but the rest laughed, said he had the wrong man and snatched as much of his stock as they could carry. Bowker took a firm grip of McConnell, who punched him in the face, while Burns thumped him with a stick and the others, naturally, joined in. Again knives were used and Bowker was stabbed in the shoulder. He woke up in hospital. All four Rippers were identified and arrested.

The Rippers also exported their violence to Bootle, where two alleged Rippers confronted a seaman named John Peterson on Derby Road and demanded money. When Peterson said he had only 6d, one of the Rippers, Thomas Gibbons, headbutted him. The second Ripper, Michael Trainor, kicked his legs away and as he staggered, the Rippers dragged him to a dark alleyway where they held him down and rifled his pockets.

Peterson's shouts of 'Murder' attracted a local woman who ran into the alley with a lighted candle, but one of the Rippers knocked the candle out of her hand. Another seaman, William White, also rushed to help, and the attackers yelled 'we'll high rip them', which may have been to frighten the helpers, or could have been a genuine gang slogan. A number of police constables arrived and, between them and White,

Gibbons was subdued and arrested. He struggled so violently that it needed five constables to carry him away as he kicked, swore and screamed 'High rip!' at the top of his voice.

Leaving his companion to fight alone, Trainor fled, but the police got him at his home the next morning. As expected, he denied any part in the robbery but claimed that Gibbons and Peterson had been fighting each other.

'A secret society known as the High Rip gang'

In October 1886 at a meeting of the Watch Committee, Chief Constable Nott-Bower spoke of the High Rip gang. He referred to rumours and newspaper reports of 'an extensive conspiracy for the purposes of assault and plunder' in the north of the city in a 'secret society known as the High Rip gang.' Nott-Bower said that this was nonsense and scare-mongering. The press also spoke of 'police incompetence' and 'few' arrests being made. Nott-Bower pointed out that there were 243 serious assaults last year, with 225 arrests, so the police were hardly incompetent and were usually successful. Other members of the Liverpool authorities also joined in the discussion.

On 19 November 1886, Mr Justice Day issued a statement in which he said that he did not believe there was an 'organisation of ruffians known as the High Rip gang.' Day was to become known as Judgement Day because of the severity of the sentences he passed down on gang members or alleged gang members who came before him. At that date, the Liverpool police had solved around 92 per cent of the crimes of violence in the city, which is a good average by anybody's standards.

Threats and pistols

Despite the apparent success of the police, the inhabitants of the north side of Liverpool knew of the danger of the High Rip. In the autumn of 1886 a number of men from the High Rip gang smashed the window of the home of a thirty-two-year-old labourer named John McShane; they hammered at the door and called him a police spy and threatened him with violence. The Ripper named Trainor, who had a reputation for violence and may have been 'captain' of the gang, said he had 'done three months and a flogging for one fellow and would do five years for you.' In response, McShane produced a pistol and left the house. There was a crowd gathered outside and he fired two shots, one of which hit an innocent man named Harold Buck in the foot.

Discipline and drama

In December 1886, the annual meeting of the Liverpool and District Teachers Association advocated technical instructions for children before they started work, and stated that if discipline and respect for authority was maintained in schools 'we should hear nothing of High Rip gangs.'

The seeming inability of the police to stamp out the gangs had an effect on popular entertainment, where in 1886 the Rotunda Theatre had its own version of *Robinson Crusoe*, with the lines:

> *Well Liverpool has its spell of crime*
> *The High Rip gang has a high old time. . .*
> *Where were the police? I'm fairly puzzled*
> *The police were catching dogs that went unmuzzled.*

After a couple of months of comparative calm, in early February 1887 the High Rip gang erupted again. As so often, they infested Scotland Road; they ran along the street with knives and a slingshot, pushed women to the ground, robbed shops and stabbed the shopkeepers. They also stabbed a young boy who happened to be present. The cry of 'knives out, lads, let's go for him' was a chilling reminder of the violence inherent in the Rippers.

Justice Day

Four of the High Rip gang were arrested and appeared before Justice Day at the Liverpool assizes in May. He was determined to stamp out this blight on Liverpool's streets and passed sentences that sent a chill of fear through the supposed hard men of the gangs.

When the Rippers were found guilty of wounding with intent as well as robbery with violence, Justice Day sentenced them to jail sentences of between fifteen and twenty-one months, plus hard labour, and reinforced the message with sixty lashes of the cat-o'-nine tails, delivered in three instalments of twenty lashes each. Day had considered a long period of penal servitude, but considered that a drain on the public purse, so chose a shorter term mixed with the cat.

The public seemed to approve, for a letter in the *Liverpool Mercury* spoke of 'the very sensible sentence' and recommended it also be used for 'wife beating and cruelty to children'. In the following assizes in August that year, there were no cases of street robbery and the High Rip gang did not figure. In their element in dealing out beatings to the innocent and unwary, the members of the gang were cowed when on the receiving end.

Jack the High Ripper

The name of High Rip still came up in the police courts from time to time, but Justice Day seemed to have knocked the spirit out of them. However, the ripples of the High Rip extended far beyond the boundaries of Liverpool. There was said to be a gang using the term 'Rip' around the Whitechapel area of London in the late 1880s, and perhaps Jack the Ripper borrowed the nomenclature from Liverpool.

The Whitechapel gang extorted money from prostitutes, so were of a slightly different stamp from their Liverpool namesakes. In Liverpool in 1889, two youths named James Mawdsley and William Baker drew knives when the police arrested them, and shouted out 'now lads, come on: high rip' but were disarmed and sent for hard labour. They used the name as a shout of defiance rather than a gang slogan.

Echoes of the High Rip

In 1893, the Watch Committee stated that 'rowdyism in the evening (so-called High Rip gangs etc) had been fairly coped with', so relegating to a footnote an aspect of Liverpool life that had once dominated the council chambers and caused questions to be asked far from the city. In 1897, a decade after Justice Day had subdued the original High Rippers, a man named Richard Owens was sent to penal servitude for seven years for assault. The Judge, Mr Justice Ridley, gave his opinion that Owen may be a leader of a High Rip gang.

There were other gangs to come as the years rolled on, but nothing like the High Rip; whether it was one gang or many using an umbrella name to cause fear, they left their mark on Liverpool as the corner men had before them. With luck their like will never be seen again. However, parts of Liverpool are still marred by gang culture.

13
Training Ship Trouble

There were many methods of dealing with delinquent boys in the nineteenth century. In the early decades they could be transported to Australia, jailed or hanged. The hanging option was reduced later, but even fairly young boys could be jailed alongside adult offenders, and there was the added option of a simple birching. If the court decided that the offender could be saved from a bad family background, they might be jailed for a few days and then sent to a reformatory school or ship for a number of years. While the reform schools trained the lads for life on land, the ships trained them for a life at sea.

Liverpool had two such vessels: *Clarence* and *Akbar*. Both were moored in the Mersey and both held their quota of troubled youths. Protestant boys were sent to *Akbar*, and Roman Catholic lads to *Clarence*, which was operated by the Catholic Reformatory Association. Despite the difference in religions, both were very similar, with strict discipline and long Sunday sermons. Not too far away HMS *Indefatigable* was moored, on which were trained the sons of seamen lost at sea and boys whose fathers were seamen but whose mothers, for whatever reason, could not look after them. Finally there was

HMS *Conway*, equally strict but home to boys who may inhabit the quarterdeck rather than the fo'c'sle: the officer class.

The boys

Of the boys on the four training vessels, those on *Clarence* were arguably the most troublesome. *Clarence* was an old man-of-war and, by the early 1880s, had been used as a reformatory vessel for many years. The people of Liverpool were used to seeing her moored in the Mersey and knew what sort of lads were on board, safe and secure. The magistrates at the Police Court were often faced with a plethora of bitter, desperate young faces, and youths who had never experienced moral guidance in their unfortunate lives. The magistrate had the choice of issuing summary punishment that would save the public from the symptoms of the child's own upbringing, or could try to help the culprit even if it seemed cruel at the time. For example, on 14 February 1877 when John McEvoy appeared before the Police Court charged with stealing timber, the magistrate called his mother to the witness box. 'That boy can neither read nor write,' he rebuked her. 'You are bringing him up like a heathen in a heathen country.' He stopped there, perhaps realising that he was wasting his time. 'I don't suppose, however, that you understand what I am saying.'

Faced with such a case of ignorance, the magistrate, Mr Raffles, sentenced McEvoy to eleven days in prison and five years on *Clarence*. It may have seemed a long time, rather like a jail sentence, but the magistrate was trying to save McEvoy from a life of crime and give him an alternative life that was better for him and for society.

Other boys had just chosen the wrong path in life, such as sixteen-year-old Charles McCarthy, who was found guilty of shop breaking and stealing £70 worth of rings and watches. He was sentenced to fourteen days in prison and five years on *Clarence*. Some were already habitual criminals, such as James Francis Mannion, who had been in and out of trouble all his young life, with a number of short sentences that seemed to have had no reformatory effect on him at all. His background was bad and his companions were all from the dregs of society when on land, so he was sent onto *Clarence*. However, within a short time he absconded. The police found him at Warrington, put him in Walton jail for a short spell and then returned him to *Clarence*.

Such was the category of inmates at a typical reformatory ship, and it was the task of the captain and crew on board to civilise them, educate them to an acceptable standard, introduce them to discipline and train them, so they could be employed at sea. It was a formidable task with hundreds of wild young boys on board, many of whom had never known any teaching and whose world was totally unregulated and uncontrolled. Yet if the training succeeded, the boys could grab the opportunity of a career at sea at a time that the British merchant fleet was the largest ever known. Quite accurately, the world would be their oyster. But first they had to learn the ropes on a reformatory ship, and many of the boys were not too happy to be on board and continued their criminal behaviour despite all that was done for, or to, them. Perhaps the fact that they were given numbers, as if they were in the army, dehumanised them a little.

Fire in the bunker

Sometimes life on board *Clarence* could be interesting, as on 9 November 1880 when a fire broke out on board as she lay in the Sloyne, a naturally deep-water channel at Tranmere. The fire started in the coal bunkers, so was potentially dangerous but two ferries, *Wasp* and *Fairy Queen*, as well as a boat from HMS *Defence* came alongside and helped quell the flames. Enquiries found that this fire was started deliberately and the culprit was fourteen-year-old James Mannion. At his trial the judge called him 'as bad a rogue as it was possible for any human being to be' and after consideration, sentenced him to a year in jail with hard labour. The captain refused to have him back on board.

Prizes

It was not all hard work on board the reformatory ships: there was an annual prize giving ceremony, with the Roman Catholic Bishop of Liverpool, the Right Reverend Dr O'Reilly distributing the prizes of ten shillings each in front of a gathering of local ladies and gentlemen. After lives of failure, neglect and crime, having something positive to strive for must have been a novelty for the boys as they displayed their prowess in reading, writing, arithmetic and Biblical knowledge. The ceremony ended with the boys showing off nautical skills and participating in a boat race.

In July 1881 Captain Algar retired after eighteen successful years in command and Captain John Hudson took over the helm. Perhaps Hudson's inexperience showed, or maybe he was unfortunate in the body of youths he inherited, for in September of 1882 there was a minor mutiny on board *Clarence*. The officers quelled it, but the ringleaders were sent to jail and others yelled out their penance over a birching block.

On 10 January 1884, there was a small fire in the ship and then on 17 January 1884 disaster struck. At that time *Clarence* was moored in the Mersey, not far off New Ferry, with 215 boys on board plus her crew. About two in the afternoon somebody smelled smoke and saw a distinctive blue cloud from forward, either from the fore magazine or, worse, from the coal bunkers that had already given trouble. Fire on a wooden ship was always a master's nightmare, but now Captain Hudson looked at the reality that coiled out in ugly spumes of smoke from beneath his deck.

As soon as he realised the danger, Hudson signalled the shore for help and began to fight the fire as best he could. He called together the crew, and many of the boys gathered together to help. Captain Saunders of HM Cutter *Margaret* brought eighteen men to *Clarence*, with Captain Vain of HM Cutter *Royal Charlotte* following soon after. They pumped up water from the sea and poured it into the hold, but still the fire spread, raging aft despite all the men and boys could do. When it reached the midships section, Captain Hudson began to evacuate the boys.

He sent some ashore in the ship's boats but the steamer *Eastham Fairy* took the majority to the New Ferry landing stage, where the boys watched their home burn until they were ushered on board *Gipsy Queen* for the night. With the boys safe, Captain Hudson ensured that all the money and anything else of value was taken out of *Clarence* and transported ashore. Then he returned to fighting the fire, but he realised that it was a battle he had already lost. The steamer *Oxton* carried a steam fire engine named *Hamilton* from the shore, with a crew of professional firefighters, and directed water onto *Clarence*. Other steamers bustled alongside and added their quota of water by using their steam pumps.

The fire was in the lower decks, with the coal and the running gear as well as the fittings of the ship being seriously affected. Although Captain Hudson was aware the masts and yards were intact and undamaged, he was less sure about the hull of the vessel. He was aware that the fire had taken hold and knew well the damage that flames could do to a wooden ship.

Hudson's fears proved well-founded. The fire had started in the hold where the stores were held, and had spread to the timbers of the ship. Dry wood burns well and the flames burned through the fabric of the ship until the damage was irreparable. *Clarence* was scuttled the next day when the Navy fired cannon at her until she sank.

With his ship taken care of, Captain Hudson had time to check on his boys. Although there were no casualties through the fire, some of the boys had been taken to the hospital at New Ferry for safety, but rather than meekly obey orders, a number took the opportunity to escape. Others murmured that they thought the fire had been started deliberately. Hudson must have felt as though the bottom had dropped out of his world.

However, the Liverpool authorities were used to dealing with recalcitrant youths and within a matter of days they located the runaways. The Reformatory Officer, Robert Wilson started the process. He knew the boys by sight and spotted fourteen-year-old Edward Ryan in Falstaff Street. Wilson picked him up and took him to the main city bridewell, where he asked if he knew how the fire had started. Perhaps it was the austere surroundings, or maybe Ryan resented being in custody when his friends were still free, but he began to boast, and hinted where the other runaways might be.

By 24 January, the police had arrested seven of the boys. Ryan claimed that he had started the fire while the others assisted him. Ryan was said to be the youngest of his group, but seemed to have a personality sufficiently powerful to persuade older boys to do as he wished. If he had kept quiet, the truth might not have been known, but he told everything. Ryan had used very simple methods to start the fire. He gathered a large quantity of paper and ordered some older boys to drag the covers off the cargo hatches. One of his followers stole some paraffin oil while others collected piles of flammable rags. One boy made a torch, but although others played supporting roles, it was Ryan who concocted the plan and Ryan who took the oil and poured it onto a coil of rope in the magazine, and Ryan who then struck a match and set it aflame.

After endangering the lives of over 200 people, the boys took the first opportunity to abscond. The police thought there might be as many as a dozen incendiaries involved, but only arrested seven. These were: Edward Ryan, aged fourteen; John Lloyd and Martin Manion, both aged fifteen, Joseph Peate, James Murphy and Christopher Sewell, all aged fifteen, and finally sixteen-year-old Anthony Banestre.

The boys had no plans except to burn the ship, and no motive except to escape. The plan was brutally simple. Sewell got the oil in an empty salmon tin and a small lamp. Manion confessed: 'I did set it on fire' as simply as that. The others agreed that they had got the materials and helped with the hatches, but said they had not actually started the fire. The people of Liverpool wondered about this obvious lack of discipline on the ship, if the boys were allowed sufficient freedom to run wild and fetch oil and matches in such a combustible environment.

The case came to the Liverpool assizes in February and Judge Butt sentenced each to five years penal servitude, which was a vicious sentence, but given the very real possibility of the death of at least some of the 200 boys on board *Clarence*, not excessive at the time.

It was not only *Clarence* that had difficulty with her boys. The reformatory ship *Akbar* also had a hard time. She was another also moored in the Mersey but for Protestant rather than Roman Catholic boys. Most of the inmates were local youths so they could see their homes from the ship, which must have been frustrating. In September 1887, the boys eventually had enough and exploded into mutiny.

Captain Symons ran a tight ship, but even a shipmaster cannot be on duty every day of the year. When he went on leave that month, some of the boys broke into his cabin and stole whatever they could find. The same boys began to stir up trouble, trying to foment a mutiny. Things were worse because a number of the ship's officers were also on leave, so there were only six on duty to control over 150 high-spirited boys.

At first the incipient mutineers had few supporters, but when the chief officer called in the police and threatened drastic action against the thieves many of the boys began to grumble. On Saturday, 24 September there were minor acts of disobedience. The situation worsened on the Sunday, and the chief officer and crew realised there was something major stirring. As the police gathered on deck in a group of blue uniforms, slightly out of their depth on board the ship, the chief and the schoolmaster tried gentle persuasion. An uneasy calm continued until teatime, with the boys glowering at the police but reluctantly obeying orders. After tea, the trouble began again with minor misdemeanours and backchat. The chaplain tried to cool the tension with reason and religion; the boys reacted with shouts and bad language and the police clumped down from the deck to use their authority. Within minutes there was uproar as the boys ran riot, yelling, shouting and vandalising.

To placate the boys, the chief officer sent the police ashore, but things just got worse. Seventeen of the boys grabbed one of the ship's boats, launched it into the Mersey and rowed ashore rejoicing. The officers had a choice: they could remain on board with the remainder of the boys or chase the fugitives; they split their numbers, with some pursuing the runaways. However, that left the ship even more shorthanded and it took over five hours for authority to be restored. Nine of the seventeen were recaptured fairly quickly and the others within a few days.

The ringleaders were aged from sixteen to nineteen and were charged with theft and absconding from the ship. Three of the boys had previously been of good character and were returned to the ship, one was given three months in jail and the others sent to the assizes. The judge, Justice Day, blamed the captain and officers for not having proper discipline on board and rather than jail the boys, he said they had already suffered two months locked up waiting for their trial, so released them to find a job.

Clarence was replaced by the perhaps unfortunately named *Royal William*, which was also destroyed by fire. The boys were transferred to land-based institutions. The idea was good: train boys for a better life, and many scores of boys would have more chance at sea than in the slums on land. The problem of youth crime, however, continues.

14
The Irish Have Arrived

When poverty forced the Irish from their homeland, or job opportunities enticed them to Liverpool, they brought with them a willingness to work and a seemingly endless supply of cheap labour. The Irish had long crossed the Irish Sea to England and Scotland to work at the harvests, to work as labourers, to work on docks and ships and to dig the canals that increased trade to inland ports. When the poor Irish emigrants arrived in Liverpool in the early decades of the century, many if not most were bewildered, hungry and lost. Many came from the rural parts of Ireland and had never been in a large city in their lives, so were unaware of the depths of depravity of which human beings were capable. One scam was used by the 'man-catchers', who lured the innocent Irish to lodge with them and robbed them blind of every penny they owned or would make in any employment they happened to find.

Religious differences

However, the Irish also brought religious differences and a desire to indulge in what were then known as faction fights, as different groups settled perceived differences with fist, boot and stick. In the 1850s, Addison Street became known as Donnybrook because of the number of times the peace was broken by sundry gangs of Irishmen.

There was always tension in Liverpool as 12 July loomed up. That was the anniversary of the Battle of the Boyne in 1690, an event celebrated in the Orange calendar as being highly significant, as Protestant King William defeated his nephew and father-in-law, the Catholic King James. Few remembered the inconvenient truths that William was allied to Catholic Spain and was backed by the Pope. In 1842, the authorities were prepared to deal with any trouble. Superintendent Whitty cancelled all police leave and had strong bodies of uniformed men on patrol in various parts of the town, making it obvious that they were ready to quell any disorder. He also had a reserve in Vauxhall bridewell, St James Market and Seel Street station house; these men carried cutlasses, which were deadly weapons in close quarter action. He added to the power of the force by having sixty mounted men to patrol the streets, but still the town held its collective breath as the 12th dawned. Shops either remained closed or kept shutters on their windows, crowds gathered to watch the fun and there were rumours and counter rumours of impending riot.

Conflict in the streets

The first hint of trouble was in Shaw's Brow, where a group of men attacked the house of a Mrs Chaddock. The police were not too surprised at the location, for there was an Orange Lodge nearby. Whitty led a party of mounted police to disperse the crowd and there were no casualties except a number of smashed windows. There were further attacks on houses in Cases Street and Houghton Street, in the former incident the householder had hung an Orange flag from the window, which served as provocation to the more volatile of the mob. Again Whitty's dispositions proved effective and the police intervened before the trouble escalated, and shuffled some of the most forward of the mob to the bridewell, out of harm's way. There was name-calling and stone-throwing in Vauxhall Street, but the police were soon there in force.

There was a more serious disturbance in Addlington Street where a crowd of some hundreds chased two men, a shipwright named Seel and a man named Pollock. A brave woman offered sanctuary and Seel and Pollock dived into her house, but a woman across the road had seen them and pointed out to the crowd where they were. The mob kicked the door in, dragged the terrified victims outside and put the boot in as the crowd cheered their approval. There were so many men trying to kick Seel that they got in each other's way. Whitty led a rescue party and arrested the ringleaders, William Ryan and James Green.

After the morning's events, the police might have been hopeful of a peaceful afternoon. There was a scuffle in Great Crosshall Street. A man named John Nicholson was arrested here: he was armed with a marline-spike, tied to his wrist. After he was arrested he slashed a policeman with the spike, but a second officer cracked him over the head with his staff and that quietened him down. Nicholson had been the leader of a mob that had rampaged through the streets.

About two o'clock, a body of Orangemen assembled at a pub at the top of Greenland Street, ensured they were all wearing sashes and orange ribbons, and headed to the Phoenix Inn at Mount Pleasant with banners, music and the drumbeat of marching boots. Whitty was not too pleased at this near-military display, so took a troop of mounted men, backed by a hundred constables, and escorted the Orange Lodge on their way. There were crowds gathered to either cheer or jeer, depending on their allegiance, but the sight of the strong body of police seemed to scare them, and there was a general rush to get as far away as possible. It took Whitty some time to calm them down, so their retreat was more orderly.

This branch of the Orange Lodge, so bold when mob-handed, was less brave later when they split into smaller parties. Some requested police protection and Whitty obliged, with the criteria that no Orange colours were displayed. The Lodge obliged and, except for one instance when a man threatened the procession with a sword, there was no trouble.

There was also an outbreak in Mount Pleasant around five in the evening. Two men, John Hill and Alex Howard, led a rush of Orangemen who shouted 'we're Orangemen; now for Orangemen – we'll have no Popery – down with the Popery Bible!'

The mob charged down Mount Pleasant, attacking anybody they thought might be a Roman Catholic, but the police pounced behind the Adelphi Hotel and arrested Hill and Howard, both Ulstermen. Hill had a large carving knife in his possession, which cost him ten days in jail.

Overall it was a successful day for the police, who also managed to round up a number of pickpockets, who always came out on such occasions. Green and Ryan appeared in court shortly after, as did a number of other men, either Orange or Green. Seel was in court to see justice done, but his face and head were so swathed in bandages that he was virtually unrecognisable. He was perhaps the worst casualty of a day that saw about a dozen men given fines or small terms of imprisonment.

There were many other Orange marches and many more confrontations between the two rival faiths in Liverpool, some more violent than others. The bright Orange banners cast an ominous shadow over the dark streets of Liverpool as people who shared the same hardships, spoke the same language with the same accent and worshipped the same God, but with different practices, vented social frustration on themselves at certain times of the year. In that, Liverpool was certainly not alone.

As a hugely important port city, Liverpool also attracted the attention of politically motivated Irishmen.

The Smoking Bag

Throughout the nineteenth century, Ireland was in a disturbed state. The country had struggled against English and then British control off and on for centuries, with plantations of mainly Protestant British in the north and a succession of alien landlords settled from north to south, taking the best there was and often relegating the native Irish to marginal land. Augmenting the aggression was the religious angle, for by the seventeenth century the majority of the alien landlords were Protestant, while the bulk of the indigenous Irish population was Roman Catholic. There was more: the British government in Ireland passed a number of anti-Catholic Acts, and the landlords pressed heavily on their tenants, who, through lack of industry and employment in the country, were forced to extreme poverty, emigration or had to sub-divide their small parcels of rented land to starvation levels.

After the horrendous famine of the late 1840s and the subsequent mass emigration, things began to slowly improve, but by then the damage had been done. The indigenous Irish were not prepared to be controlled by a country with ideas and a religion that was different to theirs. The century was peppered with outbreaks of violence, brutal murders, fierce political debate and attempts to break free of London's control. Sometimes the violence spilled out of Ireland and extended across to the sister island of Great Britain, and, as Liverpool was a major entry port, it could be a natural target for the frustrated anger of some Irishmen. When these periods of intense activity occurred, Britain was on the alert for terrorist offences, or 'outrages' as they were known at the time. In 1881, Liverpool experienced one such period of outrages.

At eight minutes to midnight on 16 May 1881, Liverpool was shaken by a sudden explosion. At that time unmarried police officers could choose to live in the police barracks, also known as the section house, at Hatton Garden, now an upmarket street near John Moore's University. A bomb had been placed at the front door, and when it exploded, it spread devastation around the lobby and smashed the outer and inner door. There were no casualties among the forty policemen inside the building but the message seemed clear: somebody did not like the Liverpool Police.

It had not been a sophisticated bomb, merely a length of gas-piping stuffed with gunpowder or dynamite, and ignited with a simple fuse, but if anybody had been near, the explosion coupled with flying glass from the door and fanlight, could have caused serious injuries. Immediately after they heard the noise, the police in the section house jumped from their beds and rushed to the scene, soon joined by the local beat policemen and men of the fire brigade whose headquarters were next door. Naturally a crowd also gathered to watch the fun, as the police cleaned the mess and tried to work out who had planted the bomb.

At first the police thought it was merely a piece of mischief by a youth, or perhaps a disgruntled man who had been arrested, but they realised the boldness of the attempt, with the bomb placed right at the front door, and they wondered if there had been a larger organisation involved. With the police and the fire brigade so close together, and the Dale Street police offices that held experienced detectives not far away, the perpetrator must have had firm nerves. A constable had entered the building at quarter to midnight without seeing anything untoward, so the bomb had been placed just a few moments before it exploded. As there were no clues, the head constable, John Greig, offered a £20 reward for 'information leading to the conviction of the offender or offenders.'

There matters rested for a while. It might have been a serious affair, but looked at in the context of a town seething with incipient violence, prostitution and theft, it was minor: the damage was slight and there had been no injuries. The police filed away their reports, kept their ears open for information and life continued as normal. And then on 10 June there was another bombing attempt in the city and the police pounced.

This time the target was the Town Hall. The perpetrators may have been emboldened by the lack of police success on the previous bombing, for rather than wait for the shroud of night, they struck in the middle of the afternoon. John Ross was driving his cab up Water Street when he saw what he thought were two seamen with a carpet bag sitting on the steps at the west entrance to the Town Hall. Hopeful of picking up a fare, he drove along Exchange Street West and waited for a couple of minutes in the hope of being hailed, but when neither appeared interested, Ross shrugged and drove to the Castle Street cab stand. It was a very minor incident that he would have forgotten if he had not heard the blast of an explosion from the direction of the Town Hall a few moments later. He turned his horse around, drove back to the Town Hall and saw a scene of confusion.

The chase

Other people had also seen the two lounging men, including the local beat policeman, Constable Read. He kept a suspicious eye on them as they stood at the top step outside the door with what he thought was a sailor's bag. When he saw the taller of the men place the bag on the ground, Read moved toward them, but when he saw a thin column of smoke coming from the side of the bag he quickened his pace. The two men noticed the uniformed policeman striding toward them and the taller one broke into a run, with the smaller hesitating for a fraction of a moment longer; he slid his hand inside his breast pocket, but seemed to change his mind and joined his companion in running like a hare. Read followed, blowing his whistle until his lungs felt like bursting and with the fugitives about twenty yards in front, but gaining distance with every step. Read was a large man and not the fleetest of foot, but he refused to give up the chase and followed, still blowing his whistle and gasping for breath.

The two men raced across the paved area known as the Exchange Flags and through the arches that led to Chapel Street, but by then

Read's whistle had summoned reinforcements. Constable Edward Creighton joined him, 'What's to do?'

Rather than ask for help in catching the fugitives, Read told Creighton to 'Go you to the Town Hall; there's a bag on the steps and a lighted fuse attached to it.'

Once Read had given the orders, he immediately resumed the chase, still blowing on his whistle. However, the time he had spent giving instructions to Creighton had allowed the fugitives time to escape and Read gave up in disgust.

Constable Peter Casey was on duty in Queen Street, but as soon as he heard the whistle he ran toward the sound, turning into Oldhall Street, where he saw two men running hard. Unfortunately, they noticed his distinctive uniform at the same time and switched direction into Edmund Street, from where they pounded under the arches of the Lancashire and Yorkshire Railway into Key Street. One glanced behind at the pursuing policeman, swore and sped up further, overtaking his companion in his frantic desire to escape. They raced into Plumbe Street, with Casey now close behind and Read not even in sight. As they entered a small close called Tinglepeg Lane, and with the Leeds and Liverpool Canal stretching ahead, the taller and slower of the two fugitives realised he could not run much further, so rolled under the belly of a lorry in the hope the police would pass him by. Unfortunately for him, Casey knew this area well. He knew that Tinglepeg Lane was a cul-de-sac and the fugitives had trapped themselves.

The arrests

Casey looked around and saw the taller man crouched under the lorry, so dived after him. They grappled for a while, with the fugitive fighting back desperately, but he was exhausted by the run and perhaps by nervous exhaustion. When it became obvious that Casey would win, the fugitive drew a Belgian ten-chambered revolver from an inside pocket. Casey grabbed his arm and for a second wondered if he was to be shot, but rather than fire, the fugitive threw the weapon over the nearest wall. It landed in a coal yard. Casey put his whistle to his mouth but the man merely said:

'You needn't whistle, I'll go quietly. You can put the handcuffs on me.'

Casey found that his prisoner's name was McKevitt, and fastened the handcuffs around his wrists. He could not see the smaller man, so bundled his prisoner over to Constable Creighton in Leeds Street. Casey could have stopped then, satisfied that he had done a good job in catching and arresting an armed man, but instead he returned to the scene of his arrest to look for the discarded revolver and the second fugitive. The first part was easy: the commotion had attracted a crowd and a workman fetched the revolver for him. Casey continued his search for the smaller man. The area consisted of the banks of the canal and a number of walled-in coal yards, but despite the time that had elapsed since he lost sight of him, Casey guessed that the second man was still hiding somewhere close by. With the police scouring the streets and a mob of interested spectators, it would be easier to hide than to flee.

Either Casey climbed the nearest wall or a workman gave him the key to Rawcliffe's coal yard, but although he searched, he found nothing. The second fugitive was not there. The search of Jackson's coal yard was equally fruitless. He asked a group of men if they had seen anybody running or hiding, but they had not. A woman advised him, 'No, but I heard a man drop onto the deck of a flat.'

Casey's next step was to check the canal side of Rawcliffe's yard, and here a workman named Anthony Nelson opened the canal bank gate of the yard. Casey looked around and saw *Alexina*, an empty coal barge, lying at the bank. Remembering what the woman had told him, he stepped on board and searched. It did not take long.

There were a number of different types of canal barges, or flats. The original Mersey flats were carvel built sailing barges that could operate in quiet coastal waters, but canal flats were generally about 70 feet long, wooden built and with a huge hold for carrying general cargo, in this case coal. When the barge was fully loaded, the bargee would stand on the ledge, which was a platform that ran around the entire perimeter of the vessel. Casey found his fugitive cowering under this ledge. He was sodden wet and his trousers were ripped from waist to ankle. Guessing the fugitive might be also be armed, Casey grabbed him by the collar and pointed the revolver at his chest.

'If you make any resistance, I'll shoot you,' Casey warned, but the man was not inclined to fight.

'I'll go quietly,' he said, 'I'm half drowned. I've had a narrow escape.' It appeared that the man had climbed the wall beside the canal, slipped and had been suspended by his trousers for a while before toppling into the canal.

Casey asked if he also carried a revolver and the man tamely replied, 'Yes, you'll find it in my pocket.'

Casey did not ask him to produce the pistol at that moment. The man gave his name as Barton and asked if Casey would let him fix his trousers. Instead Casey arrested him and escorted him away. Only when another police officer held him secure did Casey take away Barton's revolver. Barton was taken to the detective office at Dale Street, where McKevitt was already safely lodged. Both were charged with placing an explosive device with intent to murder, but McKevitt denied there was any intention of taking life.

Creighton's problem

While Casey had been dealing with the armed men, Constable Creighton had other things to contend with. He had run to the Town Hall to deal with the suspected bomb, but he had gone to the east side first, while smoke continued to issue from the bag on the steps on the west. Realising that there was nothing at the east side, Creighton ran to the west, meeting two other constables, Charles McBurney and Donald Sinclair on his way. The three policemen found the smoking bag at the top of the steps: it was making what they later described as a 'sizzling' noise that they guessed was the fuse burning toward whatever explosives were inside. Creighton hauled the bag down the steps to the kerbstone and McBurney lifted it and tossed it into the middle of the street, where it lay, gently smoking and sizzling evilly. McBurney casually produced his pocket knife and was about to slice the string that secured the mouth of the bag, but the other two police were more cautious.

'You had better mind what you are doing,' Sinclair said, but Creighton was more direct.

'Leave it,' he warned, 'it might be a bomb!'

McBurney took heed, pocketed his knife and stepped away: just in time. The explosion smashed all the windows in the Town Hall and of the Phoenix Fire office across the road. The two watchmen in the Town Hall, Matthew Swarbrick and Samuel Page, ran out to see what the commotion was, and wondered what would have happened if the bomb had gone off when they were at the front door, only a few feet away. Once again the bomb had been simple but effective, a length of gas piping plugged at both ends, with a fuse attached to a filling of what the police thought was gunpowder, but experts later thought might have been nitro-glycerine. McKevitt said that it was dynamite (a type of nitro-glycerine) but if he had known there was anybody in the building he would not have put it on the steps: 'I didn't want to have murder on my head,' he claimed. The smoke had come from the lit fuse. If Read had not ordered Creighton to take care of the smoking bag, the explosion could have cause far more damage and possibly also casualties.

The police were closest to the bomb but were miraculously

untouched. They had been positioned at either side of the bag and the explosion erupted from both ends, saving them from the worst effects.

Background stories

With the two perpetrators already under arrest, the police began to question them to find out why they had done it and if there were any more potential terrorists wandering around the streets of Liverpool. James McKevitt was a thirty-two-year-old dock labourer from Warren Point in Ireland but had been living in Liverpool since 1870. William Barton claimed to be a Glasgow man, but of solid Irish stock. He was far travelled, having worked as a steward on the Dundee and London shipping line, and then in New Orleans and New York. He had come to Liverpool less than a year previously and lived with McKevitt in Cottenham Street in the Kensington area for about a month. They bought the iron pipe near where they lived and prepared it in their own lodgings for the attempt on the Town Hall.

Fenian connections

Naturally the police searched them and found, among other things, pawn tickets, a steamboat guide, dynamite cartridges and a medal of the Irish patriot Daniel O'Connell with the words: 'Ireland for the Irish and the Irish for Ireland.' A second medal had the initials IFRB and the date 1866, possibly an allusion to the Irish Fenian Republican Brotherhood's raid on Canada that year. The Fenian Brotherhood had been founded by recent Irish Immigrants in the United States in 1858, but claimed to trace their origins to the United Irishmen of 1798. The movement was named after the *Fianna*, who were legendary bands of warriors in Ireland in the distant past. The police also found documents that linked the prisoners with the American Fenians.

The police's next step was an attempt to trace McKevitt and Barton's movements and investigate to see if they had any other contacts that might suggest a Fenian band in Liverpool. The police believed that both men were connected to the attack on the police barracks in May. George Williams, who headed the detective department of Liverpool Police, believed there was a 'party of action' among the Fenians and that a whole series of attacks were planned; he hoped to break up the gang before any more bombs were set off.

The men were kept in separate cells in the main bridewell and were well guarded before being moved to Walton jail. An escort of cabs, each containing detectives armed with Colt revolvers surrounded the prison van. Expecting a rescue attempt, the police drove at speed, avoiding the direct route, but arrived without a single incident. When McKevitt and Barton first appeared before the police court, they were described as 'Irishmen' and 'low and stupid'. Barton then confessed that his real name was William McGrath and he was thirty-one years old. He was nearly correct, his name was James McGrath.

The intense search of McGrath and McKevitt's lodgings found some interesting documents that connected them to O'Donovan Rossa, who headed the United States Fenians, as well as a list of names of other known Fenians in Britain. The police also found a chisel and saw, more piping and a piece of wood that matched the plugs that had sealed the ends of the previous two pipe bombs. Naturally there were rumours, among them that Rossa had sent American Fenians to destroy public buildings across the length and breadth of Britain. Rossa issued a public statement denying the fact. However, he did say that McKevitt was the Liverpool agent for his newspaper, the *United Irishman*, but claimed he was not a member of the Fenian organisation. Rossa also admitted that he knew of a previous attempt to blow up HMS *Doterel*.

There had been an explosion on that vessel in April 1881 that took the lives of 143 men. An enquiry in September that year concluded that coal gas was the cause and not sabotage. However, the *United Irishman* reputedly spoke of 'measure for measure and blood for blood', and asked Irishmen to 'give half your money to the Land League and give half to blow up an English ship or an English castle.' As so often in that period, the newspaper confused English with British, which reveals the lack of geographical and political knowledge of the editors. The Land League was an organisation dedicated to removing 'landlordism' in Ireland and giving the land back to the small tenant farmers.

American connection

The Liverpool case opened the public's eyes to the extent of the Fenian presence in America, and the Fenian Skirmishing Fund – an American fundraising operation intended to finance the terrorist operations in Britain. It was thought that the money for the gunpowder and revolvers came from the United States. The British government was well aware of the danger, and allegedly had a number of agents at large in America, watching the Fenians.

With two members of such a dangerous organisation in its jail, the people of Liverpool were nervous, as rumours and counter rumours were exchanged in pubs and shops. A few days after their incarceration, there was believed to be an attempt to free them from Walton Jail, and when a policeman saw a number of men walking around the vicinity and heard Irish accents, he sounded the alarm. The wardens already on duty were issued with firearms and others were summoned to help, so there was a formidable body of armed men waiting to repel an expected Fenian attack. As many were ex-military, they were quite prepared to shoot anybody who came into range. In the event, the suspicious Irishmen were merely farm labourers searching for work. Naturally, rumours of more Fenians spread across the area, with two men allegedly seen loading revolvers in Birkenhead, one of whom had a slouch hat like an 'Irish Yankee.'

On 15 June Superintendent Williamson of Great Scotland Yard

visited Liverpool to find out what was happening. Scotland Yard believed the case was of high importance and invited a number of Liverpool police to make statements to the Home Office in London. As McGrath and McKevitt awaited trial, police discovered that McGrath had also rented lodgings in Ashton Street. When they raided the rooms, they found more gas piping cut to size and plugged, but not filled with gunpowder. Main towns in England were wary, with armed detectives guarding public buildings and street lighting improved to help prevent attacks.

The court appearances

A crowd gathered at the Police Court when McGrath and McKevitt appeared to answer charges, and a large body of evidence was given against them. Their landladies spoke about a pistol being fired, about false names being used and about other Irishmen in their lodgings. More lengths of pipe were produced, and tools to shape the pipe bomb. There were witnesses who had seen McGrath making the plugs for the police barracks bomb. As always there were various rumours, including one that said the attackers had originally intended to bomb the Custom House and General Post Office, and the Town Hall was a hurried later choice.

Infernal machines

As the trial was taking place, two steamships, *Malta* and *Bavarian*, arrived in Liverpool docks from Boston, the headquarters of the Fenian organisation. When their cargoes were checked the authorities were shocked to discover that both held what were termed as 'infernal machines in great numbers and dynamite in large quantities'. Although the facts were naturally shrouded in secrecy and speculation, it seems as if the discovery was not by chance. Either one of the two prisoners had given information or British government agents in the United States had discovered that the Fenians were to send over a cargo of material for the British branch of the organisation. Whatever the truth, the authorities asked Cunard, who owned *Malta*, for permission to check the cargo. Cunard agreed at once.

One part of the cargo was a consignment of cement, which seemed strange as it was a commodity readily available in Liverpool. The barrels were taken to Huskisson Dock and opened one at a time; the police and customs officers saw a large black cross on the seventh barrel, which raised suspicions. They opened it warily, in case it exploded. Inside were a number of zinc boxes that were 'infernal machines', which were time bombs with a clockwork mechanism, a percussion cap and about three pounds weight of mixed dynamite and nitro-glycerine.

Government agents and the Customs moved the suspicious cargo to the Queen's warehouse in Liverpool, which was where anything such as smuggled or prohibited goods were stored until their final destination was determined. Shortly afterward, the Leyland Line *Bavarian* arrived with a cargo of cattle, plus passengers, but again the customs and police had advance warning. They checked her cargo manifest and confirmed she also had a few barrels of cement for the same destination as that of *Malta*. The Customs men were on her immediately and found another six of the time bombs. Rumours, possibly apocryphal, were rife that documents naming O'Donovan Rossa were also found, which would suggest a distinct lack of caution on his part. Naturally he denied all involvement. There were also rumours that the person who did send the explosives meant it as a warning and notified the government, which seems highly unlikely. All the explosives were later taken out to sea and destroyed.

Although the discovery made headline news and raised temperatures throughout the country, it did not interfere with the trial of McGrath and McKevitt. While McKevitt was only charged with the City Hall explosion, McGrath was also accused of planting the bomb at the police barracks. Both men were found guilty; McGrath got penal servitude for life and McKevitt for fifteen years.

Terrorism was only one of the guises in which crime came and the city was not alone in being a violent place. The environs of Liverpool were also home to some unpleasant people.

15
The Dangerous Countryside

While the industrial towns have gained a bad reputation for crime and violence, the countryside was not idyllic. In the late 1830s and early 1840s, the area around St Helens, a few miles north-east of Liverpool, was dangerous because of the activities of a gang known as the Long Company. This gang specialised in poaching, but were also adept at attacking lone travellers, highway robbery and any other criminal activity that could turn a profit. Because of the nature of their business, little was known about them save their name and reputation, but it was believed that there were between forty and fifty members, and it was rumoured that they could even resort to murder if they were crossed.

The Long Company

In December 1841 a local farmer named Henry Grayson was murdered near his own house at Rainford, a few miles north of St Helens. Grayson had collected a number of rents from his tenants, so was carrying a considerable amount of money as he tried to get a room for the night at the King's Head public house. It was about midnight and there was no room at the inn, so he continued his journey into the night. His body was found at five the next morning at Denton's Green, about a mile away. He had terrible head and body wounds, with the skull and ribs smashed so he was nearly unrecognisable. He had been robbed and his right-hand trouser pocket, the one in which he would carry his money, had been cut out. Grayson was about sixty-five years old.

The locals blamed the Long Company, but although the police made a number of arrests – namely Thomas Meadowcroft, Robert Wood, Charles Wood, Patrick McCoddom, William Jacques and Isaac Jacques – they could not gain a conviction. The witnesses all gave contradictory evidence, so the suspects walked free from the March assizes. Both Meadowcroft and Isaac Jacques had already clashed with the police at Grayson's farm and were suspected of being in the Long Company. The rumours added to the ferocious reputation, with travellers being attacked only on the loneliest stretches of roads where there was no possibility of assistance, or having to pay protection money in the form of drink to escape unscathed. The local farmers were frequently robbed of livestock and goods, but were too intimidated to seek help from the police. It was a reign of terror akin to that on the sixteenth century border with Scotland, or even parts of contemporary Ireland.

On Saturday, 26 November 1842, a farmer named William Basnett was travelling from Eccleston to Rainford. He stopped at Arnold's Beer House to refresh himself for the journey, and chatted to a number of his friends, but also saw men reputed to be of the Long Company in the room. He did not speak to them, nor did they speak to him, and he left quietly and quite sober to walk home.

Around midnight, as Basnett was passing a high hedge near Rainford, where Grayson had been killed, a man stepped out in front of him and another blocked his path to the rear. Without saying a word, they attacked him, but Basnett was a farmer, well used to physical labour, young, fit and strong. He matched them blow for blow and was well on top until another couple of men joined in. Still Basnett refused to give in, but he backed away, blocking their attacks and punching whenever he got the chance. However, one man cannot defeat four who are used to violence and he was eventually forced into a ditch, where the four battered, breathless men glared down on him.

'Cut the bastard's throat!' Somebody growled, and they jumped into the ditch beside Basnett.

There was the gleam of steel and the blade of a knife rasped across Basnett's throat. Luckily he was wearing a neckerchief which protected him, but while he was trying to fend off the knifeman, one of the others was going through his pockets and stealing all the money that he had with him. The four began to kick and punch at him, but this time the ditch was too constricting for full force blows and eventually they ran off, leaving Basnett bruised and bloody but still alive.

He found a long slash down the right side of his coat where one of the gang had tried to slice him open, and a few punctures, like stab wounds in the coat on the left side, while his neckerchief was nearly lacerated by the number of cuts that had been inflicted. Basnett told the local policeman, Constable Bish, who immediately began to search for the attackers. He called for reinforcements and four policemen joined him in the hunt. On the following Tuesday, the police arrested three men all with the surname of Traverse and a fourth with the familiar name of Jacques. All four were later discharged as Basnett was unable to positively identify them. The Long Company seemed to have won another round.

It was not until March 1843 before the police made a major impression on the Long Company. Superintendent William Storey decided that enough was enough. He signed up two constables specifically for the purpose of ending the careers of the Long Company, and gave them detailed instructions.

Constables Sutcliffe and Loftus pretended to be travelling Scotsmen of uncertain character and they arrived in the neighbourhood of St Helens, with the purpose of infiltrating the gang. In effect they were undercover policemen doing a very dangerous job. Their prime purpose was to try to discover the murderers of Grayson, but they did not succeed in that. However, they did gather evidence against fourteen of the gang, mainly for poaching offences.

Entrapment

In one case three men, Timothy Shaw, James Shaw and John Pendleberry, were tried for trespass, taking and selling game. It was at three in the afternoon of 2 February 1843 that Sutcliffe and Loftus were about quarter of a mile from Billinge on their way to Rainford, when they met the Shaws and Pendleberry. The three had a poaching net with a live hare trapped inside and proved very willing to sell it to the undercover police for 2s6d.

With friendly relations established, the five men entered a conversation about different poaching methods in Scotland and Lancashire, and the police said they had never tried that method of catching a hare before. Very obliging, the poachers showed the police exactly how it was done and sold the hare to them, whereupon they were arrested and found themselves in jail for two months with hard labour. On 4 March three more men, Henry Fillingham, with Thomas and George Jaques, were also lured into poaching by the undercover police. On the walk to Lord Derby's estates they met a solitary policeman and Fillingham was tempted to use his gun or throw stones, saying he would have 'given the policeman's bright hat a rattle.' They got three months.

Others were convicted of selling game to the two policemen at Holt's beerhouse at Eccleston, without a licence. They were in the midst of a sale on 15 March when Superintendent Storey walked in and scooped up the lot. Given the serious levels of crime that the Long Company were suspected of, convictions for poaching may not seem a major conviction, but it sent a jolt through the gang. They were reminded that they were not invulnerable and they faded away after that.

Poaching

One thing that is often forgotten about Victorian towns and cities is their closeness to the countryside. Although they expanded at a tremendous rate with the Industrial Revolution, they were still smaller than the urban sprawls that we inhabit today and, for most, the countryside was less than an hour's walk away. That was also true of the people: many had come straight from a rural background, so understood the workings of the land as well as, or better than, the intricacies of urban life. Liverpool was no exception and places which are today built up were then well outside the boundaries of the town.

Today, Croxteth is a suburb of Liverpool with a population approaching 20,000, but in the 1860s it was a rural area with rural crime. One of the major worries was poaching, which as a crime could be viewed two ways. There were always the minor poachers, ordinary countrymen who took a rabbit or two for the pot, or maybe lifted a fish out of season, but there were also professionals who killed game and sold it to butchers for profit. The landowners employed gamekeepers whose job it was to breed game for sport, which also added to the economic viability of the estate, and to ensure that poaching was kept to a minimum so there was sufficient game left for the official shooting season. The local gamekeeper was seldom a popular man and it was hard, demanding and often dangerous work.

On Saturday, 14 September 1867 Mr Thrasher, head keeper to the Earl of Sefton, was inspecting the lands under his care. Around ten at night, Thrasher sent four of his watchers, Charles Marsden, Richard

Bridle, Henry Saint and George Rickets to patrol the plantations and look for poachers. The watchers settled themselves in cover overlooking Craven Wood, a favoured spot for poachers. They lay still for hours, ignoring the encroaching damp of the night, and about one in the morning they heard the noise of what they called 'hares in distress', which indicated that poachers were at work.

The four watchers rose and walked carefully towards the sounds. They were used to night movement and came across the poachers before they were seen, but then stopped short. There were seven men together, all carrying dangerous heavy sticks.

Marsden stepped forward, 'What's your game?' he demanded, ignoring both the odds and the weapons the poachers carried.

'I'll soon show you what our game is,' one of the poachers said, and whacked Marsden with his stick. A second poacher joined in and landed a vicious blow that knocked Marsden to the ground.

The watchers recognised some of the men: there was William Croft and two men with the same name, Thomas Jones. The taller and more muscular of the Joneses saw the other watchers approaching and raised his voice: 'Up lads and give it to the bastards!' The words acted as a battle cry and the poachers surged forward. One of them raised his stick above his head and swung a powerful blow at one of the unarmed watchers, but thankfully a few gamekeepers had heard the commotion and hurried to the spot. One intercepted the blow with his own stick and threw himself at the poacher. The other watchers ran up and joined in the stramash, while the poachers responded with a will. A battle royale began, poachers, gamekeepers, watchers and gamekeepers' dogs all fighting together in the dark of the early morning.

At the end of the affray three of the poachers were secured: the two Joneses and William Croft, but all the combatants had been injured to a greater or lesser degree. One of the watchers had damaged knuckles where a stick had caught him, and he carried his arm in a sling for some time afterwards, while the others had bruises and cuts. William

Croft had a nasty gash above his eye and his hands were damaged; he claimed that one of the keepers' dogs had bitten the tip off one of his fingers. One of the Joneses was bleeding from cuts in his head. He later claimed that the keepers had attacked him without provocation.

When the keepers had secured the three poachers who did not run away, they searched the area and found four poaching nets and a number of hares, which had been poached. The men were jailed. But there was more than poaching to worry about in the countryside.

Troubles at Knotty Ash

Although the cities of nineteenth-century Britain earned a bad reputation, the rural areas could be equally violent. Arguably the most dangerous places to be were where the town met the country, where bands from the roughest areas of the city could bring their malice to the country and either vanish back into their aboriginal squalor, or slide into the shadows of the night.

In the winter of 1867–68, the rural outskirts of Liverpool were hit by a succession of robberies that seemed to be very well planned. In each case, the houses were robbed when the policeman was on the opposite end of his beat, which suggested the criminals knew exactly what they were doing. The police did their best, but with large beats and few officers, they were at a major disadvantage, especially when working alone. On Wednesday, 4 March 1868 Constable Robert Jolly was patrolling around Knotty Ash, now inside the city but then a few miles to the north. He was new to the area, but left the Old Swan police station and walked toward Pilch Lane, a good two miles away. Before he reached there he noticed three men standing around, doing nothing. Even in the gloom, Jolly realised that they were not local residents, so he warned the sergeant in the Knotty Ash station.

'Keep a good look-out,' the sergeant advised, and ordered Jolly to patrol another beat as well as his own. Jolly tried his best, but he was fairly new to the area and found it hard to find his way about in the dark. Rather than blunder about pointlessly through the night, he returned to his own beat. Around half past midnight, he was passing the corner of Pilch Lane and Grant Road and saw the shadowy figure of a strange man in the garden of the nearest house.

Jolly knew the owner, Henry Duckworth, by sight and immediately realised that something was wrong. Guessing that the man was a lookout, he opened the garden gate and issued a challenge, 'What are you doing here?'

But rather than be subdued at the sight of a police uniform, the man tossed back the question:

'What the hell are you doing here? I have as much right here as you have.'

As Jolly moved forward, the man gave a loud whistle and two more men appeared from the darkness. They did not say a word but launched themselves on the lone policeman. They knocked him to the ground and rained kicks and punches on him. Jolly fought back, grabbing hold of one of his attackers, but outnumbered three to one by desperate men, he had little chance. They ripped off his cape and overcoat, tore his staff from his hand and thumped him repeatedly with it. When Jolly tried to shield his head, they smashed the staff on his arm and paralysed it, then fastened his wrists with his own handcuffs.

To add insult to injury, as one of the attackers held him so tightly by the throat that he bled from the nose and mouth, the other two leisurely went through Jolly's pockets and took about fifteen shillings in change, his whistle, his knife and everything else he had. At some point Jolly passed out. When he woke it was about two in the morning and the men were long gone. It took Jolly around half an hour to stagger to Knotty Ash police station for help. Strangely, it was not all negative news, for Jolly's presence had interrupted the burglary attempt on Duckworth's house. Jolly's ripped uniform was found there, together with a discarded jemmy outside the parlour window. Jolly had a cracked collar bone, injuries to his kidneys and lost the use of an arm for some time, but after some recovery time he returned to his job. The three men were not caught.

More trouble at Knotty Ash

That year Knotty Ash was a busy place. On Saturday, 14 March a twenty-eight-year-old woman named Mary Smith came to Knotty Ash with a delivery of clothes she had made for a customer. She completed her business, spoke to her customer and walked to the Old Swan Inn, from where an omnibus ran to Liverpool. Her plan was to catch the bus to Liverpool and then the train to her home at Mossley Hill, then a village but now a suburb of Liverpool.

Mary hurried through Knotty Ash and hoped to see Mr Bulmer at the Swan Inn, but instead there was a group of men talking together and smoking their pipes, with the tobacco hanging blue and aromatic in the air. Mary asked if there was a bus to town, but they shook their collective head and one, forty-three-year-old George Barnett, told her that she had missed the last one.

'Where do you want to go?' He asked, smiling through the haze of smoke.

'Aigburth,' she told him, naming the nearest village to her home.

'I'll take you in my trap,' Barnett offered.

Mary was a country girl, and no fool, so she asked Barnett to show her the trap before she committed herself to anything. The trap was genuine, with the pony looking fit, so Mary agreed. She offered Barnett two shillings for the journey home.

'Half a crown,' he demanded at once. But Mary was adamant she would pay no more than two shillings, so they agreed on that figure and she entered his lodgings at No. 15 Swan Road, Old Swan and spent a few moments with his wife, also Mary, while he got the trap ready. At last she clambered up beside him, tucked her skirt beneath her and settled down for the journey. It was just after ten at night with the wind chill from the east, so Mary huddled into her cape and hoped to get home sooner rather than later. However, not long after they passed the village of Wavertree, Barnett pulled the trap into the side of the road and asked for his two shillings.

'I'd rather wait until we get home,' Mary said. 'My husband will pay you then,' and she added a sweetener, 'he'll give you a drink as well.'

'That won't do,' Barnett insisted, 'I'll have the money now.'

Sighing and seeing that there was no help for it, Mary fumbled in her purse and handed over a silver florin, which Barnett put away safely. They drove on, with the pony's hooves clattering on the ground, until they reached the road end at Greenbank, Aigburth, when Barnett stopped again. He put an arm around her.

'I wish I had such a wife as you,' he said. 'Give me a kiss.'

Mary pushed his arm away and looked around for help, but Barnett had chosen his spot well. It was dark and lonely, with not even the light of a house in sight. Barnett moved closer and slid his hand inside her cape. She pushed him away again and tried to dismount, but Barnett urged his horse back into motion so Mary was stuck, as he began to paw at her. Mary fought back as hard as she could, but he was strong and eager, so she overbalanced and fell out of the trap. She landed heavily, face first on the ground so she gashed open her forehead. She rolled to the side but Barnett must have panicked; rather than stop to help, he kept driving and one wheel of the trap crunched over Mary's leg and she yelled in pain and fear.

Even in the night, Mary's cry, or perhaps her earlier struggles, attracted attention and within minutes a group of men were hurrying toward the scene, calling out if anybody needed help. Barnett saw them coming, turned the trap in a wide circle and sped away, whipping on his horse. The new arrivals took Mary home, where she told her husband.

Barnett came home to his wife, but was not long in the house before he left for a few drinks. He came back drunk, which did not surprise his wife, and fell asleep.

At quarter past twelve the next day, the police called at Barnett's house and escorted him to a cell at the Old Swan police station. Sometime before one that same afternoon, he used his silk handkerchief to hang himself, as either shame or fear of the consequences of his actions overcame him.

Country living had its share of crime even in the quietest of places.

16
Liverpool Women

In the nineteenth century, women who were not prostitutes or beggars were often portrayed as one of two things: an angelic mother or a thrifty wife. They were placed on pillars and worshipped as something akin to a goddess. However, the reality often did not quite reach such heights.

When the Irish immigrated to Liverpool, they frequently carried their prejudices and troubles with them. One of the most visible was the Orange Marches that paraded through the town on 12 July. These marches could create animosity that lasted for many months as the Roman Catholic section of the town resented the memories recalled by the orange sashes and provocative banners, but sometimes the trouble was between people of the same ideology.

Feuding families

Shawhill Street was on the fringes of the Orange March in the early decades of the century, and some of the people who lived there were not on the best of terms. One of these people was Ann Dyson, who was at loggerheads with her near neighbours Jane Roberts and Thomas Stafford.

On 11 August 1819, Dyson left her house to buy butter and milk from a cart that was parked outside Roberts' door. Roberts had already verbally abused Dyson's mother, and as soon as Dyson appeared, Roberts shot out of her front door and began to shout at her, calling her every name under the sun.

'Am I worse than you?' Mrs Dyson replied, which quiet retort seemed to send Roberts into a paroxysm of fury. She sprung forward, grabbed a handful of Dyson's hair, dragged her screaming into her house and threw her onto the ground. Dyson was unable to retaliate as Roberts banged her head off the hearthstone a number of times.

'Murder!' Dyson yelled frantically, 'Murder!'

Stafford ran into Roberts' house, but rather than help, he joined in the attack on Dyson. As the unfortunate woman lay stunned on the floor, Stafford thrust a thumb under each of her ears and pushed so hard that blood spurted from her ears, nose and mouth. There is no knowing how things would have turned out had the commotion not attracted the attention of a number of other women who lived in the street.

When Jane Hinton first heard the noise she was hesitant to interfere as Roberts had a reputation of being a very violent woman. However, Dyson's screams were becoming frantic, so Hinton gathered a friend or two and they poured into the house in a flurry of skirts and indignation. They jumped on Stafford and Roberts to try and save Dyson, who was a total mess. Her hair was smeared with buttermilk, Stafford had ripped the rings from her ears and the pounding on the hearthstone had opened several cuts, so her head and face was a mask of blood. Roberts and her daughter Sarah were slapping and kicking at her while Stafford continued to squeeze under her ears.

When the women rescued Dyson they said she was 'in a state of absolute stupefaction.' Even so, the attackers were not jailed, but were only bound to keep the peace for twelve months.

'That was very wrong, you know'

Most crimes were less violent, such as the case of Mary Anne Nugent, for example, who in October 1835 appeared before the magistrates, charged with being drunk and disorderly. The mayor considered her case and told her that she had recently been discharged from Kirkdale Jail, which was her forty-sixth time locked up. As she obviously enjoyed being locked up, he said he would not send her there but reprimanded her and sent her on her way.

Other women were more inclined to use their mouths for shouting rather than drinking. Bridget Grogan was one of these: she was known as a scold, a woman who abused others, but in October 1835 she went a step too far and it landed her in court. On that occasion, the victim of her tongue was a Mrs Catherine Davison, who said that Grogan had a habit of abusing her and her family, particularly her children. That was bad enough but Grogan also encouraged other people to throw boiling water on Davison and threatened to burn down her house.

As she said that to the magistrate in her trial, Mrs Davison faced the court and solemnly declared: 'That was very wrong, you know.'

Grogan did not deny any of these charges, but instead launched a furious counter-attack by bringing in a witness, who said Davison called the Grogan family 'a parcel of damned Irish robbers.'

In return Grogan called Davison a 'damned yellow bitch.'

After hearing these pleasantries, the magistrate decided that Grogan was to blame for most of the abuse and made her find a financial bond to keep the peace.

Husband battering

Many of the crimes in nineteenth-century Liverpool were domestic: husbands attacking wives, wives attacking husbands or mothers attacking children. Although there were usually more cases of wife abuse, sometimes Liverpool wives proved more than capable of defending themselves, particularly if they had alcoholic help.

James and Mary Anne Williams lived in Back Blake Street, together with an elderly woman named Mary McAuley. On Monday, 9 September 1867, Mary had been indulging a little too freely, but alcohol had only encouraged her thirst. She came home looking for anything to drink, and remembered that her husband had a bottle of whisky in a box in his room. James was less of a drinker than Mary, and used the whisky as a medicine rather than a stimulant.

James called on her to stop drinking, but she ignored him and retreated into the tiny attached apartment in which McAuley lived. 'Come out of there,' James said, but when she refused, he followed her, but paused in the doorway and began shouting at Mary, calling her, according to McAuley, 'all the horrible names he could think of.' He demanded that Mary come out.

Mary refused to leave, so instead James asked McAuley to hand over her bottle of whisky. The elderly woman did not co-operate, so James reached inside her room and grabbed the bottle. Mary was having none of that – she took hold of the tongs from the fireside and smashed her husband over the head with them.

McAuley intervened then and snatched the tongs from Mary, but rather than act as peacemaker, she clasped both arms around James and held him.

'I've only one life to lose,' Mary said, as she took a knife and stabbed at her husband. 'If you don't leave this room, I will have your life as I have a man in the street who will keep me.'

As she tried to stab him a second time, McAuley gripped James tight, but he broke free and, bleeding from the wound, ran upstairs. In her drunken rage, Mary followed, swapped her knife for a vicious cleaver and hacked at his legs. James must have closed and barricaded the upstairs door for Mary did not follow into that room. He remained in his precarious sanctuary until he thought it was safe. When he heard Mary and McAuley talking, he slipped out of the house and informed the police. Mary Williams was jailed for her pains.

Other women also took a dislike to their husbands.

An unhappy woman

Catherine Staley was not a happy woman. She was married to Mr Staley, but her husband was not living with her on 5 June 1875. What made it worse was Mr Staley was living with another woman and they even had the audacity to claim they were married. Catherine decided that something ought to be done to remove Mr Staley from his present position and restore him to his correct abode. Accordingly she took a firm grip of her umbrella and marched to the house of Mr Staley's fancy woman in Barry Street.

Lucy Gildears was quietly sitting in her front room at about quarter to twelve when there was a terrible smash of glass and the end of an umbrella poked through one of her window panes. Gildears screamed and jumped off her chair, just as the umbrella poked again and another pane smashed inward in a shower of glass. By the time the third pane followed its predecessors, Gildears was at the front door and saw Catherine Staley lambasting her windows.

When the case came to court both women gave their sides of the story. It seemed that Mr Staley had been married to Catherine for some eighteen years, but still had time to leave her and marry Lucy Gildears. Both women had produced his children, but Catherine had the prior claim to his affection. The magistrate fined her five shillings plus six shillings for the cost of the windows, but gave Catherine advice how to charge her husband with bigamy.

But there were worse things than a cheating man . . .

Burning a woman

On the morning of 26 February 1884, Mary McNamara argued with her boyfriend of the past seven years. He was only twenty-three and his name was Robert Black, although many people knew him by his nickname of 'the Major.'

Mary was twenty-eight and sometimes worked as a prostitute. The couple lived in one room of a house in Mann Street, Toxteth Park, but many people were glad that Mary lived with Black and not them. Black was a notoriously violent man, particularly when he had been drinking. Mary also wished rid of him, but he clung to her and she was afraid to cut the knot in case he turned nasty.

On the evening of 25 February, the couple went to a friend's house and drank the night away. They came home about half past midnight and argued in the street. Black knocked her down and kicked her, so that a neighbour had to intervene, and then they returned home. In the house Black lit their only lamp. As they lacked money, the lamp had nothing but a wick, and Black said, 'Why don't you get a globe to it?'

Mary replied that there was no shop open at that time of night, and he kicked her, and then said, 'You f*** cow, I'll blind you with it!'

However, McNamara was too stubborn to let a simple kick subdue her. She refused to back down, so Black lifted the paraffin lamp and threw it at her.

The lamp crashed on the left side of her head. 'I'll hang for you yet,' Black said. The paraffin doused McNamara's head and hair and clothes as the flame spread over her. McNamara screamed and put her hands up to her face, and the paraffin burned them as well.

McNamara crumpled onto the floor and lay there, screaming as the flames spread over her back, and Black remained in the room, closing and locking the door behind him so nobody could get in to help her.

The flames burned brightly enough to attract the attention of the beat constable, Robert Fegan. He thrust open the window, climbed in and covered McNamara with a sheet to put out the flames. He saw Black 'in a stooping position' in the room; he seemed to have been watching McNamara burn, but Fegan was too concerned with trying to save the woman's life to bother about Black. Fegan ordered a stretcher and had McNamara carried to the Southern General Hospital. By the time he turned his attention to Black, he had escaped out of the back door.

The police hunted for Black and Constable Robert Johnson arrested him as he walked leisurely along Church Street about six in the evening of 27 February.

When the police took Black to the hospital for McNamara to identify him, a crowd gathered outside and yelled abuse at him, so the police had to fight to get him safely back to jail. The charge of assault against him was upgraded to murder when Mary McNamara died on 26 February. He was found guilty and sentenced to death, although he was later reprieved.

Overall, women were involved in a great number of crimes in nineteenth century Liverpool. They could be victims or vicious, but they were certainly as much part of the criminal world as men were.

17

On the Railway

The railway was a symbol of progress in Victorian Britain, with the great steam locomotives hauling goods and passengers from one end of the country to the other. Railways altered the face of the country with the never ending long steel rails that sliced through the countryside, deep cuttings, viaducts and stations, but they also facilitated travel in a way and on a scale never before seen as ordinary people could afford the fares to travel in numbers to coast and country.

Naturally railways were also magnets for criminals, with pickpockets attracted to the crowded stations and carriages, while professional gamblers infested the carriages and fleeced the unwary of their money.

The Magsmen

Swindlers and cheats could appear anywhere that crowds gathered: sporting events, political gatherings and especially ports and railways. There were a huge variety of methods by which these conmen or 'duffers' – because they preyed on the duffs or stupid people of society – could part the innocent or gullible from their money. A common trick was to sell sub-standard tobacco on the pretext that it had been honestly smuggled from the Americas: that was cigar doffing. In the 1860s, Liverpool Lime Street railway station was infested by another breed known as Magsmen.

The name originated in the old slang term for a halfpenny coin, a mag, which was the coin most used in the game of pitch-and-toss, in which many of these swindlers specialised. The term stuck and spread to any kind of sharp, from thimble-riggers to card sharps and those who threw shaved dice.

In the summer of 1866, the police decided it was time to clean up Lime Street and moved in. In June that month Detective Allinson mingled with the crowds who waited for their trains and saw a number of magsmen. He knew them by face and reputation but could not arrest them until he saw them actually committing a crime. There was no point in just moving them along, as they would just operate somewhere else where there was no police presence. As Allinson watched, two of the magsmen, very respectably dressed and nearly gentlemen in appearance, struck up a conversation with a passing traveller.

Allinson stepped closer to listen. He knew the magsmen as John Jones and John Howarth, both well-known scoundrels. He heard them find out that the traveller was going to Rochdale and tell his new friends by which train he was travelling. 'What a coincidence,' Howarth said, 'for I am waiting for that very same train.'

That was enough for Allinson. He knew that if he allowed the magsmen onto the train they would fleece their victim, so he arrested both on the charge of 'being suspicious persons.' He took both men to the nearest bridewell, where they were searched. The contents of their pockets proved interesting. Howarth had a pawn ticket for a watch, pledged at a broker in Manchester, a pack of marked playing cards used in the three card trick, a 'flash' £20 note and a forged sovereign. There was a difference between 'flash' and forged: the forged note was intended to be passed off as the real thing, while a flash note was an obvious copy, with different wording. A flash note was not illegal. They would look real to a casual observer and could be quickly produced to give the appearance of wealth, or perhaps passed off as genuine in the dark or to a drunken man.

The contents of Jones' pockets were even more interesting. He had a small leather bag that held forty forged sovereigns and a pack of cards. The police examined the cards thoroughly but they appeared genuine. Jones claimed that the coins were not to swindle people but were merely used as markers when playing billiards – an ingenious reply that brought waves of laughter from the police.

Allinson took the pawn ticket to the broker in Manchester and redeemed the watch, but Howarth could not say what name was engraved on it, which argued for a very short acquaintance with the item and to the police suggested it had been stolen.

Allinson knew these magsmen well: they were part of a gang who haunted the railway station and sometimes the docks, waiting for bewildered emigrants on their way to the Americas. Many of the emigrants were from rural areas or the continent and were not used to the wiles of such sharps; they were easy prey. Indeed, Jones openly admitted that they 'only got hold of people who were going to sea, so the police could do nothing to them.'

Although both the men were known criminals, carrying forged coins was not proof that they intended to use them, so they were only put away for a month. Allinson must have been a little frustrated, but he returned to his job and continued trying to make the streets safer.

He might have been better employed working in the carriages.

Peril on the Chester Train

On the morning of 24 November 1876, the 10.45 express from Liverpool Lime Street steamed toward Chester to catch the Irish mail.

On the approach to Frodsham Station, the train slowed for a long curve and pandemonium broke out inside one of the carriages. Passengers started as the driver blew three long blasts on his whistle to indicate an emergency, and the train abruptly slowed as they entered a short tunnel. The passengers stared up the corridor and peered out the windows to see what was happening.

They drew back, startled, when a man dived head first through a window, smashing the glass and scattering sharp shards in all directions. A second man was also hanging out of the window, with blood pouring from his hand. The first man ran down the track alongside the train and tried to enter a carriage further down. He might have succeeded had the guard, Mr Weston, not hurried after him, grabbed his collar and hauled him back.

By now, everybody in the train crowded to the windows to watch the drama. They exclaimed at each incident and exchanged views on what it all meant. They watched as the unknown man wriggled free from the guard and ran off again. He squeezed through the gap between two carriages, glanced behind him and ran along the footboard, which extended the full width of the train. The passengers dived to the opposite side of the carriages to watch, and gasped in horror as the man threw himself on the tracks in front of the engine.

For a moment the passengers thought they would be witnesses to a bloody suicide, but luckily the driver managed to stop the train and the man lay across the tracks in broken hope. The guard tried to lift him clear, but he gripped the rails and clung on until a number of passengers disembarked and prised him free.

At the same time, the man who hung out of the window was shouting in pain. In his struggle he had managed to impale his thumb on the jagged glass of the window through which the suicidal man had jumped. He was freed with difficulty and taken to hospital.

When the police arrived the story gradually unfolded. The man who was impaled was Arthur Ellis, a lithographer of Radcliffe Street in Liverpool. He had boarded the train at Lime Street and sat in a carriage beside two other men, one older than the other. There was no hint of trouble until the train approached Frodsham, when the younger man pulled out a knife and jumped on Ellis's feet.

As Ellis started and looked, the man grabbed him by the front of his coat and shouted: 'You bastard, I'll put this into you.'

Luckily his slash with the knife failed to make contact. Unwilling to chance a better aimed blow, Ellis took out his wallet and handed over £5 10/- in gold, but the attacker was obviously not interested in money, as he grabbed the coins and threw them through the window. After that Ellis and the knifeman struggled, with the knifeman's older companion trying his best to restrain him and help Ellis. Eventually the knifeman leaped out of the window. The authorities decided he was insane rather than wicked and sent him to a lunatic asylum.

Overall, the railway was an immense blessing with improved and cheaper transport for both passengers and goods, but as always, criminals could also exploit this new resource.

18
Jack Ashore

Without the sea, Liverpool would have been only a middling-sized town in the north-west of England. The sea made her important, and seamen kept the streets lively and full of character. Liverpool was a truly international port, with seamen of different colours and races mixing with the locals in relative harmony, but there was always a possibility of trouble when seamen came ashore.

What Sarah saw

Sarah Brennan was a middle-aged woman. There was nothing extraordinary about her; she was perfectly respectable, she worked and lived a normal life. About twelve o' clock on the night of Tuesday, 19 February 1856 Brennan was walking along Chisenhale Street when she saw a man and a young woman arm in arm nearby. She was an observant woman and watched them for a while, smiling at this sight of affection. The man was in his mid-forties, looked like a seaman and was a little drunk; he wore a black coat with a fur collar, black waistcoat and a cap and the woman was gaudily dressed. As Brennan passed by, the man was silent, but the woman said 'not far to go.' Brennan did not hear any more as she stepped inside a shop. When she emerged, she saw the man lying alone on the flight of steps that led to a house.

A passer-by, who Brennan thought was a coal-heaver, tried to help him, but soon gave up. Being a kind-hearted woman, Brennan tried to lift the drunken man to his feet, but he refused to be helped. She saw an acquaintance of hers, James 'Scotty' Carr, aged twenty-three, standing with a friend a few yards away and asked where he was going.

'Just around the corner,' Carr replied.

At that point the drunken man fell and Brennan tried to lift him. 'Where are you going?' she asked.

The man gave what Brennan later described as a 'saucy answer' and added he 'had money enough to pay.'

As Brennan struggled, Carr and his companion, twenty-five-year-old Philip Wall came to help. Taking one of the stranger's arms each, they cried out, 'come along, shipmate,' in a hearty fashion and lifted him to his feet. As Brennan watched, they took their comrade into a narrow and notorious passage named Knight's Buildings or Bagging Entry.

She knew Carr had a bad reputation, so warned the coal-heaver. 'They are going to do something to him,' she said.

'I'll follow them,' the coal-heaver said, but that was the last that Brennan saw of him.

The body in the lane

The next morning at about half past four, a carter named James Bryan was on his way to feed his horses. He passed along a lane between Clement Street and Chisenhale Street when he saw a man lying face up on the ground. Bryan thought the man was drunk and walked on, but when he had tended to his horses he realised that the man had not moved and tried to rouse him. There was no reply, so Bryan looked for a policeman in Vauxhall Road. Shortly afterward, a tinsmith named Hughes saw the man lying terribly still, wearing only a shirt and trousers and with a muffler, or short scarf, twisted around his neck and knotted under his right ear.

Hughes checked the man's pulse, failed to find one and searched for the police. He found Inspector John Duggan, who was marching with a section of police to the police office. As soon as Hughes told them about the body, Duggan led his men to see what had happened. A quick examination showed that there were marks of possible strangulation around the man's neck, and Duggan was sure the dead man could not have tied the muffler so tightly around his own neck. He suspected the seaman had been murdered. They ordered that the body be taken to the dead house and began their investigations.

The police discovered that the dead man was a seaman named James House, his ship was the *Charles Napier* and he came from Bristol. Although the police interviewed Hughes and Bryan, it was Brennan who was most useful with her partial description of the two men the previous night. Brennan's descriptions, plus her mention of the name Scotty Carr, led to detectives William Laycock, William Wilson and John Grisenthwaite arresting James Carr and Philip Wall. Both men were known as 'duffers' – they dressed as seamen and toured the houses around the docks selling stolen goods to the gullible on the pretext that they had been honestly – or dishonestly – smuggled into the country.

The detectives took the suspects to Central Police Station and arranged a line up. They called in Brennan, who easily picked out both suspects from an array of men with similar appearance and clothing. With their identities verified, the police searched them and found pawn tickets for a waistcoat that had belonged to House, along with sundry other items. They also found that the muffler around the neck of House belonged to Carr. Detective Grisenthwaite was sure that the

Blucher boots worn by Wall belonged to the murdered man. In the time honoured way of caught criminals, Wall put the blame on Carr by claiming he had given him the boots, but Carr denied ever seeing them before.

Detective Laycock asked Carr where he had got the muffler he wore around his neck. Carr replied he had bought it in Fleetwood.

'Why do you ask me these questions? What are we brought here for?' Carr wondered.

Laycock replied that they had been arrested for murdering and robbing a man in Chisenhale Street.

'I don't know whether we did or not,' Carr said, probably with some truth.

Inspector Kehoe was there. 'That is no answer at all,' he said, but Carr replied that he was drunk and could not remember a thing.

The police investigations continued. They spoke to Mary Fannin, who lived at No. 12 Court, Banastre Street. She had known Carr for a few weeks and was slightly acquainted with Wall. Carr and Wall had both been in her house. At about three on the Wednesday morning she was in bed when Wall, Carr and a third man came to the door. Wall wore a distinctive black coat with a fur collar and Wall a black waistcoat. While Wall and Carr came into the house, the third man merely said 'good night,' added that he had to catch a steamboat and walked away.

When Carr and Wall came into the house, Mary Fannin smelled that they had been drinking. She asked Carr to return a muffler that he had borrowed from her, but he said she could not have it, as he had put it around a man's neck and he 'expected the man was dead by this time.'

Carr asked Fannin's advice about the black coat he wore, and Wall's black waistcoat. He wondered how much he could pledge them for at a pawnshop. When Fannin said that she did not know, Carr said he 'got them off a man' and 'your muffler is now round his neck,' but he did not give the name of the man. He added that Fannin was not to tell, and finished by boasting that he had plenty of money.

Carr and Wall did not stay long, but their words remained with Fannin. When the police showed her the muffler that had been around the neck of House, she identified it as her own, and the black coat with the fur collar that House had worn was the same one, she swore, that Carr had wished to pawn.

The police also spoke to Ann Hainsworth, who, together with her husband, kept a sailors' boarding house and beer house in Chisenhale Street. On the Saturday, Wall and Carr came to look for accommodation but the house was full, so Hainsworth sent them to another place across the road. The next day Wall gave Hainsworth a pawn ticket to look after, saying it was for Carr's clothes. When Hainsworth learned of the murder she gave the ticket to the police. Detective Wilson visited Rowland's pawnbrokers at No. 181 Vauxhall Road and redeemed the black coat that had been taken from the murdered man. Thomas O'Brien, the assistant at the pawnbrokers, said that Wall and a young woman had handed in the coat and waistcoat. It was the second time the woman had tried to pledge the clothes, for O'Brien had refused her the first time as he did not believe they belonged to her. He only agreed to accept the coat when Wall had said: 'they are my clothes; you can take them in.'

A clothier name Hannon confirmed that he sold the Blucher boots to James House; he had his maker's mark on them and they were the same pair as Wall had worn. Hannon stated that House was in his shop on the Tuesday night, and that Wall and Carr were outside the shop. Hannon thought that Wall and Carr were suspicious looking men who may have intended to rob the shop.

Two policemen, constables James Beattie and Thomas Newsher had seen Wall and Carr helping House along the road. The officers had spoken to the trio, and had been assured that they were all shipmates, so let them continue. There seemed no doubt about the guilt of Wall and Carr. They were both sentenced to hang.

But there were more than just casual murderers for Jack ashore to be wary of.

Crimps

The boarding-house masters was off in a trice
A'shouting and promising all that was nice,
And one fat old crimp took a fancy to me.
Says he 'you're a fool, lad, to follow the sea.'

Chorus: And it's row, row bullies, row,
them Liverpool judies have got us in tow.

In September 1843, a meeting was held in Liverpool's Queens Theatre to try and persuade the council to grant land on which to build a Sailors' Home. Captain Hudson chaired the meeting. Hudson was very keen to have somewhere respectable for seamen to stay when their ships were berthed in the port. He spoke strongly against a 'class of men who entrapped and robbed the poor sailor, and those connected with shipping.' And 'if there was one class of the community more robbed than another, that class was the sailors, and that too by a set of men whose business was not even recognised in the directory.'

He mentioned that if a sailor fell overboard at sea there was a chance of him escaping sharks, but there was little chance of escaping the land sharks. These were the shipping masters, boarding masters, and crimps. These men took in seamen just off incoming ships, found accommodation for them in brothels or low-level lodging houses where they were fed over-priced food and drink, often paired off with grasping prostitutes who would rob them of all they had before the boarding master found them a ship, taking as payment part of the seaman's wages. Often the crimp would be hand in glove with a crooked tailor, who would supply cheap quality seagoing clothing for exorbitant prices.

Crimps based themselves in the areas where seamen congregated, the streets behind Princes Dock in the North End, and the Paradise Street and Lower Frederick Street area, known as Sailortown. Both were filled with pubs, ship's stores and perambulating seamen and their women, either gaudy and overdressed if prostitutes or haggard and relieved if wives who were just glad to have their men home for a spell. There were teenage gangs waiting for victims, seamen of all races and colours parading the streets in an example of interracial harmony that found expression in song and put the near apartheid regime on the United States' ships to shame. There was music and singing, drinking and laughter, raucous voices and, waiting in the shadows and behind the gaudy gas globes of the gin palaces, the grasping talons of the crimps.

Says he, 'There's a job as is waiting for you,
With lashings of liquor and bugger'all to do.'
What you say, lad, will you jump her too?'
Says I, 'you old bastard, I'm damned if I do.'

Rum and prostitution

Seamen did not have a good reputation. In December 1859, the Liverpool shipowner T. M. Mackay thought they were 'unfortunate wretches whose idea of home is a crimp's boarding house and whose religion is a combination of rum and prostitution.' It is a damning condemnation of a workforce on which the prosperity of the nation depended, or perhaps an indictment on the opinions of the class of people who made the accusation, blaming the victims rather than the perpetrators.

Some of the Liverpool crimps were well known. For instance there was John De Moot, who lived in Frederick Street and had once been the master of a ship, but had lost that status when he was charged with being drunk and disorderly.

In June 1860, De Moot was causing trouble in the temporary shipping office. When Mr Murphy of the local marine board tried to get him to leave, De Moot said he wished that Murphy had been inside the home when it burned and that the roof had fallen on him and he had burned to death. Murphy tried to get De Moot away quietly but De Moot refused and said he would 'do for' Murphy, and was promptly arrested.

There were other crimps with colourful names, such as Shanghai Davies who infested the Red Lion pub on Seabrow, and another remembered as John Da Costa the Yank, which gives a clue to his country of origin. There was Paddy Dreadnought, Paddy Houlihan of Denison Street, and the famous Ma Smyrden of Pitt Street, who is chiefly remembered for a possibly apocryphal tale of her once selling a corpse to a crimp on the pretence he was drugged.

The 1843 meeting agreed to try and have a sailor's home built 'as a safe retreat to the sailors from the dangers which beset them on every side.'

The meeting also highlighted some of the other malpractices the boarding masters used, including a case where a countryman requested to go to sea. The boarding master issued a signed declaration that the youth had voyaged to the Caribbean as a cook and steward, and a berth was obtained. That cost five shillings. There were boarding masters who allegedly had young boys from the country pace around a bull's horn, so they could say with complete sincerity that they had 'rounded the Horn' and were fit to sign on as seamen – with the crimp taking his fee for finding the shipmaster such an experienced sailor.

Sometimes the crimps would meet an incoming ship en masse, or even board her in small boats in order to entice the crews to their particular establishment. The boarding masters or their runners, or even the females they employed, were expert in knowing exactly how to inveigle a seaman from his place of safety to some disgusting alleyway or lodging house, where they would be fleeced of all they had. The predators knew each ship and the length of their voyage, so could judge to a penny the wages of each seaman. They would waylay him and in the few days before he was paid, help him to run up bills with women, drink and on new clothes, so when he finally drew his wages, he owed it all and more to the crimp, so was forced to sign away some of his advance pay as well. He could be robbed of months of wages in a matter of days, and sent back to sea in some hell-at-sea blood boat, hung over and without a memory of what happened.

The next I remember, I woke in the morn
on a three skys'l yarder bound south round Cape Horn.
With an old suit of oilskins and two pairs of socks
and a blooming great head and a dose of the pox.

In Spring of 1863, the council discussed the crimping system in Liverpool and explained that at the North Landing stage there were five people who appeared to be slop sellers but who in reality were crimps, and each kept a boat with two runners. The boats would meet inward bound ships. There were five more boats at the south end of the port that were ostensibly owned by tailors, but who were hand in glove with the crimps. There were another two boats the crimps used, so twelve in total, and all intent on trapping honest Jack ashore.

The runners sped out to incoming ships and gave the seamen grog, sometimes laced with drugs, so they were more than part comatose before they docked. There were often so many of these crimps and runners that they could virtually take control of the ship, in defiance of the master and mates. The crimps came disguised as riggers – experts in rigging but also able to bring ships into port. With the seamen now drunk and incapable, the riggers took the ship in, and charged huge amounts for the privilege. The crimp's boatmen took the drunken sailors ashore and charged another excessive sum, and the boarding housekeepers then had the sailor in their hands. The costs rose, the quality was poor and Jack the sailor was used, abused, robbed and half poisoned until he was bundled back to sea again, in debt and without much memory of his brief and sordid time ashore.

The Merchant Shipping Act of 1854 forbade any such person from boarding the ships, with a £20 fine for those who broke the law, but without police to regulate the act, it was a paper tiger. There was also a £5 fine for anybody who took a seaman to a lodging house without permission but, again, with scores of seamen landing in Liverpool each day, it would need an army of police to guard each man.

However, the crimps did not have things their own way. The Sailors' Home opened in Canning Place in 1848 to provide respectable lodgings for seamen. That fine move was reinforced by the Mersey Mission to Seamen in 1856, and the formation of the Liverpool River Police in 1865. But the practise of crimping continued. In 1869, the *Nautical Magazine and Naval Chronicle* mentioned specific instances of crimping where seamen fell in with crimps and were kept drunk in lodging houses until they had no money left and were sent back to sea without having given a penny of their wages to their wives.

The battle for hearts, health, minds and souls was intensified when another champion arose for the seamen in the shape of the redoubtable Rev Edward Thring, chaplain to the Mersey Seafarers from 1859 to 1867. Thring organised resistance to the crimps by holding religious services on board the ships in the Mersey and, at a time of religious revivals across the country, he advised the crews to avoid the crimps of Liverpool. He gave ships' crews the addresses of respectable lodging houses and, in 1862, he personally challenged a group of crimps in a newly-arrived vessel. As the hard-eyed men and their painted women glared at him, he had his own followers smuggle the crew's sea chests to the sailors' home. As the crimps sent their bullies and runners to interfere, the police acted as escorts and the bullies backed off, growling.

Thring's endeavours were aided by a combination of the local Marine Board and the Mersey Dock and Harbour Board, who handed over some control of the dock area to the police. The three agencies organised cab stands and porters to help escort newly-arrived seamen from the ships to an area away from the docks while the police kept the crimps and their runners away from the vulnerable, recently paid sailors. Even so, an estimated 1,279 seamen were crimped in 1869, but the worst of the system was over by then. As the authorities became aware of the problem and the Christian charities and police formed a combined front, the rule of the crimps in Liverpool diminished, although it did not disappear.

Now all you young sailors take a warning by me.
Keep an eye on your drinks when the liquor is free.
And pay no attention to runner or whore
when your hats on your head and your feets on the shore.

19

Redcross Street Murder

Wanted and reward posters were quite familiar. The police issued them and newspapers published them to alert the public to yet another murder or major robbery. However, few were as detailed as that set out in February 1895 after a murder in Redcross Street:

> *Detective Department, Liverpool, February 22nd 1895. Wanted in this city, for the wilful murder of a man early in the morning of the 19th inst., a man of the following description, viz., about thirty years of age, five foot six inches in height, thick brown moustache, occasionally twitches his mouth and winks one eye when speaking; dressed in a blue serge suit, and hard felt hat; supposed to be wearing a muffler; has the appearance of a sailor. Please cause all possible inquiry for the murderer to be made at lodging houses, shipping offices and other likely places and wire any information obtained.*

The police did not know to whom the advertisement would lead them, if indeed it evoked any response at all, but they lived in hope. By the end of the century, the police were adept at the art of detecting. They had long used a network of informers, but now also used modern technology, such as the telegraph and telephone, augmented by the press to spread information about suspected criminals, and they followed scientific methods to find their man. Although the press and penny dreadful publications tended to portray criminals as brutish, uneducated and coarse, sometimes the trail led the police to very unassuming and seemingly respectable men. Such a man was William Miller.

On the surface, Miller was a married family man who sometimes lived with his wife in Edgeware Street. The street was narrow but quiet, filled with hard-working people who mostly worked locally. His wife Sissy was a local woman with an extended family and a wide network of friends who knew and respected her as a decent mother and honest worker. Unfortunately, Miller himself did not incur the same respect. He had the reputation of a womaniser, a man who cheated on his wife. In the Victorian period, such behaviour was reprehensible but not criminal, and although all sympathy was with Sissy Miller, there was little she could do except grin and bear it or start expensive and humiliating divorce proceedings that may not have been successful.

Despite his predilection for the company of women not his wife, Miller had few other bad habits. He was quiet tempered and at a time when respectable society frowned on excess drinking, he was virtually tee-total, and on the few occasions that he visited the local pubs, he was mild, polite and retiring. He had been a seaman and knew some of the major ports of the world, but retired to Liverpool to work as a deckhand on the Woodside ferry and had done so for at least five years. His workmates said that he 'would not hurt a fly' and were all of the opinion that he was of a very inoffensive nature. If any of them knew about his womanising, they were not unduly concerned, as it did not affect his work in the slightest.

About the beginning of December 1894, Miller seemed to have

come into more money than the deckhand of a Mersey ferry boat had any right to have. He flashed around a wad of bank notes, rattled gold coins on the table and spoke about opening and running a tobacconist's shop. He had it all worked out: during the day, he would run the shop and in the evening he would help his carpenter father-in-law, while his wife looked after the business. Then he handed in his notice to Captain McQueen of the ferry and his former shipmates heard nothing more about him or the tobacconist shop. Miller vanished from the Liverpool world for a few weeks. When he appeared again, it was in the most dramatic of circumstances.

Early in the morning of 19 February 1895, a dock gateman named George Curran was walking to work along Strand Street when he saw a young man running toward him, shouting, 'a man did it . . . A man did it.' His name was George Needham and he was fifteen years old. As Needham came closer, Curran noticed that he staggered as he ran and he was bleeding heavily from his head. Curran caught hold of him before he fell, cursed as he realised the boy's clothes were sodden with blood and supported him.

'Have you seen a policeman?' Needham gasped urgently.

Curran looked around but did not see one, so he put two fingers in his mouth and blew a loud whistle to summon help.

'A man murdered my master,' the boy slurred his words as he spoke. 'He came to look at some valuable books and murdered my master.'

'Who is your master?' Curran asked.

'Old Moyse that keeps a bookstall,' the boy said.

'Where is he?' Curan asked, and no doubt glanced along the street, hoping that the police arrived soon.

'He's murdered at 26 Redcross Street.'

'Who did it?' Curran asked, but the boy just mumbled that it was a man in a blue coat and then he fainted from loss of blood.

Constables John Fahay and Edward Cashen arrived a few moments later. Fahay realised that Needham was badly injured and immediately telephoned for the Northern Infirmary's horse ambulance. There were fourteen separate wounds in Needham's head, bruises around his neck and some on his body. When he arrived at the hospital, he seemed terrified and was unable to give a coherent account of what had happened.

By that time a number of other police officers had assembled and they went in a body to the scene of the alleged murder. No. 26 Redcross Street was set back a little from the street and the police squeezed through an irregular passage around the house and into a dirty yard at the back. The house was an ancient three-storey building with the ground floor used as a hairdresser's shop and the living accommodation above. The police thundered up a rickety wooden staircase to the house and found themselves faced by a number of small rooms with tiny, multi-paned windows.

They shouted out the name of the alleged victim, but there was no answer. By that time the police had learned about Edward Moyse. He was a small-time bookseller who worked from a stall at George's Dock; he was unmarried and a very kindly Church-going man with no known enemies. Nobody knew much about him apart from that, for he had only arrived in Liverpool a couple of years previously and, apart from the customers who came to his bookstall, he did not speak to many people. Moyse was fifty-two years old, and when the police found him, he had been horribly battered to death.

Moyse lay curled up on his bed with his head on the pillow. His skull was a mass of blood, with several obvious wounds where somebody had thumped him with something sharp and heavy. Something had also cut through his right nostril, which had bled heavily onto the pillow. Apart from the obvious violence to Moyse, there was no sign of a struggle in the room, so the police believed that somebody had murdered the old man as he slept. There were a poker and a hatchet in the room, both smeared and spattered with blood, but no apparent motive for the murder.

The police began their usual rounds of enquiries, using their network of informers as well as asking questions of George Needham, the young man who had first alerted them about the murder. He had recovered sufficiently to give the police some information. He stated that a man had come to the side door the previous evening and asked for Moyse, but Needham had said the old man was out working but would return in a short while.

There were various rumours as to what had happened. One that was widespread said that Needham went to bed as normal but sometime in the early morning a man had woken him roughly by grabbing him by the throat. He had started up and asked: 'has the master been calling?'

'No, he's not,' the man said, 'don't wake him.' And he stomped away. The police wondered why the man had wakened Needham in the first place when he could have slipped away without being seen. The police also wondered how the stranger had got access to the house as there was no sign of a forced entry, no broken windows and the locks were secure.

As it happened, Needham did not heed the stranger's advice but rose from his bed and ran downstairs to see if Moyse was all right. No sooner had Needham reached the bottom of the steps when somebody – he presumed the same man – attacked him. Unfortunately, Needham was not well enough to answer questions, so much of the police work was based on speculation and detective work rather than definite knowledge.

Chief Constable Nott-Bower ordered Chief Detective Inspector Stretell, Detective Inspector Fisher and Detective Duckworth to probe into the murder and find the culprit. They started by inspecting the murder scene and tracing the movements of Moyse and Needham in an attempt to see if they had argued with anybody who might be looking for revenge. They initially ruled out robbery as a motive as Moyse's entire fortune of a few pounds was still under his pillow and surmised that one or other of the two had made an enemy.

There was some added drama in the house once the coroner had seen the remains of Edward Moyse. As soon as the cause of death was confirmed, the body was taken out of the house but as the coffin was too large for the door it was manoeuvred through the window. The watching crowd was unsettled by this final indignity to Moyse and muttered dark threats about what they would do if they caught the murderer. It was just one more problem for the Liverpool police.

The detectives tried to piece together the events of the previous night. Both the door into the passage and the door into Moyse's room had been locked and the contents were all as they should be, with no sign of a struggle except one overturned stool and a great deal of blood. There was blood beside the fireplace and a blood trail up the stairs to the boy's room and all over his bed. The police tried to equate the clues with the boy's short statement, realising that he was confused when he spoke. They thought he was attacked by the fireplace and ran upstairs to his bed before leaving to get help. The house had not been robbed – as well as Moyse's watch and chain, there was some good quality clothing that any pawnshop would have accepted like a shot.

With no clues to the perpetrator, the police rounded up all Moyse's former helpers and questioned them about any possible connection, but all were released without any charges being brought. The police worked out that Needham was attacked first with the axe and then with the poker. They decided that his story about being wakened was not correct; he may have been confused. The police made a step forward on 21 February when Needham recovered sufficiently to give some more details.

Still heavily bandaged and lying in his hospital bed, Needham gave an account of what he remembered. He said that Moyse and he returned home from the bookstall around six in the evening, but while he remained in the house, Moyse went back out to Myrtle Street to look at more stock. Shortly after, the visitor knocked at the door and claimed he wanted to buy some valuable books. When Needham told him that Moyse was out, the man said he would return about nine. Instead, he was back at eight and insisted on waiting for Moyse.

The man did not give his name but Needham got the impression that he had known Moyse for a long time. He had an odd twitch in his face when he spoke, and asked how much the old man earned with his book stall and where he kept his money. When Needham said that he did not know, the visitor said that was a 'very odd thing' and if anything happened to Moyse 'no one would know where to find his money.' He spoke about the old man as a 'noisy, funny sort of fellow', who was 'very queer in his ways and talk.'

Needham agreed that he was queer but repeated that he had no idea about Moyse's money.

'Does he have a bank?' the visitor asked and spoke about giving Moyse some money to bank. It was about five to ten when Moyse entered, and shook hands with the visitor like old friends.

'I didn't expect to see you back so soon,' Moyse said. He told Needham that he had had 'the gentleman for a lodger before' and he would sleep on the sofa that night, and would take the best room after that. Needham agreed and went to bed, leaving the two to talk the night away. It was about five in the morning before he heard somebody coming up the stairs toward his bedroom. It was the visitor and he carried a flickering candle.

'Are you not going to get up?' the man asked. 'I can't wake your master.'

'Has he called me yet?' Needham asked, but the stranger said he had not.

'Is he awake?' Needham asked.

'No,' the stranger replied, 'aren't you going to get up and make the fire?'

Needham said he was and asked the man to get the hatchet from the kitchen and break up some firewood and sticks. After Needham got dressed he saw the man rubbing his hands along the floor, and then he set up a chair under the access hatch to the loft. As Needham watched, the man looked into the loft, but came down when Needham laughed at him. Needham withdrew to his bedroom and the man followed, blew out his candle, grabbed Needham by the throat and cracked him over the head with the hatchet.

'For God's sake, don't kill me!' Needham screamed and struggled to escape. He got free and ran downstairs but the man followed into the kitchen, lifted the poker from the fireplace and continued to beat him.

'Hold your noise,' the man shouted as he battered the boy over the head.

Unable to run away, Needham came closer, so he was inside the swing of the poker, but now it was the turn of the stranger to get out of the way.

'Don't put blood on me,' he said, and pushed Needham to the ground. 'You can now go and wake the old man.' The stranger turned before he reached the door. 'If you follow me,' he said, 'I'll kill you.'

Not surprisingly, Needham needed a few moments to recover, and when he checked on Moyse he saw that he was dead and covered in blood. The youth ran from the house and gave a garbled account to Curran the dock gateman.

After giving his story, Needham was questioned as to the man's identity but could not help much. 'I never saw the man before,' he said, 'and I never heard my master mention his name.' However, Needham thought he looked like a sailor, mentioned the twitch when he spoke and said he talked about bringing 'a bird and some tobacco next time.'

At first the police did not believe Needham's assertion that the intruder had been in the loft above his bedroom, but when they examined the loft, they found bloody handprints and wondered if the murderer had left that way. They had no motive, but now wondered if the murderer may have intended robbery, and thought that Moyse kept a store of valuables in the loft.

Needham described the stranger as a sailor of about twenty-nine years old, five foot five with a moustache and a thin pale face. He thought the man was respectable and noticed he had a Liverpool accent.

On Saturday, 23 February 1895 the police made an arrest. When they had circulated the description of their chief suspect, a woman in Liverpool immediately recognised him; she had been in his house that very day. The police acted at once: they listened to the woman's story and moved to William Miller's house in Edgeware Street. While the uniformed police guarded the exits, Stretell led the detectives inside and found Miller sitting in the parlour with his pregnant wife and children.

'We have come to make inquiry about a rather serious matter and you had better be careful how you answer.'

When Detective Sub-Inspector Fisher arrested him, Miller remained very calm and made no resistance. He had stains on his shirt, but had told his wife that he had been working in a slaughterhouse. The police asked him questions about his movements on the night of the murder, but they did not believe his replies that he had been in a number of cocoa houses, and bundled him inside a closed cab. With three policemen to ensure he did not escape, the cab growled to Dale Street Detective Office.

It was not long before news of Miller's arrest spread and a crowd gathered outside the police station, as he was bundled back out again and into another cab. Strettell and Moss, the prosecuting solicitor, accompanied Miller to the Northern Infirmary. The police rounded up another four men who resembled him and formed an identity parade, with Needham, still heavily bandaged and lying on his hospital bed, asked to identify the man who attacked him.

Without any hesitation, Needham indicated that Miller was the man, and the police took him away to Dale Street and charged him with murder, there and then. The police asked about the stains on his shirt and he said he had been assisting in slaughtering cattle in

Trowbridge Street on the Saturday. However, the manager of the slaughterhouse told them that no cattle had been slaughtered that day. Although Miller constantly denied the murder, the police were sure they had their man. They found two witnesses who had seen him in the vicinity of the murder on the night in question, one of whom thought he had been drunk.

Miller's story

It was after his arrest that details of Miller's less respectable side became known. His womanising was on a grand scale: grubby one-night-stands in seedy lodging houses were not for him. He chased women, promised them the world and left them shaken, disillusioned and betrayed. If the stories were anything like the truth, Miller had left his wife on two occasions to live with another woman, and returned home both times. The first occasion was only a few months previously, when he had become very friendly with an attractive Liverpool widow named Goss, who worked as a domestic servant for a very high class family. She was described as around twenty-seven, dark haired and with a fresh complexion. Even better for Miller, the woman had around £130, not a huge sum, but about two years wages for a skilled man. Even although he was the chief wage earner and his absence would leave his wife and family virtually penniless, Miller abandoned them and ran off with the attractive Mrs Goss.

They spent around £30 on a ship to the United States and settled in Philadelphia, where Miller broke open her cash box, and filched the contents. He did not marry the dark haired woman and left her to fend for herself in Philadelphia instead. He wrote to his wife, saying she could join him in America, and promised to send her money. He also wrote to his father-in-law, asking him to 'kiss the children' for him. After taking his lover for all she had, he returned to his wife, dressed as a gentleman of leisure and with kid gloves covering his new gold ring.

His lover told the British Consul, who notified the Liverpool police. Miller might have been more concerned when the woman he had wronged and robbed turned up at his house and demanded satisfaction. Naturally there was a lot of shouting, his wife was upset, the neighbours were interested and Miller first threatened suicide and then fled the scene, leaving his wife to pick up the pieces once more.

Despite his threat to kill himself, Miller preferred to live the high life. He took the packet ship to Dublin, then sailed to Glasgow, booked himself into the Lorne Temperance hotel, wrote a letter promising suicide to his wife, then once again pretended to be a gentleman. Perhaps his pretence was more believable than his morals, for another young woman fell for him and rumours said they ran off to Edinburgh together. Once there, he robbed her of her money and everything else of value. Once she was milked, he left her and scampered back to Liverpool and his long suffering wife. Left destitute, the abandoned woman complained to the Edinburgh police, who began a search, helped by their comrades in Glasgow, for Miller had neglected to pay his hotel bill.

Either Miller was a spendthrift or was monumentally greedy, for he returned back to the family home, said he was broke and spoke again of suicide, but once again left and slept a few nights in a cocoa shop at Great Charlotte Street, near the docks. On the Tuesday morning, around seven o' clock, he was seen calmly drinking cocoa in that shop. He had also written to the owner, a Mr Robinson, saying he and his wife would take over the running of a Scotland Road coffee shop and rooms that were presently empty. On the night of the murder he again returned home, but this time he had a bottle of laudanum, which his wife discovered and smashed, throwing the contents onto the fire.

Mrs Goss's story

In the meantime Mrs Goss, with whom Miller had eloped, had not been idle. Abandoned penniless in Philadelphia, she proved she was a woman of resource by raising the money for her return voyage by selling most of her clothes. As soon as she reached Liverpool, she had called in to Dale Street Police Station and told the police about him, but they could do nothing to help as the offences had been committed outside the UK. However, she called back, again and again until the police knew her face very well. When she was not pestering the police, this persistent woman was following Miller and finding out all she could about his life and movements. Some people believed that as soon as she saw the description of the murderer of Moyse, she was said to have hurried to the bridewell at Olive Street and told the officer on duty that Miller was his man. If that was true, it was fitting closure to Miller's amorous escapades.

The trial

When Miller appeared before the magistrates at Dale Street Police Station, a crowd had gathered to watch the proceedings, but the police had expected this and kept the doors firmly locked until the initial hearing began. From the Police Court, Miller was sent to the assizes, where the jury heard the evidence. Miller used a defence of alibi and mistaken identity, but it took the jury only twenty minutes to find him guilty of murder and assault. The judge donned the customary black cap and sentenced Miller to death.

Miller achieved instant notoriety with the then famous Reynold's Exhibition, showing a waxwork effigy of him at their Lime Street rooms. He had been composed throughout his trial and only when his wife and children came to see him for the last time in his cell did he show emotion. On a bright sunny 4 June, he was hanged at Walton Jail despite a petition to save his life. Even after being so cruelly betrayed, his wife stood by her man and firmly believed him innocent.

Epilogue

So that was Liverpool in the nineteenth century. It was an enigma, a typical port city but yet a town like no other, a city built on shifting trade, but with a population intensely loyal, a city with problems but a warm heart that welcomed outsiders. There was violence and theft, there were riots and vice, there were robberies and gambling, and places where no sane man or woman would venture alone unless he or she was searching for trouble; there were pimps and bullies and crimps and criminals, but there was always character.

That may be the defining theme that drives Liverpool: it is a city both of great character and great characters. If there were dangerous streets and areas where it was best not to venture, there were also men and women ready to stand up for themselves and their neighbours, usually a friend in need and always laughter beneath the tears. That was Liverpool: there through the good times and the bad times, and if the city has less contact with the sea just now, then the sea has not forgotten Liverpool. The Packet Rats and the sea shanties and the tales and legends and songs still resonate and will do for many decades.

Despite the crime, the brutal murders and sordid assaults, it is the song of Liverpool that survives, and that is something that transcends any negative image the city may have had in the nineteenth century.

Select Bibliography

Aughton, Peter,(2008) *Liverpool: A People's History*, Lancaster, Carnegie Publishing

Belchem, John, (2012) *Liverpool 800: Character, Culture and History*, Chicago, University of Chicago Press

Briggs, Asa, (1963, 1968) *Victorian Cities*, London, Penguin

Chesney, Kellow (1970) *The Victorian Underworld*, London, Maurice Temple Smith Ltd

Dell, Simon Patrick, (2004) *The Victorian Policeman*, Colchester, Shire Publications

Emsley, Clive, (2010) *The Great British Bobby: A History of British policing from 1829 to the present*, London, Quercus

Emsley, Clive, (1996) *The English Police: A Political and Social History*, Hove, Routledge

Fraser, Derek, (1979), *Power and Authority in the Victorian City*, Oxford, Basil Blackwell

Godfrey, Barry and Lawrence, Paul (2005), *Crime and Justice 1750–1950*, Devon: Willan Publishing

Gray, Adrian, (2011), *Crime and Criminals of Victorian England*, Stroud, The History Press

Griffiths, Major Arthur, (2010) *Victorian Murders: Mysteries of Police and Crime*, Stroud, The History Press

Hughes, Robert (1987), *The Fatal Shore*, London, Vintage

Jones, David (1982), *Crime, Protest, Community and Police in Nineteenth Century Britain*, London, Routledge & Kegan Paul

Jones, Steve, (1992), *Capital Punishments: Crime and Prison Conditions in Victorian Times*, Nottingham, Wicked Publications

Knepper, Paul (2007), *Criminology and Social Policy*, London, Sage Publications

Lees, Andrew, (2011), *The Hurricane Port: A Social History of Liverpool*, Edinburgh, Mainstream Publishing

Lubbock, Basil, (1977), *The Western Ocean Packets*, Glasgow, Brown, Son and Ferguson Ltd

Macilwee, Michael (2007), *The Gangs of Liverpool: From the Cornermen to the High Rip The Mobs that Terrorised a City*, Preston, Milo Books

Macilwee, Michael, (2011), *The Liverpool Underworld: Crime in the City 1750-1900*, Liverpool, Liverpool University Press

Parry, David, (2011), *Murder in Victorian Liverpool*, Lancaster Palatine Books

Rafter, Nicole (2009), *Origins of Criminology: A Reader*, Abingdon, Routledge

Samuels, Samuel, (2012) *From Forecastle to Cabin*, Barnsley, Seaforth Publishing

Tobias, John Jacob (1972), *Nineteenth Century Crime Prevention and Punishment*, Newton Abbot, David and Charles

Tulloch, Alexander (2008), *The Story of Liverpool*, Stroud, The History Press

Newspapers

Liverpool Mercury
The Times

Websites

http://liverpoolcitypolice.co.uk/